STOPPING POWER

Pulpless.Com™ Books by J. Neil Schulman

Novels
Alongside Night (trade edition forthcoming)
The Rainbow Cadenza (trade edition forthcoming)

Nonfiction
The Robert Heinlein Interview and Other Heinleiniana
The Frame of the Century?
Stopping Power: Why 70 Million Americans Own Guns
Book Publishing in the 21st Century,
Volumes One and Two

Short Stories
Nasty, Brutish, and Short Stories
(trade edition forthcoming)

Omnibus Collection
Self Control Not Gun Control

Collected Screenwritings
Profile in Silver and Other Screenwritings
(trade edition forthcoming)

J. NEIL SCHULMAN

STOPPING POWER

WHY 70 MILLION AMERICANS OWN GUNS

FOREWORD BY CRIMINOLOGIST AND CIVIL-RIGHTS LAWYER DON B. KATES, JR.

AFTERWORD BY CRIMINOLOGIST GARY KLECK

PULPLESS.COM, INC.
775 East Blithedale Ave., Suite 508
Mill Valley, CA 94941, USA.
Voice & Fax: (500) 367-7353
Home Page: http://
www.pulpless.com/
Business inquiries to
info@pulpless.com
Editorial inquiries & submissions to
editors@pulpless.com

First published by Synapse˜Centurion, June, 1994
Pulpless.Com™ HTML Edition May, 1996
Revised Pulpless.Com™, Inc. Editions July, 1999.
Library of Congress Catalog Card Number: 99-60343
Trade Paperback ISBN: 1-58445-057-6
Acrobat PDF ISBN: 1-58445-058-4
HTML ISBN: 1-58445-059-2

Cover designed by CaliPer, Inc.
Cover Illustration by Eugene C. Herrera

To L. Neil Smith

Who Made Me Ashamed to Be Unarmed

Author's Acknowledgements

Authors get all the credit, but they usually have help. Considering the many hours in which I have been educated on the subjects of history, liberty, morality and ethics, justice, criminal justice and law enforcement, firearms, and criminology, I would be remiss if I did not pay acknowledgements to the personal instruction I received from the following individuals: Sean Barrett, Alan Brennert, Steve Clar, Culver City Police Chief Ted Cooke, Charles Curley, Robert Durio, Art Eisenson, Harlan Ellison, Dan Feely, Elizabeth and Justin Feffer, Manuel Fernandez, John Ferrero, Dennis Foley, David Friedman, James Gatlin, Alan Gottlieb, Helen Grieco, Stephen Halbrook, Sylvia Hauser, Robert and Virginia Heinlein, Steve Helsley, Randall Herrst, Karl Hess, Ray Hickman, John Hosford, Phill Jackson, Dan Gifford, Sal Grammatico, T.J. Johnston, Don B. Kates, Jr., Keith Kato, Bill Keys, Gary Kleck, Peter Lake, Wayne LaPierre, Robert LeFevre, Rick Lowe, Elodie McKee, Michael McNulty, John Milius, Armando Miranda, Andrew Molchan, Jerry Pournelle, Dennis Prager, Leroy Pyle, Pat O'Malley, Paxton Quigley, Ayn Rand, Robert Ray, Michael D. Robbins, Rep. Dana Rohrabacher, Fred Romero, Murray Rothbard, Jim Saharek, Randy Shields, Jay Simkin, Culver City Police Lt. Owen Smet, Thomas Glenn Terry, Lance Thomas, Linda Thompson, Cathy Tolley, Luis Tolley, Kent Turnipseed, Jim Waldorf, Aaron Zelman, and, of course, my parents and family.

Additionally, for their direct guidance and help on this book, I'd like to thank Léon Bing, John Douglas, Larry Freundlich, Kent Hastings, Dafydd ab Hugh, Keith Kirts, Neal Knox, Victor Koman, Samuel Edward Konkin III, Richard Kyle, Jared Lobdell, Tanya Metaksa, Kate O'Neal, Ave Pildas and the students of the Otis Design Group at Otis College of Art and Design, Dori Smith, and Albert Yokum.

And, finally, a very special thank you to Brad Linaweaver and Randy Herrst for assistance at the penultimate hour.

I know that some of the people I'm thanking disagree with my views as expressed in this book. Tough. They have my gratitude anyway.

—JNS, 1994

Contents

Foreword

BY DON B. KATES, JR.

While still a student at Yale Law School, Don B. Kates, Jr., did civil rights work in the South, was a law clerk for William Kuntsler, and drafted civil-rights legislation for the House Judiciary Committee. From 1966 to 1975 he held various administrative positions with California Rural Legal Assistance and was deputy director and director of litigation for the San Mateo County Legal Aid Society, providing free legal representation for the poor. He specialized in major constitutional litigation and police misconduct litigation. In 1970 he was denominated the nation's outstanding legal services lawyer by the National Legal Aid and Defender Association. He has also been a member of the California Advisory Committee to the United States Civil Rights Commission.

Professor Kates has acted as a police legal advisor to departments in California and Missouri and has been a consultant on firearms, firearms legislation, and civil rights legislation to police departments and state and federal legislative committees. His articles on firearms have appeared in police and firearms technical journals; and his articles on firearms laws and "gun control" in general have appeared in *Harper's*, *The New York Times*, the *Christian Science Monitor*, the *Civil Liberties Review*, the *Criminal Law Bulletin*, the *Washington Post*, the *Los Angeles Times*, the *St. Louis Post Dispatch*, and various law reviews and other publications. He is the author of *Guns, Murder, and the Constitution*, and books he has edited include *Restricting Handguns: The Liberal Skeptics Speak Out* and *Firearms and Violence*.

Professor Kates has taught constitutional and criminal law

at St. Louis University and as a criminologist is currently associated with the Pacific Research Institute. He maintains a largely constitutional law practice in San Francisco and has recently been litigating constitutional issues regarding California's gun laws.

— JNS

Most Americans, including most gun owners, support reasonable gun controls. As a criminologist, so do I — with the caveat that even the best controls can only have marginal effects because the real determinants of violence are cultural and socioeconomic. The reason gun control remains a controversy is that the gun "control" movement has no interest in control, and no interest in working with the millions of gun owners who support control. The gun-control movement is dominated, rather, by prohibitionists whose ideologically motivated program obstructs society's ability actually to control guns.

Exemplifying that obstruction is Washington D.C.'s ban on handgun sales, passed at the urging of Handgun Control, Inc. (HCI) and the National Coalition to Ban Handguns (NCBH). This ban just drove the traffic underground, destroying the limited real control-value gun laws can have. When gun sales are legal, they're concentrated among gun dealers who can be required to register or conduct background checks on buyers, and refuse sales to prohibited persons such as felons and juveniles. Banning guns created a thriving business, with black marketeers obtaining scores of handguns in adjoining states and selling them on D.C.'s streets to anyone with the money to buy.

The situation will be even worse if HCI and NCBH attain their goal of a federal handgun ban. In addition to importing millions of handguns, the black marketeers will produce modern handguns in pot-metal copies. Though such a gun could only fire perhaps 300 shots before exploding, any competent machinist can fabricate one using tooling no more sophisticated than that found in millions of home workshops. Pot-metal guns would actually be less expensive than commercially manufactured guns are today — being produced without safeties, serial numbers, and brand names — by businesses free from costs such as taxes, record keeping, and likelihood of product liability suit. Similarly, "rotgut" sold for less during Prohibition than good liquor had before it.

The issue of licensing good citizens to carry concealed guns further illustrates the anti-gun movement's indifference to, and retardation of, actual control. Under California law, the police are required to license adults who have good cause and good character. The City of Los Angeles has more population than Connecticut which, as of mid-1993, had 110,000 licenses statewide. Yet at the behest of HCI, NCBH, and their ally the virulently anti-gun *Los Angeles Times*, as of mid-1993 the City of Los Angeles hadn't issued a handgun concealed-carry license in 18 years.

Predictably, however, that didn't mean no one was carrying concealed guns. A May 17, 1992 *Los Angeles Times* poll found 250,000 people admittedly carrying handguns without a license. Think of that: 250,000 uncontrolled people carrying concealed guns around — their identities, training, and qualifications completely unknown to the police! Now, of course, criminals wouldn't seek licenses even if they were freely available to good citizens. But the law-abiding would — whereby society would have notice of their identities and the power to condition licensure on training and testing. That is pragmatic gun control. The program of the *LA Times*, Handgun Control *et al.* is prohibitionist myopia.

But they don't care that their program is non-pragmatic and ineffective. Their real goal is a law symbolically affirming their deeply held moral belief that people should depend on the police for defense and never be prepared to defend themselves. Nationally syndicated columnist Garry Wills, a distinguished cultural historian, calls those who own guns for family defense "anti-citizens," "traitors, enemies of their own *patriæ*," arming "against their own neighbors." Ramsey Clark calls defensive gun ownership "anarchy, not order under law — a jungle where each relies on himself for survival." The *Washington Post* deems "The need that some homeowners and shopkeepers believe they have for weapons to defend themselves" to be among "the worst instincts of the human character." Likewise, representatives of the Presbyterian Church regularly seek a handgun ban because their church's "General Assembly has declared in the context of handgun control that it is opposed to 'the killing of anyone, anywhere, for any reason.'"

The Presbyterians distinguish long guns, which they see as intended for sporting use only, from handguns which they seek to outlaw as primarily intended for self-defense. The National Council to Ban Handguns (of which the Presbyterian Church USA is a charter member) changed its name to Coalition Against Gun Violence to clarify that it seeks prohibition also of long guns that are especially adapted for self-defense rather than sport. That is the real basis of the campaign against so-called assault rifles.

The law NCBH and HCI got Washington D.C. to pass (and which they see as the basic minimum gun control) doesn't just ban sale of handguns. To preclude the use of any firearm for self-defense, it prohibits householders from keeping even long guns assembled or loaded. NCBH was founded, and is still sponsored, by the Board of Church and Society of the United Methodist Church. Its rationale for gun "control" is explained by the editor of its publication *Engage-Social Action*, Rev. Allen Brockway. He is so deeply opposed to self-defense that he solemnly informs women that it is their Christian duty to submit to rape rather than do anything that might imperil a rapist's life. Rhetorically posing the question "Is the Robber My Brother?" Rev. Brockway answers "yes" for, though the burglary victim or the "woman accosted in the park by a rapist is [not] likely to consider the violator to be a neighbor whose safety is of immediate concern ... [c]riminals are members of the larger community no less than are others. As such they are our neighbors or, as Jesus put it, our brothers..."

Theological considerations aside, the Methodist Board and the YWCA condemn the mere possession (not just the unlawful use) of defensive firearms as "vigilantism." HCI and the other dominant forces in the gun "control" movement (quoted above) concur in condemning gun ownership for self-defense on purely secular moral grounds. As Illinois anti-gun activist and University of Chicago professor Robert Replogle puts it, "The only legitimate use of a handgun that I can understand is for target shooting." HCI's Sarah Brady, in an interview from the *Tampa Tribune* of October 21, 1993, agrees that "the only reason for guns in civilian hands is for sporting purposes."

Concomitantly, on August 15, 1993 the *New York Times* quoted Sarah Brady as saying that HCI proposes federal gun licensing under which self-defense would not be accepted as a ground for gun ownership. Only sportsmen would be allowed to own guns. Of course the *Los Angeles Times,* in an editorial from October 22, 1993, agrees. So does NCBH, though it also seeks to have all handguns (even target .22s) banned and confiscated. And, again, both HCI and NCBH insist that all firearms be kept unloaded and disassembled to make it impossible to use them for self-defense.

If only to appeal to those who disagree with their anti-self-defense moral premises, HCI and NCBH do avow pseudo-criminological arguments for such laws. Thus, when he was HCI Chairman, Pete Shields in his book *Guns Don't Die, People Do* advised that women submit to rapists and never physically resist in any way: when attacked by criminals "the best defense against injury is to put up no defense — give them what they want or run." In fact, however, it is only victims who run away or resist barehanded or with some weapon less than a gun who increase their danger of injury. Though the submissive are only half as likely to be injured by criminals as are victims who resist without a gun, criminological data show victims who submit are still twice as likely to be injured by criminals as are victims who resist with a gun — not to mention that the submissive are much more likely to be raped or robbed.

HCI and NCBH try never to acknowledge or mention these facts, which have been established by the leading American authority on guns and crime, Prof. Gary Kleck of Florida State University's School of Criminology and Criminal Justice. Kleck also finds that each year handguns are used by good citizens three to four times as often in self-defense as they are misused by criminals in committing crimes. Of course this research has also escaped the notice of the *Washington Post*, New York and LA *Times*, and the rest of our ignorant and highly biased media. Fortunately, it has not gone unnoticed by others. It is responsible for changing the minds of many criminologists who started out, as did Kleck, believing that gun ownership even by good citizens promotes crime. In 1993, the American Society of Criminology awarded Kleck's book *Point Blank: Guns and Violence in America* its coveted Hindelang Award for the most important research in criminology over the past several years.

HCI, NCBH, and gun prohibitionists in general ignore Kleck's work because, at bottom, their position is not criminological, but rather non-pragmatically "moral" and ideological. Yet that position is morally bankrupt because it can only be urged upon the American people by active and consistent deceit. Consider what I call The Parable of the Fox, the Rabbit, and the Porcupine: While our society is ravaged by foxes, HCI, NCBH, and their allies urge us to disarm and cower in our holes like rabbits. In contrast, gun owners imitate the porcupine. But HCI, NCBH, and their allies obscure the truth by pointing to the slain rabbits and shrieking, "It's the porcupines' fault! The porcupines are eating the rabbits!"

Note: Readers wishing more detailed verification for the facts cited above can refer to Kates' "Bigotry, Symbolism, and Ideology in the Battle Over Gun Control," 1992 *Public Interest Law Journal* 31; also his "The Value of Civilian Arms Possession as Deterrent to Crime or Defense Against Crime," 18 *American Journal of Criminal Law* 113 (1991); also his "Handgun Banning in Light of the Prohibition Experience" in *Firearms and Violence* 1984 (Kates is editor); my own interview with Gary Kleck, later in this book; and other sources referenced throughout or recommended at the end of this book — **JNS**

Preface

"Buy a gun. Learn to use it safely and appropriately. Carry it with you at all times. Be prepared to defend yourself, your loved ones, and your neighborhoods,"

—J. Neil Schulman on ABC TV *World News Tonight,* May 2, 1992, during the Los Angeles Riots

Yes, I admit it: the title of this book is a bad pun.

Technically speaking, "stopping power" is a measurement of the ability of a firearm or a round used by a firearm to incapacitate an attacker.

But I also mean it as the ability of an armed citizenry to stop tyrannical power.

This book contains my writings on firearms-related topics, although it expands out from there into issues of criminology, political history, and theories of justice.

I'm not what you'd call a gun nut. When I started writing in defense of firearms, I didn't even own a gun.

I shot my father's .22 rifle in the back yard of our house in Natick, Massachusetts once or twice, got an NRA marksmanship certificate with an air rifle when I was 12 or so, and didn't shoot again for another two decades.

I only bought my first firearm, a .380 Colt Government Model semi-automatic pistol, in late summer, 1991. Since that time I've bought two more semi-auto pistols, have taken California police reserve training, and have received a license to carry a concealed firearm in California and Massachusetts. I've also become a pretty decent marksman, though not up to competition standards.

The reason I started writing about guns is that I'm interested in justice — not to mention life, liberty, and the pursuit of happiness — and I don't believe any of these things are possible if the government and criminals are well-armed and the people aren't.

In this book I'm going to try to explain two things. I hope I'm explaining them to people who have never owned, or even considered owning, a firearm.

The first thing I'm going to try to explain is why 70 million Americans — about half the adults in the United States of America — already own at least one firearm, and many Americans own a veritable arsenal of them.

The second thing I'm going to try to explain is why — despite a barrage of anti-gun propaganda by virtually the entire institutional establishment in this country — these 70 million American gun owners are morally, historically, legally, and politically justified in their choice to be armed.

That is about as far as the National Rifle Association would take you. I'm going to go farther. I'm going to give reasons why the other half of the adult population in the United States — the half who *aren't* armed — are the reason this country suffers from the epidemic of violent crime that it does.

This is not a textbook. I'm not a professional historian, nor am I a constitutional lawyer or a criminologist. I'm a novelist, screenwriter, and journalist. In other words, I'm a self-appointed pundit.

That should make me at least as qualified to write about guns as other self-appointed pundits such as Sarah Brady of Handgun Control, Inc. Aside from ideology, the emotional difference between Sarah Brady's and my view of guns is that Sarah Brady's husband was badly hurt by a gun in an assassination attempt on President Reagan, and my father, a concert violinist, saved his life from muggers several times because he was carrying a gun.

I'm not going to present you with a systematic defense of gun ownership. I'm going to give you a bunch of things I wrote over the last few years. Some were published as newspaper opinion pieces and magazine articles, and others presented as editorial replies, letters, computer bulletin-board arguments, broadsides, speeches, polemics, and proposals. Everything you're going to read in this book was written in the heat of battle, as I responded to wave after wave of anti-gun hysteria on television and radio, and in prestigious newspapers and journals that should know better.

If you don't have any interest in what a self-appointed pundit has to say on this subject, and you're looking for more systematic or academic presentations on the issues I cover in these articles, I include a recommended list for further reading in the back of the book. I'll forgive you for flipping to the back of the book, writing down some of those other titles, and putting this book back on the shelf. Just don't let the bookstore clerk catch you.

We live in an age of soundbytes. Maybe you're not in the mood to read a whole book on this subject. Okay, the next time you get into an argument about guns, here's all you need to know:

- Every 13 seconds an American gun owner uses her or his firearm in defense against a criminal. If you're only counting handguns, it's every 16 seconds.
- Women use handguns 416 times each day in defense against rapists, which is a dozen times more often than rapists use a gun in the course of a rape. Handguns are used 1145 times a day against robbers. Handguns are used 1510 times a day in defense against criminal assaults.
- A gun kept in the home for protection is 216 times as likely to be used in a defense against a criminal than it is to cause the death of an innocent victim in that household.
- The U.S. cities with the strictest gun-control laws also have higher homicide rates than U.S. cities with less gun control. Switzerland and Israel both have highly armed civilian populations, and have extremely low rates of gun-related homicides.
- Gandhi once said, "Among the many misdeeds of the British rule in India, history will look upon the Act depriving a whole nation of Arms as the blackest." (M. Gandhi, *An Autobiography or The Story of my Experiments With Truth*, Volume 2, Published 1927, M. Desai, Translator, Page 666)
- Hitler once said, "The most foolish mistake we could possibly make would be to allow the subject races to possess arms. History shows that all conquerers who have allowed their subject races to carry arms have prepared their own downfall by so doing." (*Hitler's Secret Conversations – 1941 - 1944*, Farrar, Straus and Young, 1953, Page 345)

I enjoyed quoting this to my liberal Jewish relatives right after they first saw *Schindler's List*.

And no list of soundbytes would be complete without a bumpersticker: "When guns are outlawed, only liberals *won't* have guns."

This, then, is the case for the civilian population to be better armed than the government. **— JNS**

Introduction
As American as Guns

"You know why there's a second amendment? In case the government doesn't obey the first one."

— Rush Limbaugh, August 17, 1993

Advocates of the right to keep and bear arms in the United States usually base their arguments on the Second Amendment: "A well-regulated Militia being necessary to the security of a free State, the right of the people to keep and bear Arms shall not be infringed."

But what if the Second Amendment were repealed? Would the people's right to keep and bear arms still exist?

If we do not have a basic understanding of the nature and source of rights in general, as did the Framers of the Constitution, then it is near-impossible to discuss whether the people's right to keep and bear arms exists only as a collective right, or as an individual right; and whether it would disappear if the "well-regulated militia" mentioned in that amendment is ruled to be under state jurisdiction rather than the adult civilian population at large, as it was thought to be at the time of the amendment's passage.

The answers to both questions must rest on prior examination of what constitutes rights and individual liberty to begin with.

In its most fundamental aspect, the concept of liberty is that of a society organized on the basis of universal individual rights — rights which are equally held by every individual in that society.

What do we mean by a "right"? Here's a working definition: a right is the moral authority to do something without needing prior permission from another to do it.

In Biblical times, it was assumed that only God has rights, and that He grants them only to a specific chosen few. He liberated the nation of Israel from bondage to the Egyptians by a series of plagues imposed upon the Egyptians. Was God violating the Egyptians' rights? Not according to the Biblical writers, who viewed the Egyptians as merely God's property, to do with as He will.

Later, God ordered the Israelites, under the command of Joshua, to evict everyone from Canaan, killing every man, woman, and child among them and take the land for themselves, as His exclusively authorized tenants.

The Biblical writers assumed that God had the rights of a landlord to do so, and the Canaanites had no rights to live there: only the nation of Israel, to whom God granted an exclusive, long-term lease.

Still later in Biblical accounts, the nation of Israel petitioned God to have a king, so they could be like other nations. Reluctantly, God agreed, and thus was born the concept of the divine right of kings. The king appointed by God had an exclusive moral authority to take actions in that society, answerable only to God Himself. Everyone else was under the King's authority and had no rights of their own — no rights to their own lives, property, or freedom of action. All these were owned by the king, who dispensed them to his favored few.

There were historical variations, of course. Often kings found that they needed to share power with military men in order to keep their turf — thus the birth of aristocracy. The ancient Greeks vested much authority in military leaders, and experimented with popular government without much success. Ancient Rome experimented with a republican form of government, in which certain classes of people had greater rights than others, ranging from the patricians, to the plebeians, to slaves — even women had certain rights. Later, when Rome became an empire, we find one of the oddest reversals of rights being that of the Roman Emperor's right not only to rule on earth with absolute authority over all that he conquered, but to create new gods as well.

In any event, as history progresses, there is a tendency to disperse rights among larger and larger groups of people. There were a number of forces at work to produce this. One of them was the Reformation's transfer of biblical interpretation from the Church to the individual. Another was the greater importance of trade making even kings and emperors dependent on private merchants to one extent or another. Still another was the necessity of kings requiring wide dispersal of arms to as many of their subjects as could handle them, to discourage other kings from invading.

Ideas began percolating in the English Leveller's movement in the 1640's which by the 18th century, largely due to John Locke's 1690 "Two Treatises on Government," started gaining popularity among many Englishmen, particularly those living in America: that rights are not invested by God in a single King, but exist in every single individual.

In Europe, however, the theory of rights took a different road — based on extreme egalitarianism — particularly in the French revolution. Instead of rights being seized from the king and given to the individual, it was given to new collectives of revolutionaries. Thus the idea of revolutionary communism and revolutionary socialism was born. The moral authority to act without permission was shifted from the king to the governing council or party. Because this idea granted the people a moral sense that it was proper to kill the old kings and aristocracies and grab their lands and property, it became popular — popular until it became evident to everyone that all that had happened was the transfer of power from an old aristocracy to a new one called by a different name. The new aristocracy was just as hard to overthrow as the old ones, and it is only well into the 20th century that there has been any success at it.

This history lesson has a point. No matter what the institutions are of a given society, or what names they are called, the fundamental question is whether rights in that society are universally held by all the people, or whether they are reserved to those with the political power to get their own way.

"Getting your own way" can take a number of forms.

One of them is institutional politics. This can take the form of a political party, or a political lobby, or a class of people who are well-organized enough to require those in power to take their desires into account. It can be the ability to convince politicians to grant favors — sometimes by cash payoffs, sometimes merely by a promise that you will support their next campaign for office. Sometimes it can be something as silly as being a popular actor or TV personality whom people are willing to pay attention to.

But underneath all this civilized horse-trading is the question of, when push comes to shove, who has the raw force to win the day?

Historically, the king's rights meant nothing if his soldiers wouldn't act on his orders, or if others could overthrow him by force of arms.

What is true for the rights of kings is just as true for the rights of the people. Rights are only as secure as the ability to wield sufficient force to defend them.

In a free society which recognizes the moral authority of individuals to act for their own good — to make decisions about their lives, lifestyles, and property without prior permission from a king, political party, or even their neighbors — individuals are the sovereign, the kings. Whatever compacts such sovereigns make with one another to keep from violating each other's boundaries only have the moral authority which is first held by the individuals themselves.

America is a culture historically different from any other in the history of the human race, and still largely different from any other elsewhere on this world. What has distinguished American civilization from all others is the doctrine of universal individual sovereign rights. This unique difference made the American civilization superior to any previous or foreign civilization in the known universe.

I carefully said "made" in the previous sentence rather than "makes." Reactionary forces for the last century have been working hard at eliminating those qualities that made the American civilization unique, and America is a long way on the road back into the quicksand of European and Asian barbarism from which it once freed itself.

In every previous civilization, the individual was finally the servant of the polity, whether that polity was the tribe, the religious order, or embodied in the person of a king or emperor. Even in such decentralized polities as existed in ancient Ireland or Iceland, an individual pledged fealty to a king above himself, regardless of his ability to change his mind and switch kings.

The American civilization, which was born on July 4th, 1776, utterly rejected this doctrine for the first time in human history, in its founding document, the Declaration of Independence:

"We hold these truths to be self-evident, that all men are created equal, that they are endowed by their Creator with certain unalienable Rights, that among these are Life, Liberty and the pursuit of Happiness. That to secure these rights, Governments are instituted among Men, deriving their just powers from the consent of the governed, — That whenever any Form of Government becomes destructive of these ends, it is the Right of the People to alter or to abolish it, and to institute new Government, laying its foundation on such principles and organizing its powers in such form, as to them shall seem most likely to effect their Safety and Happiness."

In an historical instant, all previous conception of the relationship between the individual and the polity was reversed. From then on, each individual held sovereignty as a birthright: not a king's claim to rule others and sit in judgment on them, but a free man's sovereignty to determine his own destiny, rule his own life, and dispose of his own property as he saw fit. For the first time in human history, a polity declared itself a nation — a single people — by an act of will rather than by an accident of geography or history or religion or language.

It is true that the structural implementation of this doctrine of universal individual sovereignty was decidedly flawed. At the outset, the implementation excluded women, Africans, and native tribes, and favored landed property owners. In practice, rights were held only by white Protestant male property owners. These were hangovers from the Old World way of doing things. But the rhetoric was universalist. The power of this rhetoric of universal rights acted as a moral goad, in the United States, first to rebellion against the King, then later to wider and wider dispersal of rights, until chattel slavery of Africans was abolished and full legal rights accorded to them; property qualifications for franchise were eliminated; and full citizenship rights were granted to women as well.

While the principles propelled the culture to progress toward closer and closer approximations of extending universal rights, reactionary forces were working to destroy the concept of sovereign rights entirely. In the twentieth century we have seen the doctrine of universalism triumph while the doctrine of individual powers is nearly extinguished.

The Constitution of the United States in 1787 was the first attempt in human history to forge a government of individual sovereigns, in which the exercise of individual powers was considered an essential check on governmental power. The Articles of Confederation before it was not: it was merely a confederation of states with varying degrees of individual versus state sovereignty. From the perspective allowed by 207 years of observation, it is clearly an imperfect attempt in that it provided no reliable institutional mechanism, short of revolution, to enforce punishment upon magistrates, legislators, and executives who usurped the people's rights and powers.

But it did preserve the option of revolution as a final means of enforcement of the people's rights and powers, and it did that in the Second Amendment to the Constitution's Bill of Rights, the Preamble of which declared the Bill of Rights' purpose: "The conventions of a number of the States having at the time of their adopting the Constitution, expressed a desire, in order to prevent misconstruction or abuse of its powers, that further declaratory and restrictive clauses should be added ..."

The "militia" referred to in the Second Amendment — supported by debates at the time and enabling legislation — was the people as a whole. It was the expectation of the Constitution's Framers that the people would train to arms and be available both for defense against foreign enemies and as a posse comitatus (Latin for "power of the county") against domestic enemies. The constitutional debates now known as the Federalist Papers, largely written by Madison and Hamilton, clearly distinguished the militia from both a standing army and "select" militias. The revolutionaries had had experience with both, courtesy of the British, and wanted the people armed and ready as a protection against them.

Today, 203 years after the Second Amendment was made part of the Constitution, the right of the people to keep and bear arms is under attack as the final barrier to the triumph of statism's conquest of America, but two centuries of that right's existence has left us a living legacy from its authors. In spite of an extreme hostility toward civilian arms from every powerful organized institution in this country, half the homes in this country still maintain a private arsenal, and two-thirds of Americans have said to Louis Harris pollsters that they have no intent of surrendering their arms, even if they are both bribed and threatened by the law.

Gun control, so-called, is a fraud perpetrated by those who are fundamentally opposed to the doctrine of universal individual sovereignty: individual liberty. Its proponents are either philosophical pacifists or statists, or both. Its stated purpose of reducing crime and violence has never succeeded in doing either, no matter how thoroughly it has been tried; as good a case can be made that it disarms only the innocent and increases violent crime overall. While the purposes for which it is proposed are dubious, its function is clearly to deinstitutionalize, once and for all, the doctrine of universal individual sovereignty in this country by depriving the people of their final means of resisting incursions upon their lives, property, and liberty: armed force.

Arms are the power of the sovereign, whether that sovereign is one man or a billion.

If the doctrine of universal individual rights is to triumph on this planet, "the last, best hope of earth" — the United States of America — must preserve the power of its people to defend the rights of its people.

Sorties into Enemy Territory: the *LA Times* Op-Eds

Southern California has only one newspaper that is widely distributed throughout the state: the *Los Angeles Times*. Its editors like to compare themselves only to *The New York Times*.

In January, 1992, when the Op-Ed page of the *Los Angeles Times* published the first of four opinion pieces of mine putting forth a defense of civilian firearms, it had probably been over a decade since the last time they had published an article with this viewpoint. The editor of the editorial pages, Thomas Plate, doesn't believe in the Second Amendment — he has referred to it in a letter to the NRA's Sacramento lobbyist as a "blip on the Constitution" — but when a subscriber pointed out to him the *Times*'s lack of balance on this subject, he felt chastened and promised the subscriber to do something about it.

The *Times* subscriber was Dafydd ab Hugh, a fellow novelist and firearms-rights activist. I had unsuccessfully submitted three articles to the *Times* at that point. When Dafydd told me of Mr. Plate's promise to him, I decided to submit again.

An incident at a Shoney's Restaurant in Alabama gave me the opportunity to update one of my articles, and I made my first sale to the *Times* Op-Ed page.

That article got me on two major Los Angeles radio talk shows, and started a friendship with the most-respected talk show host in Los Angeles, KABC's Dennis Prager. My article was the final straw that convinced Dennis to abandon his opposition to civilian arms, and to embrace a philosophy of citizen self-defense that includes both widespread gun ownership and what he sees as necessary gun regulations.

During the almost-two-years that I was selling articles to the *Times* Op-Ed page, the *Times* Editorial Page was calling for what it self-described as only modest gun-control measures.

But on Friday, October 15, 1993, only three weeks after the Second Amendment Foundation gave me their James Madison Award for my fourth *Times* Op-Ed piece, published on September 20th, the *Los Angeles Times* Editorial Page began a series of weekly half-page editorials called "Taming the Gun Monster."

In these editorials, the *Times* editors called for a national ban on handguns and any semi-automatic firearm that could be lumped into the undefined category of "assault weapons," and denied that there were any insuperable legal or constitutional barriers to doing so.

I probably didn't do my career any good when I organized a demonstration against the *Los Angeles Times* which took place the Monday morning following the first of the editorials. A dozen other firearms-rights activists and I, dressed in business suits, handed out copies of articles in front of the *Times* offices to anyone going in or out who would take one. The hand-outs included several of my articles — both from the *Times* Op-Ed page and the *Times*'s nearest rival, the conservative *Orange County Register* — and additional articles refuting the *Times* editorial contention such as a *Times* news article from May 20, 1992, titled "Assault Rifles Are Not Heavily Used in Crimes."

Thomas Plate "balanced" these editorials by running several excellent pieces by pro-firearms criminologists and Second-Amendment scholars on the Op-Ed page.

But I wasn't invited to be one of the balancers, and my one submission to the *Times* since the demonstration was rejected. I believe that the *Times*'s editor of the Op-Ed page, Bob Berger, likes my articles. I suspect his boss, Mr. Plate, has overruled him.

I can't say I blame Mr. Plate. I had bit the hand that was feeding me.

But Thomas Plate's hand was attempting to destroy the most important of the Bill of Rights.

It deserved to be bit.

—JNS

The following article appeared in the January 1, 1992 *Los Angeles Times.*

A Massacre We Didn't Hear About

This is the story you saw on the evening news:

At lunch hour on Wednesday, Oct. 16, George Jo Hennard of Belton, Tex. smashed his Ford pickup through the plate glass doors of Luby's cafeteria in Killeen, injuring some patrons immediately. While other patrons rushed toward the truck believing the driver was a heart-attack victim, Hennard calmly climbed out of his pickup, took out two 9-millimeter semi-automatic pistols, and started shooting people in the cafeteria's serving line.

Hennard continued shooting for 10 minutes, reloading five times. One of his pistols jammed repeatedly, causing him to discard it. There would have been plenty of opportunity for any of the cafeteria's customers or employees to return fire. None did because none of them were armed. Texas law forbids private citizens from carrying firearms out of their home or business. Luby's employee's manual forbids employees from carrying firearms.

Police officers were inside Luby's within minutes. But before they were able to corner Hennard in the cafeteria's restroom, where he turned his gun fatally on himself, Hennard had killed 15 women and 8 men, wounded 19 and caused at least five more to be injured attempting to flee.

The Killeen massacre was ready-made excitement for the media: a madman with a gun, lots of gruesome pictures. CBS News devoted an entire "48 Hours" Dan Rather report to it. Sarah Brady of Handgun Control Inc. capitalized on it in a nationally published column to call Congress cowardly for voting down more stringent gun laws the next day.

Now here's a story you probably didn't see:

Late at night on Tuesday, December 17, two men armed with recently-stolen pistols herded 20 customers and employees of a Shoney's restaurant in Anniston, Ala., into the walk-in refrigerator, and locked it. Continuing to hold the manager at gunpoint, the men began robbing the restaurant.

Then one of the robbers found a customer who had hidden under a table and pulled a gun on him. The customer, Thomas Glenn Terry, legally armed with a .45 semi-automatic pistol, fired five shots into that robber's chest and abdomen, killing him instantly.

The other robber, who was holding the manager at gunpoint, opened fire on Terry and grazed him. Terry returned fire, hitting the second robber several times and wounding him critically.

The robbery attempt was over. The Shoney's customers and employees were freed. No one else was hurt.

Because Terry was armed, and used his gun to stop two armed robbers who had taken a restaurant full of people hostage, there was no drawn-out crisis, no massacre, no victims' families for Dan Rather to interview. Consequently, the story hasn't received much coverage.

Among those who rely on national news media for their view of the country, the bloody image of Luby's Cafeteria is available to lend the unchallenged impression that guns in private hands serve only to kill innocent people. The picture of 20 hostages walking out of Shoney's refrigerator unharmed, because a private citizen was armed that night, is not.

As we celebrate the bicentennial of the Bill of Rights, it's worth noting that the Framers wrote the Second Amendment so the people's defense would be in our own hands, and we wouldn't have to rely on a "standing army" or "select militia" for our security. Though no police departments existed in America then, there's no historical doubt that the Framers had considered centralized public defense, and considered it not merely ineffective, but itself dangerous to public safety. Recent vigilante-type police attacks, such as the beating of Rodney King, lend credence.

Yet, it's fashionable to relegate constitutional protections to the dustbin of history. Judges sworn to defend the Constitution ignore its clear provisions, as do legislators. Virtually every major organ of society — both political parties, the media, the American

Bar Assn., the ACLU — urges them to do so.

Today's "consensus reality" asserts that private firearms play no effective role in the civic defense, and that firearms must be restricted to reduce crime. The media repeat these assertions as a catechism, and treat those who challenge them as heretics.

Yet, we have before us an experiment showing us alternative outcomes. In one case, we have a restaurant full of unarmed people who rely on the police to save them. The result is 23 innocent lives lost, and an equivalent number wounded. In the second case, we have one armed citizen on the scene and not one innocent life lost.

How can the choice our society needs to make be any clearer?

It's time to rid ourselves of the misbegotten idea that public safety can be achieved by unilateral disarmament of the honest citizen, and realize that the price of public safety is, like liberty, eternal vigilance. We can tire ourselves in futile debates on how to keep guns out of the wrong hands. Or we can decide that innocent lives deserve better than to be cut short, if only we, as a society, will take upon ourselves the civic responsibility of defending our fellow citizens, as Thomas Glenn Terry did in Alabama.

My account of Thomas Glenn Terry's actions in this article was based on an Alabama newspaper account. I later interviewed Terry for a weekly radio program I was hosting and discovered that the account was mistaken on several points.

Postal clerk Terry was finishing a late-night dinner with his wife when the robbers came in and took over the restaurant. Terry hid his .45 Colt Government Model under his sweater, not seeing any immediate opportunity to use it. Terry's wife was captured with the other customers and herded off to the cooler, where one of the robbers proceeded to collect wallets and jewelry.

Terry did not hide under a table; he had separated himself from the other customers and managed to get to a back door in the Shoney's to see if it was open so he could escape and call the police. The door was chained shut. At that point one of the robbers discovered him and when the robber drew on him, Terry pulled his own handgun from under his sweater and returned fire, incapacitating this robber, who ultimately survived. The second robber heard the exchange of gunfire and also drew on Terry; it was the gun fight between Terry and this second robber which resulted in the robber running out to the parking lot, where he died from his wounds. It was at this point that Terry told the store manager to phone the police, informing them that an armed customer was present; Terry then proceeded to the cooler and released his wife and the other customers.

Both robbers whom Terry shot had previous armed robberies on their record, and one had murdered a motel clerk just a few days earlier. A third robber escaped as soon as Terry exchanged gunfire with the first robber.

The only national media outlet to cover this incident as news, just two months after the Killeen restaurant massacre, was the *Christian Science Monitor.* **—JNS**

The following article appeared in the *Los Angeles Times* of June 8, 1992.

Joining Forces against a Common Foe

There are about 200 million guns in America in the hands of about 60 million Americans. The sale of guns nationwide following the Los Angeles riots has reached record levels, many of them to first-time buyers. Firearms training classes are filled to capacity. The National Rifle Association currently has 2.8 million members — ten times the membership of the American Civil Liberties Union — and expects to exceed 3 million by the end of 1992.

Both advocates of gun control and advocates of gun rights agree that there is an epidemic problem with the criminal use of guns in America. But every time a gun-control advocate points to the latest atrocity committed with a firearm, the gun-rights advocate will surely ask: why was there no armed citizen who could have tried to stop the criminal?

The difference between the advocate of gun control and the advocate of gun rights lies in a perception of the cause of the criminal use of a gun. Those who advocate gun control think the cause is wide and easy availability of guns. The advocates of gun rights think the cause is a legal system which leaves criminals free to prey on a public which is socially discouraged, and often legally forbidden, from using guns for personal defense.

The war over gun control is fought with news reports. Advocates of gun control have no shortage of reports that prove guns in the hands of criminals are a plague on our society. Advocates of gun rights find, however, that the use of firearms to prevent or stop a crime is often left unreported by media which are worried that reporting gun defenses will encourage irresponsible vigilantism.

The war over gun control is fought with statistics. The number of gun attacks in the United States is easy to compile: just count up the thousands of bodies in the morgues, and the hundreds of thousands of gunshot victims treated in hospitals. The number of times a gun is used for defense, however, has a built-in problem:

the use of a firearm to deter, prevent, or stop an attack is unrecorded, overwhelmingly because the defense was accomplished without pulling the trigger, and less often, because the person using the gun for self-defense was legally forbidden to be in possession of it at that time or place, and thus did not report it.

The war over gun control is fought with historical debates about the intent of the Second Amendment. Those who advocate gun control say the Second Amendment has no Supreme Court ruling which defines the Second Amendment as protecting an individual right of the citizenry to keep and bear arms for personal defense. Those who advocate gun rights say that the intent of the authors of the Second Amendment, and the Fourteenth Amendment which would apply it to the states, is indisputable, and it is a politicized Supreme Court which does not have the courage to enforce it.

It's likely that the only other issue with such polarized and deeply felt world views is abortion. Oddly, those who advocate the right of choice on abortion are often the same people advocating eliminating the right to choose firearms as a defensive option.

It's also likely that a final Supreme Court ruling on the Second Amendment would fail to end the issue. A ruling in favor of an individual rights interpretation of the Second Amendment would probably coalesce gun-control advocates into a movement to repeal the amendment. A ruling against an individual rights interpretation of the Second Amendment would alienate and radicalize the millions of Americans who believe in that right as firmly as the advocates of abortion rights believe in theirs.

As long as the advocates of gun control write laws and court rulings that abridge the right of private citizens to buy, own, and carry the firearms they feel are theirs by right to have for defensive and sporting use, gun owners will continue to be alienated and radicalized, and become more and more willing to engage in civil disobedience against such abridgements.

Advocates of gun control need to realize that passing laws that honest gun owners will not obey is a self-defeating strategy. Gun owners are not about to surrender their rights or their guns, and only the most foolish of politicians would risk the stability of the government by trying to use the force of the State to disarm the people.

If gun-control advocates do not acknowledge the right of the people to keep and bear arms for individual and civic defense before they attempt to remove guns from the hands of those who abuse them, then sensible gun laws will be out of reach, and the criminal plague of gun victimizing will continue.

Can't advocates of gun control see the advantage of recruiting gun-rights advocates to a joint cause of eliminating gun tragedies? We can all agree that guns need to be kept out of the hands of the violent criminal and the lunatic. We can agree that the solution to gun accidents is safety training. We can agree that those who own and carry firearms for protection must take responsibility for knowing how to use them safely and appropriately.

Surely, instead of fighting one another, we can join forces to fight our common enemy: the armed criminal?

The following article appeared in the *Los Angeles Times* of October 27, 1992.

Gun Fight at the 4 'n 20 Pie Shop

Here's another story you didn't see on the network news.

At midnight on Friday, September 18th, 1992, former top-ranked boxer Randy Shields was sitting at his usual table at the 4 n 20 Pie Shop in Studio City, writing a screenplay. Suddenly, two masked robbers burst in with a shotgun blast and handgun fire. Shields dropped to the floor; the robbers immediately shot at him, winging his leg. Dragging himself into the darkened back room, Shields watched as the robbers pistol-whipped a busboy to get him to open the cash register, then shot through his shoe when he couldn't do it. "Somebody's gonna die tonight!" one of the robbers yelled, then opened fire toward several customers and waitresses, ordering them to hand over their wallets.

Shields saw his opportunity to fire without endangering bystanders. He pulled out his concealed .380 Walther PPK/S pistol, which he carries licensed as a part-time private bodyguard, and opened fire on the robbers, wounding them. They ran out to the parking lot where their driver was waiting; Shields put a couple of bullets into the getaway car, then ran out of ammunition. The robbers opened fire on him again and he dived back into the restaurant. The robbers squealed out to Laurel Canyon then pulled a U-turn so they could fire a few extra rounds into the restaurant.

Aside from Randy Shields's minor leg wound, and the busboy's bruises, none of the restaurant's employees or customers were hurt. The robbers called an ambulance to treat their gunshot wounds, claiming to be victims of a drive-by shooting. But the bullets Randy Shields put into their getaway car — and a bullet hole Shields had put in a wad of money from two previous robberies they'd committed that night — were enough for police to make an arrest.

Even an advocate of restricting civilian carry of handguns would find it hard to argue against the effects of Randy Shields being armed that night.

But that advocate of handgun restriction will undoubtedly argue that this incident is mere anecdotal evidence, useless in deriving any public-policy conclusions regarding the value of issuing civilians concealed-carry weapons permits to deter crime. Surely, carrying a gun is no guarantee that others will be as brave and clear-headed as Randy Shields when faced with armed criminals. Further, since no criminal justice agency in the United States compiles statistics on anti-crime gun use by civilians, the gun-restrictionist's objection is difficult to answer.

Difficult but not impossible. Criminologist Gary Kleck, professor at Florida State University, has compiled survey data that American civilians successfully use handguns for defense about 645,000 times each year, without wounding anyone 99% of the time. A 1986 National Institute of Justice survey of 2,000 felons in ten state prisons documents that 34% of felons have been "scared off, shot at, wounded or captured by an armed victim," and 57% agreed that "Most criminals are more worried about meeting an armed victim than they are about running into the police." Professor Hans Toch of the State University of New York School of Criminology at Albany concludes, "[F]indings suggest that high saturations of guns ... inhibit illegal aggression."

But even granting possible deterrence against crime, doesn't the danger of even licensed, concealed firearms in the hands of civilians outweigh the benefits?

No. To begin with, criminologist Don Kates of the Pacific Research Institute said, "Instances of citizens using guns with excessive force or against innocent persons they have misidentified as criminals are negligible."

And while the California Department of Justice doesn't compile records on firearms licenses revocations, a few states do. After rigorous tracking, the Florida Department of State reports that of 129,049 licenses issued since October 1, 1987, under that state's mandatory license issuance to all qualified applicants, it has revoked 222 licenses (1 in 581)) but only 115 for a crime (1 in 1122) and only 17 licenses have had to be revoked for a crime utilizing a firearm: 1 in 7591. Meanwhile, according to FBI crime reports, the homicide rate in Florida dropped 20% between 1986 and 1991, while the U.S. homicide rate increased 14% during that same period.

Indiana, which has 220,623 licenses outstanding, doesn't break down its reasons for revoking licenses, and reports 349 licenses revoked between 1989 and 1991 (1 in 632), with most revocations being one year for unnecessarily brandishing a firearm.

By comparison, California Department of Motor Vehicles reports a rate of 1 in 368 drivers' licenses revoked for all causes in 1991 alone — a higher rate of revocation than Florida or Indiana has for firearms licenses.

Any sensible public policy demands that hysteria and demagoguery not bury the facts. Firearms carried by responsible, competent civilians present no danger to the public, and both survey data and dramatic examples such as Randy Shields provide us good reason to believe that they save lives.

If anyone wants more proof than that, then they will have to demand that the criminal justice agencies that track the evil that people do with firearms also track the good that they do as well.

The following article appeared in the *Los Angeles Times* of September, 20, 1993.

If Gun Laws Work, Why Are We Afraid?

It's almost funny that under existing laws a successful merchant can't be sure of selling anything legally. If you sell a product for less than your competitors, that's "cutthroat competition" or "dumping." If you sell at the same price, it's "price-fixing." And if you sell for more, that's evidence of "monopolistic advantage."

In olden days, this was called a Mug's Game.

The pundits who promote gun control, though, have stacked the cards even colder.

If you buy a handgun which is inexpensive, small, and low-caliber, it's a Saturday Night Special. If you want a handgun which is more expensive, larger, and higher caliber, it's "the weapon-of-choice of drug dealers." Whatever qualities a particular handgun has, gun-controllers don't want it allowed. Heads they win, tails you lose.

If a rifle is magazine-fed and semi-automatic, it's a deadly "assault weapon." If a rifle is bolt-action, it's a "sniper rifle." Again, all possibilities are covered.

A favorite media practice is to focus only on the bad things firearms are used for. If a handgun is used for murder or mayhem, it's headline news. If that same handgun is used by a restaurant patron to stop a takeover robbery, the story is buried.

Another gun-controller's game is to tell us how successful the last gun-control law they got passed is, while simultaneously telling us how "gun violence" is unchecked by current laws.

Examples are California's 15-day waiting period on firearms, and the Roberti-Roos Assault Weapons Act. If these laws had reduced violent crime, why would we need new gun-control laws? Since crime continues upward, why should we believe gun-controllers when they say we need more of the same?

Here's another. New York City has strict gun-control laws and a high rate of violent crime; Virginia less-strict gun laws and a lot less violent crime. Supposedly, criminals were buying guns in Virginia (using fake Virginia ID's) and smuggling them into New York for black-market sales. Political pressure was placed on Virginia to limit gun purchases to one a month; the law passed over National Rifle Assn. protests that it impacted only honest gun owners, because criminals could obtain black-market ID's anyway.

So if New York's laws are so unsuccessful that guns can be smuggled in anyway, what good is New York's gun control? And if Virginia, with easily-obtainable firearms, has less crime than does New York, why didn't New York take a lesson from Virginia and loosen its gun laws instead? Do criminals know something about attacking armed people that New York politicians don't?

But my favorite trick is the one which says that the reason gun owners keep guns around is that they're paranoid and fearful.

We're shown videotape of Rodney King being excessively beaten by Los Angeles police. We read Ventura County Prosecutor Michael Bradbury's report about how even rich, white Donald Scott was killed by a Los Angeles County Sheriff during a drug raid trumped up in an attempt to steal Scott's Malibu estate using the asset forfeiture laws. We see an acquittal of Randy Weaver for defending himself from the U.S. marshals who killed his wife and son, and see videotape of ATF agents opening fire on David Koresh's followers in Waco, Texas, with no return fire from the Branch Davidians visible. Then we're told gun owners are paranoid for not wanting to rely on tainted police authorities for protection against criminals.

Day after day, the news media tell us every time a gun is used in a murder, a carjacking, an ATM robbery, or a drive-by shooting, and we're told it's unreasonably fearful to think we're in enough danger that we need to arm ourselves.

LA Assistant City Attorney Byron Boeckman, in discussing LAPD's new policy of issuing concealed-carry-weapons licenses for the first time since 1974, tells us that the danger of violence to Los Angeles residents is exaggerated.

Well, which is it? Either America today is so peaceful, well-ordered, and efficiently protected by its police that there is no "gun violence" in the first place, and the rationale for gun control is based on a non-existent problem, or we are surrounded by heavily-armed psychopaths terrorizing our society, in which case being better armed than the criminals is the rational response of decent citizens who wish to preserve their civilization; and our laws should encourage, rather than discourage, civilians to train in, keep, and carry firearms.

Gun-control advocates constantly contradict themselves because gun control has never been shown as an effective solution for reducing violence. And in the absence of a provable case, all they have left in their stage magician's trunk is old, worn-out tricks.

Which gun owners know better than to fall for.

Some Practical Arguments for an Armed Civilian Population

Most of the time you hear gun owners defending their guns, they're talking about "the right to keep and bear arms." That is, of course, an important argument to make, but it's not the one that will appeal to those among us who are swayed only by arguments regarding social utility.

I've never believed there is any great divide between good theoretical arguments and good practical ones. If something is correct in theory, it should necessitate practical consequences. If something works in practice, it should be generalizable into a theory. How can something be moral if it isn't practical? How can it be practical if it produces destruction?

I'll focus more on political theory later in this book. But for now, here are some empirical arguments in favor of keeping and bearing arms. **— JNS**

A Time to Kill

Maybe you haven't noticed it, but the Star-Spangled Banner has been replaced by the dove of peace. Attorney General Janet Reno and Senator Paul Simon condemn the portrayal of violence on television. Surgeon General Joycelyn Elders wants to ban toy guns. The *Los Angeles Times* wants to ban real guns. The latest Clint Eastwood movie, *A Perfect World*, is not Dirty Harry ending the career of some maniac, but a buddy movie about a fatherless boy and the sympathetic psychopath who takes him under his wing. The federal Center for Disease Control, backed by the American Medical Association, has declared violence to be a national health crisis.

There is without doubt a national crisis when automatic-teller-machine hold-ups, carjackings, and serial rapes are commonplace; when our celebrities are a woman who cuts off her husband's penis and the husband who sells T-shirts commemorating it; when youth gangs don't even have the courage to rumble — they just do drive-by shootings.

But it's not a national health crisis. It's a national moral crisis.

The King James Bible tells us that the Sixth Commandment is, "Thou shalt not kill." Any biblical scholar will tell you that's a mistranslation from the original Hebrew. It should instead read, "Thou shalt not *murder*."

In Ecclesiastes Chapter 3, Verse 3, the Bible also tells us that there *is* a time to kill.

We have lost our ability to distinguish between justified and unjustified violence. We no longer feel certain about the difference between good guys and bad guys. We no longer know when it's time to kill, or whom.

A time to kill would have been when Patrick Purdy walked into a schoolyard in Stockton, California and started shooting at children. But we place our children in the care of defenseless teachers, so there was no one able to kill Patrick Purdy in time.

A time to kill would have been when George Hennard walked into a Luby's cafeteria in Killeen, Texas and began shooting diners. But Texans may no longer legally carry six-shooters on their hips, so there was no one able to kill Hennard in time.

A time to kill would have been when Gian Luigi Ferri walked into a San Francisco law office and began shooting at attorneys, secretaries, and clients. But not one lawyer kept a Smith & Wesson in her desk, so there was no one able to kill Ferri in time.

A time to kill would have been when Colin A. Ferguson began shooting passengers on the Long Island Railroad. There were men on the train with the courage to tackle and capture Ferguson even though they were unarmed — but not before Ferguson had shot dozens of people. If only one person had been armed, innocent people might be alive and Ferguson dead.

A recent article in *The Public Interest* by Jeffrey Snyder — lauded by George Will in *Newsweek* — suggests that we have become "a nation of cowards" in our willingness to submit peaceably to crime and rely on police to protect us. But is it courage that we lack, or moral certainty?

We have become a nation of deer facing oncoming headlights, paralyzed with moral ambiguity. Like Clint Eastwood's stymied Texas Ranger in *A Perfect World*, we declare, "I don't know a damn thing anymore."

The currently fashionable condemnation of violence is based on morally untenable premises, either pacifistic or statist. We civilians are told to be peaceable either because violence does not solve problems, or because only people in uniforms are entitled to use violence.

Certainly violence does not solve all problems. But there is one sort of problem that violence is indispensable to solve: stopping violent evildoers.

Certainly we don't want to live in a nation of lynch mobs. There is a clear distinction between self-defense and proactive law enforcement. But with the examples of the ATF siege in Waco, the unindicted murder of Randy Weaver's wife and son by federal agents, and the looming threat of well-armed police enforcing civilian gun bans, isn't Janet Reno's condemnation of violence more than a little hypocritical?

Violence is not of itself always wrong. Sometimes committing an act of violence is a right and a moral necessity. When violence is righteous, it is glorious. If we do not understand this and ready ourselves with arms and training for the rightful violence that is necessary to defend the innocent, then the random violence eating away at our nation's substance is just what we have coming to us.

140,000 LA County Gun Owners Have Used Firearms Defensively

In new data on defensive use of firearms by private citizens, a *Los Angeles Times* poll published Sunday, May 17, 1992, indicates that 9% of Southern California gun owners have used a firearm in personal self-defense, resulting in an approximation of between 135,000 to 145,000 gun owners who have personally defended themselves with a gun in Los Angeles County alone. The poll question excluded defensive use of a weapon in the military or while on the job.

Out of those who say they have used a gun in self-defense, only 2% say they actually fired the gun, signifying that the deterrence value of the firearm without being fired was approximately 98%.

The poll, conducted by telephone between April 9-15, 1992, interviewed 2,619 Southern Californians 18 or older — 878 gun owners and 1,741 non-gun-owners, and the *Times'* pollsters, using demographic weighting, estimate the number of gun owners in Southern California as approximately 24% of the population. Because of the size of the sample, the *Times'* pollsters give a 4% margin of error in their results.

The 1990 U.S. Census gives the 18-and-older population of Los Angeles County as 6,537,054.

The *Times'* poll data is particularly useful, inasmuch as it can be directly correlated with other statistical information on crime drawn from the polling.

While 9% of Southern California gun owners report use of their weapon in defense against crime, 13% of Southern Californians report that a member of their household has been a victim of a violent crime or act of violence in the last two years, with 13% also reporting having personally witnessed a crime or act of violence.

This data, when correlated, indicates that among the subset of the population that owns a firearm, the firearm stands a significant chance of preventing a crime or act of violence when it occurs. Just how high the deterrence effect is can not be correlated exactly because the *Times*' poll did not specify that the defense in question needed to be within the last two years, as the crime or act of violence in question was.

Further, the highest rates of victimization are among African-Americans, at 20%, and Latinos, at 17%, while 11% of Anglos and 9% of Asian Americans are victimized. With the exception of the Asian-American community, this victimization rate approximates an inverse proportion to the rate of firearms ownership in each community, with 43% of Anglos having at least one gun in their home or garage, 33% of African-Americans, and 25% of Latinos. The anomaly is the Asian-American community which has a 19% rate of firearms ownership and a relatively low rate of crime and violence.

The *Times*' poll data tends to reinforce the findings of the study by Gary Kleck, Ph.D., a criminologist from the School of Criminology and Criminal Justice, Florida State University, Tallahassee, Florida, which he summarized at the August 29 through September 1, 1991, Annual Meeting of the American Political Science Association, as follows:

"Each year," Kleck stated, "about 1500–2800 criminals are lawfully killed by gun-wielding American civilians in justifiable or excusable homicides, far more than are killed by police officers. There are perhaps 600,000 –1 million defensive uses of guns each year... People who use guns for self-protection in robberies and assaults are less likely to have the crime completed against them (in a robbery, this means losing their property), and, contrary to widespread belief, are less likely to be injured, compared to either victims who use other forms of resistance or to victims who do nothing to resist. (Criminals take the gun away from the victim in less than 1% of these incidents.) The evidence does not support the idea that nonresistance is safer than resisting with a gun."

The *Los Angeles Times* poll compiled other interesting data relating to firearms ownership:

- While 75% of all homicides in Los Angeles County are gun-related, 33% of homicides in Los Angeles County are gang-related — either the shooter or the victim is gang-member.
- The chances of being shot in Los Angeles county: 1/1000 (.1%) — (same odds as getting lung cancer).
- Over the last five years, California Department of Justice records show 466,543 handguns sold in Los Angeles County.
- The vast majority of firearms in Los Angeles are owned by ordinary citizens rather than criminals or gang-members.
- 29% of Southern California homes have guns compared to 43% nationally, however most Southern Californians have guns for self-protection rather than sporting use, compared to opposite elsewhere.
- Most Southern California gun owners possess more than one gun. 70% own at least one handgun. 70% own a shotgun or rifle.
- Most firearms owners in Southern California have received formal firearms training, and firearms classes are booming, especially for women.
- Even though it is a misdemeanor, 25% of gun owners admit to sometimes carrying a loaded gun either in their car or on their person. 20% of gun owners admit to carrying a loaded gun in their car, and 11% admit to carrying a concealed loaded gun on their person.
- 12-1/2% of Southern California residents are planning to buy a gun in 1992 — 75% for self protection. In a follow-up survey conducted in Los Angeles after the riots, 5% of LA City residents said they will buy a gun as a result of the riots.

Do Guns Do More Harm or More Good?

One of the greatest problems in determining any sort of social policy is comparing that which is seen, and therefore directly quantifiable, to those effects which are unseen, and therefore must be inferred by other means.

Such is the problem in comparing the number of people killed or wounded by firearms, with the number of times a gun is used to prevent or stop an act of violence.

The number of gun homicides are more or less tracked. Minus those bodies which are encased in cement overshoes and end up at the bottom or the East River or in the foundation of a new office building, most people who die from gunfire end up in a morgue where the homicide is statistically recorded.

Likewise, for non-fatal gunshots, most are treated at hospital emergency rooms which are legally required to report them to police agencies. Often, as the *LA Times* has reported is the case in Los Angeles, there is no further investigation; nonetheless, the figures can be collected and entered into databases.

The *Los Angeles Times* reported on Sunday, May 17, 1992, that in Los Angeles County in 1991 there were 1554 firearm-related homicides (no breakdown given between wrongful homicides and those which are either excusable by reason of self-defense or justifiable in the attempt to prevent or stop a violent attack), 489 gun-related suicides, and 32 accidental shooting deaths. Additionally, 8050 firearms wounds were treated in local hospitals in 1991.

Minus the uncounted "excusable" and "justifiable" shootings, fatal or not, this gives us a more-or-less quantifiable database of undesirable shootings.

Suicides we can eliminate from our analysis of gun-effects immediately. *The American Journal of Psychiatry* from March,

1990 reported in a study by Rich, Young, Fowler, Wagner, and Black that all gun-suicides which were statistically reduced by Canada's handgun ban of 1976 were substituted 100% by suicides using other methods. Therefore, eliminating firearms does not eliminate suicide: it merely shifts the suicide to other causes, and no rational public policy can conclude that the existence or availability of firearms is a causative factor.

Since the quantity of gun suicides to gun homicides is approximately 31%, it's fair to assume that some significant percentage in non-fatal shootings is likewise an incomplete suicide rather than an incomplete homicide. It would be tempting to assume that 31% of the 8050 gunshot wounds are botched suicides, but this strikes me as counterintuitive: I suspect that most people who choose a firearm for suicide aim at a vital target, and are more-or-less successful at achieving fatality.

This suspicion gains weight from the *Time Magazine* of July 17, 1989, which says that, "But one study has found that when people use a gun, the rate of death is 92%. Says Tulane University sociologist James Wright: 'Everyone knows that if you put a loaded .38 in your ear and pull the trigger, you won't survive.'"

Therefore, for the purpose of this statistical exercise, I will assume that 8% of non-fatal shootings are incomplete suicides rather than incomplete homicides.

As far as quantifying excusable or justifiable shootings and firearm homicides, we are on less certain ground. The FBI Unified Crime Reports for 1990 reported only 215 homicides out of 11,700 to be justifiable. However, the FBI classifies a homicide as justifiable only if it is so ruled in the first police report; if a homicide is later ruled by investigation or judicial procedure to be excusable or justifiable, those figures are not figured in by the FBI's statistical methods.

We must therefore go to inferential methods. The study by criminologist Gary Kleck, Ph.D., of Florida State University estimates that private citizens account for between 1500 and 2800 excusable and justifiable homicides in a year. If we use Kleck's figure, we get a ratio of criminal homicides to excusable or justifiable homicides between 7.8: 1 (87.2% criminal to 12.8% excusable or justifiable) and 4.2: 1 (76.2% criminal to 23.8% excusable or justifiable) a year. This would quantify the Los Angeles County homicide figures so that of the 1554 firearm-related homicides reported in 1991, between 198 and 369 were likely excusable by reason of self-defense, or justifiable in the prevention or stopping of a criminal attack.

It is reasonable to assume that a similar ratio would apply to non-fatal shootings, which would mean that of the 8050 gunshot victims treated at Los Angeles hospitals in 1991, between 1030 and 1916 were persons who had been excusably or justifiably shot while they were in the process of committing a crime or other violent attack.

The real problem of comparing criminal use of firearms to defensive use of firearms only really begins at this point, though, because of the unseen deterrence effect of firearms which prevent a criminal attack without even having been fired. According to a *Los Angeles Times* Poll conducted April 9-15, 1992 of 2619 Southern Californians (878 gun owners and 1741 non-owners), "9% of firearms owners in Southern California say they have used their guns to thwart burglaries, car thefts, or other crimes." The *Times*' poll question specifically excluded gun defenses in the military or while on the job, which leaves a sizable number of gun defenses in convenience stores, pawnshops, jewelers, banks, etc., uncounted in this data. More problematic for the purposes of comparison is that the *Times*' Poll did not ask how many times the poll respondent had used a firearm in self-defense, or set a time frame within which this defensive act had occurred.

Out of this 9%, in the *LA Times*' poll, only 2% report having fired their weapon in the course of the defense, leaving 98% claiming successful defenses without the necessity of their gun being fired. It would be tempting at this point to assume that we have quantified a 98% passive deterrence rate when a firearm is available for defense, but we run into a problem which makes this figure questionable.

Time Magazine, in its January 29, 1990 issue, published the results of a telephone poll of 605 gun owners for *Time*/CNN made from December 15-22, 1989 by Yankelovich Clancy Shulman.

In response to the poll question, "Have you ever fired your gun?" 9% of those polled by Yankelovich Clancy Shulman stated that they had done so for "self-protection," while 7% stated they had fired their gun "to scare someone."

Either the *LA Times*'s sample of gun owners is much more effective at scaring someone away without having to fire their guns than the Yankelovich Clancy Shulman sample — which seems unlikely — or Los Angeles gun owners are afraid to tell of pulling the trigger for fear of later repercussions, or the form of the *LA Times*'s question is creating some ambiguity.

Further, accepting the *LA Times* rate of deterrence without trigger-pulls leads to the absurdity of an estimated number of justifiable or excusable homicides which is greater than the estimated number of times a trigger *is* pulled to stop or end a criminal attack.

We will therefore leave open the question regarding the rate of passive versus active deterrence.

Both the *Time*/CNN poll and the *LA Times'* poll data, however, tend to confirm data from a nationwide poll conducted by Peter Hart Research Associates, Inc., for the National Alliance Against Violence, which found that 4% of households reported the use of a handgun in self-defense within the 5 years preceding the survey (including cases when the handgun was only displayed, not fired). The Hart study did not count defenses with shotguns or rifles. Including shotguns and rifles, one can easily, with no fear of overestimation (and a strong suspicion of underestimation), raise the gun-defense figure by 20% to 5% within the preceding five years, which gives us a horseback estimate of 1% of households having a member who uses a firearm — handgun, shotgun, or rifle — for defensive purposes in any given year.

We now have a reasonable percentage for firearm defenses that we can quantify with reference to census, police, and poll data, and compare to known figures for criminal homicides and wrongful non-fatal shootings.

For Los Angeles County in 1991

Firearms homicides: 1554

Number of homicide victims estimated to be excusable or justifiable: 198-369

Mean estimated excusable or justifiable homicides in 1991: 283

Mean estimated wrongful homicides for 1991: 1271

Number of non-fatal gunshot wounds treated in 1991: 8050

Number of gunshot–wound victims estimated to be attempted suicides: 645

Number of gunshot–wound victims estimated to be excusable or justifiable shooting: 1030-1916

Mean number of estimated excusable or justifiable shootings: 1473

Estimated number of non-fatal gunshot victims caused by wrongful attack in Los Angeles in 1991: 5772

Number of wrongful gunshot victims (fatal and nonfatal) in Los Angeles in 1991: 7043

1990 U.S. Census figures for 18-and-older population of Los Angeles County: 6,537,054

Percentage of 18-and-older persons who own a firearm in Los Angeles County according to *LA Times*: 24%

24% of 6,537,054 = 1,568,893 gun owners in Los Angeles County

1% of Los Angeles County gun owners who are estimated to use a firearm for self defense in a year: 15,689

[Percentage of gun owners whose firearm defense is passive: 98% — *LA Times*]

[Estimated number of Los Angeles County firearm-defenders in a year who use a gun for defense without the gun having to be fired: 15,375 — derived from *LA Times* poll data]

[Estimated number of Los Angeles County firearm-defenders in a year who use a gun for defense with the gun having to be fired: 314 — derived from *LA Times* poll data]

Comparison of wrongful gunshot victims in Los Angeles County to firearm defenders: 7043 to 15,689 or 1: 2.2

Conclusion: **For every wrongful gunshot victim in Los Angeles County, it is reasonably estimated that two persons are able to use a firearm to deter a violent crime or attack.**

It must also be noted that the percentage of firearms ownership in Los Angeles is considerably lower than the nation as a whole: 24% as compared to 43% nationally. Whatever defensive uses we note in Los Angeles would therefore be considerably amplified elsewhere.

What is clear is that the unseen and unrecorded effect that firearms play in protecting the public from armed criminals is extremely likely to be equal to or greater than the number of victims created by firearms in the hands of criminals.

This statistically significant defensive and deterrent effect of firearms in the hands of private citizens must be given a wider hearing in public policy debate on the role of firearms in society.

The following article appeared in the *Orange County Register* on Sunday, September 19, 1993, and was reprinted in the October 1, 1993 *Gun Week*.

Q & A on Gun Defenses

Gary Kleck, Ph.D. is a professor in the School of Criminology and Criminal Justice at Florida State University in Tallahassee and author of *Point Blank: Guns and Violence in America* (Aldine de Gruyter, 1991), a book widely cited in the national gun-control debate. In an exclusive interview, Dr. Kleck revealed some preliminary results of the National Self-Defense Survey which he and his colleague Dr. Marc Gertz conducted in Spring, 1993. Though he stresses that the results of the survey are preliminary and subject to future revision, Kleck is satisfied that the survey's results confirm his analysis of previous surveys which show that American civilians commonly use their privately-owned firearms to defend themselves against criminal attacks, and that such defensive uses significantly outnumber the criminal uses of firearms in America.

The new survey, conducted by random telephone sampling of 4,978 households in all the states except Alaska and Hawaii, yield results indicating that American civilians use their firearms as often as 2.5 million times every year defending against a confrontation with a criminal, and that handguns alone account for up to 1.9 million defenses per year. Previous surveys, in Kleck's analysis, had underrepresented the extent of private firearms defenses because the questions asked failed to account for the possibility that a particular respondent might have had to use his or her firearm more than once.

Dr. Kleck will first present his survey results at an upcoming meeting of the American Society of Criminology, but he agreed to discuss his preliminary analysis, even though it is uncustomary to do so in advance of complete peer review, because of the great extent which his earlier work is being quoted in public debates.

[Note: Gary Kleck updates this interview in the afterword to this edition. — **JNS, 1999**]

The interview was conducted September 14-17, 1993.

Readers may be interested to know that Kleck is a member of the ACLU, Amnesty International USA, and Common Cause, among other politically liberal organizations. He is also a lifelong registered Democrat. He is not and has never been a member of or contributor to the NRA, Handgun Control Inc., or any other advocacy group on either side of the gun-control issue, nor has he received funding for research from any such organization.

Schulman: Dr. Kleck, can you tell me generally what was discovered in your recent survey that wasn't previously known?

Kleck: Well, the survey mostly generated results pretty consistent with those of a dozen previous surveys which generally indicates that defensive use of guns is pretty common and probably more common than criminal uses of guns. This survey went beyond previous ones in that it provided detail about how often people who had used a gun had done so. We asked people was the gun used defensively in the past five years and if so how many times did that happen and we asked details about what exactly happened. We nailed down that each use being reported was a bona fide defensive use against a human being in connection with a crime where there was an actual confrontation between victim and offender. Previous surveys were a little hazy on the details of exactly what was being reported as a defensive gun use. It wasn't, for example, clear that the respondents weren't reporting investigating a suspicious noise in their back yard with a gun where there was, in fact, nobody there. Our results ended up indicating, depending on which figures you prefer to use, anywhere from 800,000 on up to 2.4, 2.5 million defensive uses of guns against human beings — not against animals — by civilians each year.

Schulman: Okay. Let's see if we can pin down some of these figures. I understand you asked questions having to do with just the previous one year. Is that correct?

Kleck: That's correct. We asked both for recollections about the preceding five years and for just what happened in the previous one year, the idea being that people would be able to remember more completely what had happened just in the past year.

Schulman: And your figures reflect this?

Kleck: Yes. The estimates are considerably higher if they're based on people's presumably more-complete recollection of just what happened in the previous year.

Schulman: Okay. So you've given us the definition of what a "defense" is. It has to be an actual confrontation against a human being attempting a crime? Is that correct?

Kleck: Correct.

Schulman: And it excludes all police, security guards, and military personnel?

Kleck: That's correct.

Schulman: Okay. Let's ask the "one year" question since you say that's based on better recollections. In the last year how many people who responded to the questionnaire said that they had used a firearm to defend themselves against an actual confrontation from a human being attempting a crime?

Kleck: Well, as a percentage it's 1.33 percent of the respondents. When you extrapolate that to the general population, it works out to be 2.4 million defensive uses of guns of some kind — not just handguns but any kind of a gun — within that previous year, which would have been roughly from Spring of 1992 through Spring of 1993.

Schulman: And if you focus solely on handguns?

Kleck: It's about 1.9 million, based on personal, individual recollections.

Schulman: And what percentage of the respondents is that? Just handguns?

Kleck: That would be 1.03 percent.

Schulman: How many respondents did you have total?

Kleck: We had a total of 4,978 completed interviews, that is, where we had a response on the key question of whether or not there had been a defensive gun use.

Schulman: So roughly 50 people out of 5000 responded that in the last year they had had to use their firearms in an actual confrontation against a human being attempting a crime?

Kleck: Handguns, yes.

Schulman: Had used a handgun. And slightly more than that had used any gun.

Kleck: Right.

Schulman: So that would be maybe 55, 56 people?

Kleck: Something like that, yeah.

Schulman: Okay. I can just hear critics saying that 50 or 55 people responding that they used their gun and you're projecting it out to figures of around 2 million, 2-1/2 million gun defenses. Why is that statistically valid?

Kleck: Well, that's one reason why we also had a five-year recollection period. We get a much larger raw number of people saying, "Yes, I had a defensive use." It doesn't work out to be as many per year because people are presumably not remembering as completely, but the raw numbers of people who remember some kind of defensive use over the previous five years, that worked out to be on the order of 200 sample cases. So it's really a small raw number only if you limit your attention to those who are reporting an incident just in the previous year. Statistically, it's strictly the raw numbers that are relevant to the issue.

Schulman: So if between 1 percent to 1-1/3 percent of your respondents are saying that they defended themselves with a gun, how does this compare, for example, to the number of people who would respond that they had suffered from a crime during that period?

Kleck: I really couldn't say. We didn't ask that and I don't think there are really any comparable figures. You could look at the National Crime Surveys for relatively recent years and I guess you could take the share of the population that had been the victims of some kind of violent crime because most of these apparently are responses to violent crimes. Ummm, let's see. The latest year for which I have any data, 1991, would be about 9 percent of the population had suffered a personal crime — that's a crime with personal contact. And so, to say that 1 percent of the population had defended themselves with a handgun is obviously still well within what you would expect based on the share of the population that had suffered a personal crime of some kind. Plus a number of these defensive uses were against burglars, which isn't considered a personal crime according to the National Crime Survey. But you can add in maybe another 5 percent who'd been a victim of a household burglary.

Schulman: Let's break down some of these gun defenses if we can. How many are against armed robbers? How many are against burglars? How many are against people committing a rape or an assault?

Kleck: About 8 percent of the defensive uses involved a sexual crime such as an attempted sexual assault. About 29 percent involved some sort of assault other than sexual assault. Thirty-three percent involved a burglary or some other theft at home. Twenty-two percent involved robbery. Sixteen percent involved trespassing. Note that some incidents could involve more than one crime.

Schulman: Do you have a breakdown of how many occurred on somebody's property and how many occurred, let's say, off somebody's property where somebody would have had to have been carrying a gun with them on their person or in their car?

Kleck: Yes. We asked where the incident took place. Seventy-two percent took place in or near the home, where the gun wouldn't have to be "carried" in a legal sense. And then some of the remainder, maybe another 4 percent, occurred in a friend's home where that might not necessarily involve carrying. Also, some of these incidents may have occurred in a vehicle in a parking lot and that's another 4 percent or so. So some of those incidents may have involved a less-regulated kind of carrying. In many states, for example, it doesn't require a license to carry a gun in your vehicle so I'd say that the share that involved carrying in a legal sense is probably less than a quarter of the incidents. I won't commit myself to anything more than that because we don't have the specifics of whether or not some of these away-from-home incidents occurred while a person was in a car.

Schulman: All right. Well, does that mean that approximately a half million times a year somebody carrying a gun away from home uses it to defend himself or herself?

Kleck: That's what it would imply, yes.

Schulman: All right. As many as one-half million times every year somebody carrying a gun away from home defends himself or herself.

Kleck: Yes, about that. It could be as high as that. I have many different estimates and some of the estimates are deliberately more conservative in that they exclude from our sample any cases where it was not absolutely clear that there was a genuine defensive gun use being reported.

Schulman: Were any of these gun uses done by anyone under the age of 21 or under the age of 18?

Kleck: Well we don't have any coverage of persons under the age of 18. Like most national surveys we cover only adults age 18 and up.

Schulman: Did you have any between the ages of 18 and 21?

Kleck: I haven't analyzed the cross tabulation of age with defensive gun use so I couldn't say at this point.

Schulman: Okay. Was this survey representative just of Florida or is it representative of the entire United States?

Kleck: It's representative of the lower 48 states.

Schulman: And that means that there was calling throughout all the different states?

Kleck: Yes, except Alaska and Hawaii, and that's also standard practice for national surveys; because of the expense they usually aren't contacted.

Schulman: How do these surveys make their choices, for example, between high-crime urban areas and less-crime rural areas?

Kleck: Well, there isn't a choice made in that sense. It's a telephone survey and the telephone numbers are randomly chosen by computer so that it works out that every residential telephone number in the lower 48 states had an equal chance of being picked, except that we deliberately oversampled from the South and the West and then adjusted after the fact for that overrepresentation. It results in no biasing. The results are representative of the entire United States, but it yields a larger number of sample cases of defensive gun uses. They are, however, weighted back down so that they properly represent the correct percent of the population that's had a defensive gun use.

Schulman: Why is it that the results of your survey are so counterintuitive compared to police experience?

Kleck: For starters, there are substantial reasons for people not to report defensive gun uses to the police or, for that matter, even to interviewers working for researchers like me — the reason simply being that a lot of the times people either don't know whether their defensive act was legal or even if they think that was legal, they're not sure that possessing a gun at that particular place and time was legal. They may have a gun that's supposed to be registered and it's not or maybe it's totally legally owned but they're not supposed to be walking around on the streets with it.

Schulman: Did your survey ask the question of whether people carrying guns had licenses to do so?

Kleck:: No, we did not. We thought that would be way too sensitive a question to ask people.

Schulman: Okay. Let's talk about how the guns were actually used in order to accomplish the defense. How many people, for example, had to merely show the gun, as opposed to how many had to fire a warning shot, as to how many actually had to attempt to shoot or shoot their attacker?

Kleck: We got all of the details about everything that people could have done with a gun from as mild an action as merely verbally referring to the gun on up to actually shooting somebody.

Schulman: Could you give me the percentages?

Kleck: Yes. You have to keep in mind that it's quite possible for people to have done more than one of these things since they could obviously both verbally refer to the gun and point it at somebody or even shoot it.

Schulman: Okay.

Kleck: Fifty-four percent of the defensive gun uses involved somebody verbally referring to the gun. Forty-seven percent involved the gun being pointed at the criminal. Twenty-two percent involved the gun being fired. Fourteen percent involved the gun being fired at somebody, meaning it wasn't just a warning shot; the defender was trying to shoot the criminal. Whether they succeeded or not is another matter but they were trying to shoot a criminal. And then in 8 percent they actually did wound or kill the offender.

Schulman: In 8 percent, wounded or killed. You don't have it broken down beyond that?

Kleck: Wound versus kill? No. Again that was thought to be too sensitive a question. Although we did have, I think, two people who freely offered the information that they had, indeed, killed someone. Keep in mind that the 8 percent figure is based on so few cases that you have to interpret it with great caution.

Schulman: Did anybody respond to a question asking whether they had used the gun and it was found afterward to be unjustified?

Kleck: We did not ask them that question although we did ask them what crime they thought was being committed. So in each case the only incidents we were accepting as bona fide defensive gun uses were ones where the defender believed that, indeed, a crime had been committed against them.

Schulman: Did you ask any follow-up questions about how many people had been arrested or captured as a result of their actions?

Kleck: No.

Schulman: Did you ask any questions about aid in law enforcement, such as somebody helps a police officer who's not themselves an officer?

Kleck: No. I imagine that would be far too rare an incident to get any meaningful information out of it. Highly unlikely that any significant share of these involved assisting law enforcement.

Schulman: The question which this all comes down to is that we already have some idea, for example from surveys on CCW license holders, how rare it is for a CCW holder to misuse their gun in a way to injure somebody improperly. But does this give us any idea of what the percentages are of people who carry a gun having to use it in order to defend himself or herself? In other words, comparing the percentage of defending yourself to the percentage of being attacked, does this tell us anything?

Kleck: We asked them whether they carried guns at any time but we didn't directly ask them if they were carrying guns, in the legal sense, at the time they had used their gun defensively. So we can probably say what fraction of gun carriers in our sample had used a gun defensively but we can't say whether they did it while carrying. They may, for example, have been people who at least occasionally carried a gun for protection but they used a gun defensively in their own home.

Schulman: So what percentage of gun carriers used it defensively?

Kleck: I haven't calculated it yet so I couldn't say.

Schulman: So if we assume, let's say, that every year approximately 9 percent of people are going to be attacked, and approximately every year that 1 percent of respondents used their guns to defend against an attack, is it fair to say that around one out of nine people attacked used their guns to defend themselves?

Kleck: That "risk of being attacked" shouldn't be phrased that way. It's the risk of being the victim of a personal crime. In other words, it involved interpersonal contact. That could be something like a nonviolent crime like purse snatching or pickpocketing as well. The fact that personal contact is involved means there's an opportunity to defend against it using a gun; it doesn't necessarily mean there was an attack on the victim.

Schulman: Did you get any data on how the attackers were armed during these incidents?

Kleck: Yes. We also asked whether the offender was armed. The offender was armed in 47.2 percent of the cases and they had a handgun in about 13.6 percent of all the cases and some other kind of gun in 4.5 percent of all the cases.

Schulman: So in other words, in about a sixth of the cases, the person attacking was armed with a firearm.

Kleck: That's correct.

Schulman: Okay. And the remainder?

Kleck: Armed with a knife: 18.1 percent, 2 percent with some other sharp object, 10.1 percent with a blunt object, and 6 percent with some other weapon. Keep in mind when adding this up that offenders could have had more than one weapon.

Schulman: So in approximately five sixths of the cases somebody carrying a gun for defensive reasons would find themselves defending themselves either against an unarmed attacker or an attacker with a lesser weapon?

Kleck: Right. About five-sixths of the time.

Schulman: And about one-sixth of the time they would find themselves up against somebody who's armed with a firearm.

Kleck: Well, certainly in this sample of incidents that was the case.

Schulman: Which you believe is representative.

Kleck: It's representative of what's happened in the last five years. Whether or not it would be true in the future we couldn't say for sure.

Schulman: Are there any other results coming out of this which are surprising to you?

Kleck: About the only thing which was surprising is how often people had actually wounded someone in the incident. Previous surveys didn't have very many sample cases so you couldn't get into the details much but some evidence had suggested that a relatively small share of incidents involved the gun inflicting wounds so it was surprising to me that quite so many defenders had used a gun that way.

Schulman: Dr. Kleck, is there anything else you'd like to say at this time about the results of your survey and your continuing analysis of them?

Kleck: Nope.

Schulman: Then thank you very much.

Kleck: You're welcome.

How Does Japan Get That Low Crime Rate, Anyway?

Today's *Los Angeles Times* has an article that illuminates the difficulty of citing Japan's low crime rate as evidence that gun-control is a factor.

In a Column One story titled "Victims of a Safe Society," the *Los Angeles Times* details how the relatively low rate of private criminality in Japan is achieved by massive police criminality: beating suspects so severely that they are permanently crippled in order to obtain confessions, a massively high rate of false executions and imprisonment, and virtually no penalties for police who commit these crimes.

"Many foreign people think Japan is a highly developed, advanced, democratic country, and it is," says Hideyuki Kayanuma, an attorney for an American entertainer who was permanently crippled by Japanese police who suspected him of drug possession. "But especially in the field of criminal justice, it's a Third World country. There are no human rights."

Civil-rights attorney Kensuke Onuki says, "It's almost like *Midnight Express.*"

In addition to beating of suspects, sleep deprivation to achieve confessions, and common torture of arrestees, the article describes a Japanese criminal justice system with virtually no bail, strip searches for traffic violations, and a conviction rate of 98% — about that of Stalinist USSR. In contrast, of 12,615 complaints of torture and abuse filed against police over the last 40 years, only 15 cases were tried, and only *half* of that 15 resulted in punishment for police officers.

Citing "a typical example," of Japanese justice, the article tells of a day laborer released after 16 years in prison. The laborer was coerced into a false confession during six months of detention in three different police stations outside Tokyo. During that time, the laborer says, "officers beat him on the head with fists, trampled his thighs, and ordered him to 'apologize' to a photo of the dead woman as they burned incense for her spirit in the interrogation room. They interrogated him for a total of 172 days as much as 13 hours a day."

Other methods of interrogation, according to the *Times* article, involve telling suspects that their families will suffer if they don't confess or that an interrogation won't end without a confession. The article cites human rights attorneys who have estimated forced confessions to be as high as 50%. Suspects may be held in custody for up to 23 days with no charges, bail, right to an attorney, or court supervision.

Nor is there much objection to this brutality by the Japanese public. The Japanese Civil Liberties Union has only 600 members, as compared to 280,000 ACLU members. Instead, says the *Times* article, "most Japanese place a high degree of confidence and trust in police and assume that suspects under arrest probably committed the crime."

Those who wish to cite Japan's low murder rate as proof that gun control works, had better think again. And if after reconsidering the issue they still advocate the Japanese approach, those Americans who value the concepts of fairness and justice would do well to understand what the goal of those who advocate gun control actually is: the importation of fascism to America.

— February 27, 1992

An Overview of the Statistical Case

In June, 1993, I responded to a message in the Gun Rights "echo" on the Fidonet personal computer network. The following is a slightly edited version of the stimulus and my response.

From : NEIL SCHULMAN
To : CHRISSY M Date: 06/04/93 11:04a
Subject : Weapon permits
Conf : 003 - GUN RIGHTS

NEIL> Guns don't encourage more murders. That is fallacious
NEIL> reasoning.

NEIL> Guns in the hands of bad people are used to do bad
NEIL> things.

NEIL> Guns in the hands of good people are used for the good
NEIL> purpose of stopping bad people from doing bad things.
NEIL> Pacifism is based on the premise that if good people
NEIL> surrender to bad people, good will prevail. Wrong. Dead
NEIL> wrong. If good people do not conquer bad people when
NEIL> bad people use violence to do bad things, then innocent
NEIL> people suffer.

CHRIS> Geeeeee, Am I getting slammed or what?? <grin> I
CHRIS> realize this. But in *MY* opinion, I don't think it
CHRIS> should be MANDATORY to have a gun in our homes. It
CHRIS> should be that person's decision. And you hafta admit,
CHRIS> that guns DO in fact increase the crime rate. A small
CHRIS> percentage, but it does.
CHRIS> Chris.

No, Chris, I do not admit that guns increase the crime rate. Your opinion is not in accordance with known facts.

Switzerland and Israel have two of the most heavily armed civilian populations on Earth. Both have an extremely low rate of violent crime and homicide — some of the lowest anywhere.

According to *The Jewish Week* for Dec. 11-17, 1992, the Israeli homicide rate for 1992 was 1.96 per 100,000 persons. One in ten Israeli civilians carries a firearm.

In Switzerland, every male between 20 and 50 is required to keep a fully-automatic assault rifle in his home, and the Swiss regularly carry these full-auto rifles to ranges on public transportation and on bicycles for practice. There are 4 million weapons in private hands including 220,000 pistols in a nation of 6.5 million people, which gives Switzerland about 3,400 pistols/100,000 Swiss citizens; and there are 4 million weapons in private hands, for a ratio slightly less than the ratio in the United States (61,500/100,000 in Switzerland compared to 83,300/100,000 in the US). I don't have the overall Swiss homicide rate handy, but they had 91 handgun murders in 1990 — for a population of 6.8 million, this works out to a Swiss handgun-related homicide rate of .00014%.

Analyzing American Homicide Rates

(Source: FBI Unified Crime Reports)

U.S. cities (1990):		**U.S. states** (1990):	
Washington D.C.	78 per 100K	New York	14.5 per 100K
Miami	39 per 100K	Florida	10.7 per 100K
Houston	35 per 100K	Pennsylvania	6.7 per 100K
New York City	31 per 100K	Montana	4.9 per 100K
Los Angeles	28 per 100K	Minnesota	2.7 per 100K
Denver	14 per 100K	Vermont	2.3 per 100K
Phoenix	13 per 100K	South Dakota	2.0 per 100K
Seattle	10 per 100K	New Hampshire	1.9 per 100K
El Paso	7 per 100K	Iowa	1.7 per 100K
Colorado Springs	3 per 100K	North Dakota	.08 per 100K

Several things become immediately obvious. Washington, D.C. and New York have extremely strict gun laws; Houston and Miami less so. Gun control doesn't seem to be a factor.

Next, laws — not just gun control laws, but all laws — are not a controlling element in the homicide rate, period. Houston and El Paso both are subject to the same Texas laws; yet Houston has five times as many murders per 100,000 residents as El Paso. Denver, Colorado has 4.7 times as many murders per 100,000 residents as Colorado Springs, which has the same laws.

Perhaps looking at the United States homicide rate for this century will also be useful:

Murder Statistics from Statistical Abstract of the United States,

U.S. Department of Commerce

The murder rate from 1870 to 1905 was slightly under/over 1 per 100,000. Except for New York City's Sullivan Law and Reconstruction-era laws against blacks carrying guns without permission, U.S. has virtually no gun laws.

1900: 1.2
1901: 1.2 Sept. 6: President McKinley shot; dies 9/14.
1902: 1.2 Theodore Roosevelt elected president.
1903: 1.1
1904: 1.3 Upward trend in homicide rate begins.
1905: 2.1
1906: 3.9 T. Roosevelt reelected.
1907: 4.9
1908: 4.8
1909: 4.2 William H. Taft assumes presidency.
1910: 4.6
1911: 5.5
1912: 5.4
1913: 6.1 Woodrow Wilson assumes presidency.
1914: 6.2 World War I begins in Europe.
1915: 5.9
1916: 6.3
1917: 6.9 April 6: US enters World War I
1918: 6.5 WWI ends; troops return; influenza epidemic.
1919: 7.2
1920: 6.8 Prohibition starts.
1921: 8.1 Harding presidency begins.
1922: 8.0
1923: 7.8 Harding dies; Coolidge becomes president.
1924: 8.1

1925: 8.3
1926: 8.4
1927: 8.4
1928: 8.6 Herbert Hoover elected president.
1929: 8.4 Oct. 29: Stock market crash
1930: 8.8 Beginning of Great Depression
1931: 9.2
1932: 9.0 FDR elected first time
1933: 9.7 Prohibition repealed.
1934: 9.5 National Firearms Act restricts machine guns
1935: 8.3
1936: 8.0
1937: 7.6
1938: 6.8
1939: 6.4 World War II begins in Europe
1940: 6.3
1941: 6.0 December 8: US enters WW II
1942: 5.9
1943: 5.1
1944: 5.0
1945: 5.7 WW2 ends; troops return home, many w/ weapons.
1946: 6.4 Beginning of baby boom.
1947: 6.1
1948: 5.9
1949: 5.4
1950: 5.3 June 25: Korean War begins.
1951: 4.9
1952: 5.2
1953: 4.8 July: Korean Armistice; troops return home.
1954: 4.8
1955: 4.5
1956: 4.6
1957: 4.5
1958: 4.5

1959: 4.6
1960: 4.7
1961: 4.7
1962: 4.8 October: Cuban missile crisis
1963: 4.9 Nov. 22: JFK assassinated; LBJ takes office.
1964: 5.1 Gulf of Tonkin resolution; LBJ elected.
1965: 5.5
1966: 5.9 Vietnam War escalates; anti-war demonstrations
1967: 6.8
1968: 7.3 Nixon wins; King & RFK murd'd; 1968 GCA passed
1969: 7.7 Jan. 20: Nixon takes office.
1970: 8.3
1971: 8.6
1972: 9.0 Nixon reelected
1973: 9.4 Watergate scandal; US troops pull out of Vietnam.
1974: 9.8 Nixon resigns; Ford assumes presidency.
1975: 9.6 April: fall of Saigon to Communists
1976: 8.8
1977: 8.8 Jan. 20: Carter takes office
1978: 9.0
1979: 9.7
1980: 10.2 Reagan elected. Dec. 8: John Lennon murdered.
1981: 9.8 Reagan takes office Jan 20; shot by Hinckley 3/20
1982: 9.1
1983: 8.3
1984: 7.9 Reagan re-elected
1985: 7.9
1986: 8.6 McClure-Volkmer Gun Act passes, easing gun laws.
1987: 8.3
1988: 8.4 Bush elected
1989: 8.7 Jan. 20: Bush takes office
1990: 9.4
1991: 9.8
1992: 9.3 Apr 29: widespread riots. Nov: Clinton elected.

Analysis: It's hard to draw specific conclusions on the causes of the increases and decreases in homicide. It's tempting to blame an increase on the passage of Prohibition or World War I, except the upward homicide trend begins in 1904, before either event. The repeal of Prohibition in 1933, however, does seem to begin a gradual lowering in homicide rates (one can't attribute it to the 1934 National Firearms Act because that law focuses only on machine-guns, a minor part of the body count), until the period beginning in 1963-64 with the JFK assassination and the escalation of the Vietnam War, when rates start sharply upward again. There is a short spurt in homicides at the end of World War II which is not repeated at the end of the Korean War. The period from 1949 to 1963 is fairly low on domestic homicide. Nor, judging from the Great Depression, can poverty be used to explain increasing homicide rates: after a brief peak in 1931, the U.S. homicide rates falls by about a third over the Depression decade.

The most severe federal gun control passed is the 1968 Gun Control Act, which outlaws buying guns through the mail or transferring them interstate without a federal dealers' license. The law has no observable effect on increasing homicide rates. Nor does the easing of some 1968 restrictions by the McClure–Volkmer Firearms Owners Protection Act in 1986, while outlawing ownership of new full-auto weapons, seem to produce any observable impact on the national homicide rate.

One set of comparisons are not included in the time-series homicide rate chart and probably should have been. The increase in domestic homicides seems to compare closely with the increase in immigration.

Also, if you were to statistically isolate the inner-city black population in the United States, the rest of the homicide rate drops down to that of the low-end-homicide-rate states. Black criminals murdering other blacks is the largest single statistical homicide grouping in this country, and throws all the other statistics out of whack.

As with regional comparisons of gun control, time-series observations do not seem to offer any reason to believe that increasing restrictions on firearms have any positive effect on reducing homicide rates.

All in all, I'd say anyone who is trying to make a case for or against gun control by linking availability of firearms with homicide rates is going to find it impossible to do so with any credibility.

Now let's get to the other side of the equation: gun defenses. When a pharmaceutical company markets a drug, they must check to see whether or not it is (1) safe; and (2) effective. Let's apply the same tests to firearms in the hands of the civilian population to see whether guns are safe and effective means for private citizens to defend themselves against crime.

Let's look at safety first.

First, what about gun accidents? Let's begin by comparing gun-related accidental deaths with accidental deaths from other causes.

Source: National Center for Health Statistics
(1991, latest official estimates)

Motor Vehicle*	47,575
Falls	12,151
Poisoning (solid, liquid, gas)*	6,524
Fires and Flames*	4,716
Drowning (incl. water transport drownings)	4,716
Suffocation (mechanical, ingestion)*	4,491
Surgical/Medical misadventures*	2,850
Other Transportation (excl. drownings)*	2,160
Natural/Environmental factors*	1,816
Firearms	1,489

(includes estimated 500 handgun and 200 hunting accidents)
*1989, latest official figures

In other words, firearms-related accidents are a comparatively small cause of death as compared to most other accidental causes.

And just to put this in context, accidental death from firearms is down 40% from ten years ago, and down 80% from fifty years ago.

Now that we've established that firearms accidents aren't a major problem, let's look at the overall safety of an armed citizenry.

Vermont in the only state in the union to allow any citizen to own or carry a gun, concealed or unconcealed, without any sort of license or permit. What is the homicide rate in Vermont? It's 2.3 per 100,000 — one of the lowest in the nation.

Now let's go to a state with a high homicide rate: Florida, with a homicide rate of 10.7 per 100,000. Florida licenses the carrying of concealed firearms to any U.S. resident who isn't disqualified by reason of being a convicted criminal, or a drug addict, or a mental patient. You have to pass a fingerprint background check and show some sort of proof that you're competent to carry a gun: any 8-hour NRA basic firearms handling & safety course will do.

Here are the statistics on Florida's concealed-carry-weapons program:

SEP-10-1993 07:54 FROM DI 4122446062ING TO 63108397653 P.02

FLORIDA DEPARTMENT OF STATE
Jim Smith
Secretary of State
DIVISION OF LICENSING
Post Office Box 6687
Tallahassee, Florida 32314-6687

CONCEALED WEAPONS/FIREARMS LICENSE
STATISTICAL REPORT FOR
PERIOD 10/01/87 - 7/31/93

		TOTAL
o Applications Received:		170,532
New	125,020	
Renewal	45,512	
o Licenses Issued:		164,404
New	119,234	
Renewal	45,170	
o Licenses Valid		96,608
o Applications Denied:		916
Criminal History	538	
Incomplete Application	378	
o License Revoked:		319
Clemency, Rule Change or Legislative Change	66	
Illegible Prints With No Response	10	
Crime Prior To Licensure	63	
- Firearm Utilized --4		
Crime After Licensure	164	
- Firearm Utilized --16		
Other	16	
Reinstated		40*

*Statistics regarding number of licenses reinstated were not maintained prior to January 1990.

We see here that among the 119,234 persons Florida has licensed to carry a concealed firearm, there have been only 16 cases where a licensee has subsequently used a firearm in violation of Florida law — and most of those are simply carrying into prohibited places such as a bar or airport.

We have established the safety of civilian carry of firearms beyond a doubt. Now let's look at effectiveness of civilian carry of firearms in fighting crime.

Gary Kleck, professor of criminology at Florida State University at Tallahassee, has examined data from 8 separate studies, and has concluded with a 95% certainty interval (assuming one defense per survey respondent in the last five years — a highly conservative assumption) civilians in the United States use firearms over a million times a year in defense against crime. My own analysis of data compiled in a study by the *Los Angeles Times* leads me to believe that Kleck's analysis is in fact an underestimate. **[Note:** I was right. The figure is now updated to *2.45 million* defenses. See *Q & A on Gun Defenses* **—JNS]** My own figures show that for every time a criminal uses a gun to commit a violent crime, there are two uses of a firearm by a private citizen to stop, prevent, or deter a crime.

Additionally, let's look at some comparisons between police use of firearms and civilian use:

Comparisons between Civilian and Police Use of Firearms

(Source: Civil Rights Attorney Don Kates, St. Louis University School of Law, in *Restricting Handguns: The Liberal Skeptics Speak Out, Firearms and Violence*, and "Gun Control and the Subway Class." The first two are books; the last is an article in the January 10, 1985 *Wall Street Journal*.)

Percentage of privately owned handguns used in crime: 0.4%

Number of times a year private handguns successfully used in defense: 645,000

[Note: Now estimated at 1.9 million defenses yearly.**—JNS]**

Percentage of times armed police have succeeded in wounding or driving off criminals: 68%

Percentage of times armed private citizens have succeeded in wounding or driving off criminals: 83%

Percentage persons who are innocent of a crime shot by armed police: 11%
Percentage of persons who are innocent of a crime shot by armed private citizens: 2%

Now, let's look a Florida's crime rate. We already know that Florida concealed-carry-weapons licensees aren't a problem. But is there any other change in the Florida crime statistics since they instituted their new carry law?

Not a dramatic or conclusive one, but the crime trend in Florida is reversing. Note the following:

Crime in the United States, the FBI's Uniform Crime Report.

Murder and Non-Negligent Manslaughter

Florida

Year	Total	% Change	Rate/100,000	% Change
1990	1,379	–1.9	10.7	–3.6
1989	1,405		11.1	
1989	1,405	–.8	11.1	–2.6
1988	1,416		11.4	
1988	1,416	+3.3	11.4	——
1987	1,371		11.4	
1987	1,371	——	11.4	–2.6
1986	1,371		11.7	
1986	1,371	+5.8	11.7	+2.6
1985	1,296		11.4	

Which shows that homicide, the most serious of the offenses, has been in a downward trend in Florida during the period when the number of private persons legally carrying firearms is increasing.

Handgun Control, Inc., responded by charging that the homicide figures weren't telling, because rape and assault were still rising.

Well, they aren't anymore. The trend has started to reverse.

Verbatim Statistics on Violent Crime in Florida,

1991 Annual State Report:

Murder	DOWN	8.0%
w/Handguns	DOWN	3.9%
w/firearms	DOWN	15.4%
w/knives	DOWN	5.2%
w/hands/fists/feet	DOWN	14.1%
Other	DOWN	17.9%
Robbery	DOWN	1.7%
w/Handgun	UP	0.6%
w/firearms	DOWN	10.3%
w/knives	DOWN	6.6%
w/hands/fists/feet	DOWN	0.6%
Other	DOWN	4.6%
Aggravated Assault	DOWN	1.7%
w/handgun	DOWN	5.9%
w/firearms	DOWN	9.4%
w/knives	DOWN	3.4%
w/hands/fists/feet	UP	5.5%
Other	UP	1.3%
Burglary	DOWN	3.8%
w/forced entry	DOWN	2.0%
no forced entry	DOWN	9.5%
Attempted entry	DOWN	5.3%
Purse Snatching	DOWN	7.3%

Now lets look at some Non-Violent Crimes from the same 1991 Annual Report:

Larceny	UP	3.1%
Pocket Picking	UP	1.0%
Shoplifting	UP	4.8%
Theft from Coin Machines	UP	11.4%
Motor Vehicle Theft	UP	1.5%
Drugs: Sale Overall	UP	11.0%
Cocaine sale	UP	11.3%
Marijuana sale	UP	34.3%
Fraud	UP	0.7%
Credit Card/ATM	UP	16.2%
Impersonation	UP	9.0%
Welfare	UP	45.5%
Wire (telephone fraud)	UP	87.5%

Crooks in Florida do seem to be avoiding occasions where they might run into an armed citizen. I would say that while it is not conclusive, there is as much statistical weight at this point to the proposition that increasing the number of firearms being carried by the civilian population inhibits violent crime, as there is to the statistical linkage between cigarette smoking and heart disease or emphysema.

It is indisputable that the Florida concealed-carry firearms law has not turned Florida into the Gunshine State, as HCI and CBS News predicted in 1986.

It is indisputable that making CCW-licenses available to anyone who wants one and can pass an ordinary background check showing no criminal or psychological disqualification does not endanger the public.

And it is getting statistically strong that increasing the ability of the civilian population to carry firearms reverses rising crime trends as well.

What can we conclude from all this?

1) Restricting firearms does not reduce the homicide rate. Look at Scotland and Washington D.C.

2) Proliferating firearms does not increase the homicide rate. Look at Switzerland, Israel, New Hampshire, and Vermont, and the concealed-carry-weapons licensees in Florida.

3) Civilians carrying firearms are more safe and effective at deterring crime than are professional police.

My bottom line is my tagline:

Gun Control = Victim Disarmament & Increases Violent Crime!

Neil

It's Time to Take a Second Look at Murder

If there is any fundamental precept of Western Civilization, it's the injunction from the Ten Commandments that tells us, "Thou shalt not murder."

But perhaps we in the United States today, suffering from one of the worst crime waves in our history — a crime wave that causes us to hide in our homes behind elaborate security systems — need to ask ourselves whether we are making a mistake in basing the laws of a secular society on the clearly sectarian religious precept that murder is wrong. Shouldn't we, rather, take a more empirical approach to murder and first assess whether the actual practice of murder produces greater harm to society or a net social benefit?

There is plenty of good reason to believe that murder benefits society more than it harms it.

The Detective Division of the Chicago Police Department has analyzed all 940 murders that took place in Chicago in 1992, and issued a report titled *Murder Analysis*. In it we discover not only that 72.39% of the 1992 Chicago murderers had a prior criminal history, but *65.53% — virtually two-thirds* — of the 1992 murder *victims* in Chicago had a prior criminal history as well.

That means that for every time an innocent person in Chicago was murdered, two criminals lost their lives. Six hundred and sixteen criminals were killed in Chicago alone in one year.

It is, of course, unfortunate that innocent people are dying from murder, but clearly murder is eliminating criminals from society twice as often as it is eliminating good people. Shouldn't this make us begin to question whether we are making a mistake by placing the selfish interests of a few individuals to hang onto their lives for a few extra years above the clear social benefits of removing criminals whose destructive acts are destroying the fabric of our society?

Despite its sinister reputation, it appears that far more often than not, murder is a natural market reaction to the failure of our criminal justice system to punish criminals. Between 1968 and 1992, there were only 143 executions in the United States. During that same period, the United States had about 531,000 murders. If we apply the Chicago study's percentage of 65.53% murder victims having a criminal history, we come up with a figure of about 350,000 criminals killed during that 25-year period. This is over *2400 times* as many criminals killed in the private sector as all the criminals executed in all the states.

With trials, appeals, and lengthy death-row waits before a criminal can be executed in the United States — almost always at taxpayers' expense — executing a single criminal costs the taxpayers well over a million dollars on average. Further, our antiquated laws only allow us to execute murderers, and not even all of them — there has to be "special circumstances."

Yet, the private sector executed over 350,000 criminals at a fraction of the cost that the government's criminal justice system did in one twenty-five year period. If the justice system had executed these criminals, it would have added *350 billion dollars* to the federal debt.

But the taxpayers' savings in bypassing official executions are only the beginning. The average criminal can be expected to commit about half-a-million dollars-a-year in economic crime, and hundreds of thousands of additional dollars in property destruction and physical harm to victims. Considering the revolving-door nature of our criminal justice system, one can estimate that over a twenty-five-year span, a criminal will spend about half his time in prison — at taxpayers' expense, of course — and the other half on the street, committing robberies, assaults, burglaries, car thefts, carjackings, and rapes.

A simple automobile burglary for a car stereo can cost an insurance company almost a thousand dollars to repair broken windows and the dashboard console, and to replace the stolen equipment.

A simple assault can cost tens of thousands of dollars in medical bills, lost wages, and psychological counseling.

Shoplifting causes stores to hire security personnel to watch us instead of sales clerks to help us.

The thousands of dollars we spend each year in insurance premiums and higher prices reflect the costs of living in a criminal-infested society.

How can we, as a society, even *begin* to calculate the immense social benefit that permanently removing even one criminal from society has, much less the 15,000 or so criminals that private-sector killing is eliminating each year? If a single criminal is responsible for several million dollars in losses over a career, isn't murdering them at the rate of 15,000 or so a year producing a benefit to society several times that of the entire yearly federal deficit?

In 1729, Jonathan Swift, Dean of St. Patrick's Cathedral in Dublin, and best-known today for his *Gulliver's Travels*, wrote a satire called *A Modest Proposal*, in which he suggested that the children of the poor could benefit Ireland by being eaten.

Mark Twain said in his autobiography, "There are three kinds of lies — lies, damned lies and statistics."

And in 1983, my satirical novel *The Rainbow Cadenza* was published, in which I portrayed a future that had "eliminated" rape by drafting women into a three-year hitch of public sexual service, and legalized hunting of draft-evaders for free sex.

The statistics quoted above are true. It is true that the Chicago Police Department's *Murder Analysis* determined that twice as many persons with a criminal history were murdered in Chicago in 1992 than those without criminal histories.

It would have been just as easy for me to write an essay using real statistics, proving that since most crime in America is committed by young African-American males, therefore abolishing slavery was a bad idea, or that we could reduce our homicide rate to that of England's by the simple expedient of shipping blacks back to Africa.

We are living in a society which has come down with a bad case of a disease we can dub "statisticitis": the uncritical use of statistical soundbytes to influence public policy.

So-called experts at the federal Environmental Protection Agency have used statistics to claim that second-hand smoke is killing half a million of us each year.

Former Surgeon General C. Everett Koop once claimed in the *Journal of the American Medical Association* that guns are killing a million American children each year.

In fact, the national death rate from all causes is two million or so per year, with heart disease and cancers alone accounting for about two-thirds of the deaths.

Now a new study in the *New England Journal of Medicine* is claiming that you are three times more likely to have one of your loved ones murder you with a handgun you keep for protection than that the handgun will scare off, or actually defend you from, a burglar. But the doctor who made that claim didn't even look at the question of how many times a year a firearm is used defensively without killing or wounding anyone.

We can't all be experts in all the technical fields of knowledge necessary to make political judgments nowadays. There are just too many of them. But is it too much to ask, when someone wants to engineer public policy on the basis of what's statistically "good" for society, whether it wrongs actual individuals who have to live in that society?

There is never shortage of good arguments for instituting a public policy that would benefit the greater good at the expense of some selfish few. These are the arguments we hear nowadays in favor of limiting your choice of legal medical treatment to those allowed by government-controlled "health alliances," or limiting the portrayal of violence on television to what may be suitable only for children, or restricting firearms only to people who wear uniforms.

But without a moral sense of the dignity and rights of the private individual placing overriding limits on what governmental power may do to benefit society, what is to stop every ambitious social experimenter from enslaving each of us in reality, to "all of us," in their wildest fantasies?

The War to Bear Arms in the City of the Angels

No one should have to choose between carrying the means for defending themselves and their loved ones against the criminally insane among us — and risking criminal charges — or obeying the law by leaving their means of defense at home and therefore being defenseless. This is the choice that people in most American cities have to make. Here in Los Angeles, I decided to do something about it. **— JNS**

Remarks to the Los Angeles Board of Police Commissioners

July 16, 1991

After Schulman identifies himself as speaking for the Committee to Enforce the Second Amendment:

Madam President and Members of the Commission, I do not sit before you seeking to make it easier for criminals and mental incompetents to carry firearms. They find it too easy already — far easier than I do, for they are not afraid of the law, and I am.

But the Los Angeles Police Commission's guidelines for issuing licenses to carry concealed firearms is in clear opposition to the words of the Second Amendment to the United States Constitution.

Let me quote both:

The independent clause from the fourth paragraph of the "Board Policy Concerning Licenses to Carry Concealed Weapons" states, "[I]t is the policy of this Board that 'good cause' for the issuance of any concealed weapons license would exist only in the most extreme and aggravated circumstances."

And, the independent clause from the Second Amendment is, "the right of the people to keep and bear Arms, shall not be infringed."

The Second Amendment does not say the right of the militia, or police, or the National Guard. It says "the right of the *people*."

The Founding Fathers, in their good sense, knew that a free society requires its citizens — the people themselves — to take responsibility for the defense of themselves, their loved ones, and their neighbors, and that such responsibility requires being armed to fulfill it.

We live in a city where violent crime is epidemic and the police are incapable of protecting the citizens from it. Your own former police chief, Ed Davis, said as much in a well-publicized speech.

When you deny a citizen a firearms permit because in your opinion there is no "extreme and aggravated circumstance," you take upon yourself a discretion that the Constitution does not permit you. The Constitution says you may not infringe the right of the people to keep and bear arms. I think we can agree that leaves out convicted criminals and mental incompetents. Use your discretion all you can to keep *them* from getting and carrying guns.

But the Constitution forbids you from denying the right to carry firearms to the people — we honest, law-abiding citizens.

California Penal Code Section 12050 authorizes you to issue a license to carry a concealed weapon provided that the person is of good moral character and that good cause exists for issuance of the license. The "good cause" is the requirement of the Second Amendment that the people's right to carry arms not be infringed.

I am calling upon you to fulfill your obligation under California law, and most specifically the highest law of the land, the U.S. Constitution, to revise your policy for issuing licenses to carry firearms, so that any sane, adult citizen may carry firearms for the protection of her or his life, loved ones, and neighbors.

Thank you.

The Case for a Concealed Weapon's License in Los Angeles

A Refutation of the Los Angeles Board of Police Commissioners' Policy Concerning Licenses to Carry Concealed Weapons

I originally wrote this immediately after the April, 1992 Los Angeles riots as my personal case to the Los Angeles Board of Police Commissioners for a license to carry concealed weapons. Later, I updated it and eliminated arguments applicable only to myself personally, so it could be used by other applicants. I have edited it for the current book to eliminate some duplication of arguments found elsewhere in it. **— JNS**

The Los Angeles Board of Police Commissioners takes the position that the private citizen can be adequately protected on the streets of Los Angeles without the need for carrying firearms for personal protection. This position is reflected in the Board Policy Concerning Licenses to Carry Concealed Weapons, which reads as follows:

> By operation of California law, Penal Code Section 12050, the Board of Police Commissioners has the discretionary authority to issue a license to carry a concealed weapon to a resident of the county provided that the person is of good moral character and that good cause exists for issuance of the license.
>
> However, experience has revealed that concealed firearms carried for protection not only provide a false sense of security but further that the licensee is often a victim of his own weapon or the subject of a civil or criminal case stemming from an improper use of the weapon.
>
> It is the Board's considered judgment that utilization of standard commercial security practices furnishes a security which is both more safe and more sure than that which obtains from the carrying of a concealed weapon.

> For these reasons, considering the dangers to society resulting from possession and use of concealed weapons, it is the policy of this Board that 'good cause' for the issuance of any concealed weapons license would exist only in the most extreme and aggravated circumstances.

First, I will argue that the Board's policy regarding what constitutes "good cause" under PC 12050 is based on a set of incorrect facts and assumptions in general; and in specific, that the Board's prior requirements regarding "good cause" are further inapplicable following the riots, murders, lootings, and torchings following the Rodney King beating verdict;

Second, I will demonstrate that the Board's policy proceeds on a misunderstanding of the discretion regarding "good cause" that the Board is allowed under PC 12050, as that law must be interpreted according to the California Constitution; and

Third, I will demonstrate that for the average person there are no reasonable alternatives to firearms for defense.

I. Good Cause

In satisfying my first argument, let me analyze the Board Policy in detail.

A. The Board Policy states, "However, experience has revealed that concealed firearms carried for protection not only provide a false sense of security but further that the licensee is often a victim of his own weapon or the subject of a civil or criminal case stemming from an improper use of the weapon."

The first statement is that concealed firearms carried for protection provide a "false sense of security."

The studies by Gary Kleck, Ph.D. [detailed throughout this book — **JNS**] document the frequency with which firearms are used in defense by the civilian population.

The Board's position can additionally be refuted by reference to three incidents involving individuals I have personally interviewed where concealed firearms carried for protection have provided real protection, rather than a false sense of security.

The first case is that of Montebello, CA Reserve Police Officer

Justin Feffer. After changing to plainclothes and going off-duty, in a 1991 incident, Officer Feffer drove to his home in Los Angeles County when he was attacked by a gang of "follow-home" robbers who did not know that he was a police officer and was carrying a concealed .45 caliber semi-auto pistol. Officer Feffer was confronted by the robbers, and successfully defended himself against them by drawing his weapon and firing at them, fatally wounding one of the attackers, and driving the others away. I have interviewed Officer Feffer, and it is his judgment that his police training gave him no special advantage over any private citizen who is trained in the use of firearms, in the circumstances of defending himself against attack.

The second case is that of Thomas Glenn Terry. [See *A Massacre We Didn't Hear About*. — **JNS**]

The third case took place at midnight on Friday, September 18th, 1992. [See *Gunfight at the 4 'n 20 Pie Shop*.— **JNS**]

Numerous other examples of successful use of a firearm in self-defense have been compiled by the National Rifle Association, drawn from published newspaper accounts, and republished in the NRA's "Armed Citizen" column in *American Rifleman* and *American Hunter*. Since 1977, the "Armed Citizen" column has begun with the following statement, which is verified by the thousands of accounts that column has published, "Mere presence of a firearm, without a shot being fired, prevents crime in many instances as shown by news reports sent in to The Armed Citizen. Shooting usually can be justified only where crime constitutes an immediate, imminent threat to life or limb, or in some circumstances, property. The accounts are from clippings sent in by NRA members. Anyone is free to quote or reproduce them." Many of these accounts have also been republished in the book *The Armed Citizen*, edited by Joseph B. Roberts, Jr.

Finally, in sworn testimony to a legislative committee of the Texas legislature, Dr. Suzanna Gratia, a survivor of the restaurant massacre of 23 people in Killeen, Texas on October 16, 1991, who lost both of her parents in that massacre (as reported by the *San Antonio Express-News* of Feb. 13, 1992) said, "I'm not saying that

I could have stopped this guy, but I would have had a chance." According to the *Express-News*, Dr. Gratia had left her gun in her car because it was a crime to carry it in her purse and she didn't want to be arrested. "The point of this is," Dr. Gratia said, "someone legislated me out of the right to protect myself and my loved ones."

B. The second claim in the Board Policy "that the licensee is often a victim of his own weapon or the subject of a civil or criminal case stemming from an improper use of the weapon," is likewise false.

[The Kleck study provides the first refutation.— **JNS**]

Since the City of Los Angeles has not issued a license to carry a concealed firearm since 1974, it is impossible to provide current statistics for Los Angeles, beyond the clear statement that with no licenses available, there has been no possible licensed use of concealed firearms by private citizens, proper or improper. Similarly, since so few licenses are issued by other similar-sized municipalities in California — Santa Monica has also issued no licenses for over 25 years, and the County of Los Angeles currently has fewer than 400 licenses out — one must go to another populous state for a sizable database, which disproves the Board's claim.

For the past five years, Florida has had a liberal policy on issuing concealed-carry-weapons permits: a citizen who can pass a background check and prove competency in firearms safety and usage, can get a license.

According to the Division of Licensing, Florida Department of State, out of 133,852 applications received between October 1, 1987 and July 31, 1992, 476 were denied for criminal history and 93,541 licenses were issued. Revoked for crime after licensure: 84 (9 one hundredths of 1%). Revoked for a crime utilizing a firearm: 17 (2 one hundredths of 1%). Revoked for "other": 12 (1 one hundredth of 1%). These statistics show that there is no significant danger to the public from the misuse of firearms by holders of concealed-carry weapons permits in Florida, and it would be odd indeed if the Board were to hold that the citizens of Florida are in any sense more prudent or careful than the citizens of California.

C. The Board policy claims that, "It is the Board's considered judgment that utilization of standard commercial security practices furnishes a security which is both more safe and more sure than that which obtains from the carrying of a concealed weapon. This judgment is in accord with the view of the California Peace Officers Association — expressed formally on two occasions in 1968 and 1973 'that all permits to carry concealed weapons by private individuals in the State of California be revoked and that the legislation authorizing the issuance of such permits be repealed.'"

"Standard commercial security practices" are entirely inapplicable and inappropriate to the discussion of individual self-defense, in that (1) it presumes that a private individual has the resources to hire an armed, uniformed guard to provide security to an individual while on the street; (2) such a presumption could only apply to the wealthy businessperson who could afford, or whose company could afford, to provide such protection, and such presumption is discriminatory against all but the wealthy; (3) it presumes that armored vehicles capable of withstanding armed assault are possible or appropriate transportation for private citizens, which is discriminatory against all but the wealthy; and (4) it presumes that any emergency response system which is capable of summoning either police or armed guards is available to a private citizen who is alone on the street, and that even with an available telephone, a private person on the street would be able to evade an attacker in order to call for help, or persuade an attacker to cease attack while the victim calls police for help. All of these assumptions are highly improbable and useless for a realistic discussion of personal defense of the ordinary person against violent attackers.

Regarding the opinion of the California Peace Officers Association from 1968 and 1973, it is not in accord with the views of police officers as collected in a survey conducted in 1991.

In a survey of 25,000 subscribers to *Law Enforcement Technology* Magazine, the results of which were published in the July/August 1991 issue of that magazine, 92.7% of chiefs, sheriffs, and top police management, 91.1 percent of police middle management, and 94.5% of street officers, responded "Yes" to the question, "Should private citizens use handguns for personal protection?" In addition, 60% of chiefs, sheriffs, and top police management, 68% percent of police middle management, and 73% of street officers, responded "No" to the question, "Do you support a ban on concealed weapons?"

D. The Board's policy has presumed either that violent criminal attack is infrequent enough that the ordinary person is unlikely to need protection or that in the event of an attack that the ordinary person can safely rely on the emergency response system to summon police quickly enough for effective protection against such an attack.

1. Starting with the general and moving to the more specific, the report of the 4th National Poll of America's Police Chiefs for the Year 1991, which polled every sheriff and chief of police in the United States, provided the answer that 72.3% of those police personnel polled responded "Yes" to the question, "Would you agree with the statement that because of a lack of police manpower that you can no longer provide the type of service and crime prevention activities that you did ten years ago?"
2. Moving the question specifically to Los Angeles, 64% of Los Angeles residents felt that their city was unsafe, according to a Gallup poll conducted in 1990.
3. Los Angeles has 229 police officers per 100,000 residents — lower than Washington D.C., (658), Detroit (458), Chicago (396), Philadelphia (379), Atlanta (356), Boston (352), New York (351), Dallas (248), or Houston (239), and in 1989 (latest available statistics) had 9,272 crimes per 100,000 residents (sixth in the nation), including 25 homicides per 100,000 (ninth in the nation).

Clearly, Los Angeles residents have had a reason to feel unsafe on the streets. An increase in violent crimes such as follow-home robberies, automobile theft at gunpoint, and crimes where individuals were robbed when auto accidents were staged requiring victims to exit their vehicles to exchange licenses, speaks clearly to that lack of safety, even during "normal" times. The Board's underlying assumption about the lack of necessity for concealed weapons was questionable even before the riots, looting, and hate crimes following the Rodney King beating trial verdict caused the city to erupt into civil unrest.

After the events following the Rodney King beating trial verdict, there can be no further question. As of May 3, 1992, we saw thousands of buildings either burned or destroyed by looting; we had over 50 deaths, most by gunfire, and several thousand injuries — several hundred of them critical injuries.

It took four nights of city-wide curfews, 5,000 of Los Angeles Police, 2,370 California Highway Patrol, 2,195 outside agency law-enforcement personnel, 7,000 National Guard, 1,000 Federal law-enforcement personnel, and 4,500 U.S. Army and U.S. Marine Corps troops — an armed force of approximately 22,065 to pacify the city. But for the first two days of violence, police and National Guard manpower was almost entirely incapable of providing any sort of protection of life or property to the population of Los Angeles, Long Beach, Compton, and other areas of Los Angeles County.

A significant number of the attacks were racially-motivated hate crimes. Matthew Haines of Long Beach, described in a *Los Angeles Times* report as a "white 32-year-old mechanic," was, according to the *Times*, "gunned down after he was stopped by a mob of black men and teenagers as he and his nephew, Scott Coleman, 26, rode Haines' motorcycle to a friend's apartment in Long Beach."

Reginald Denny, a trucker, was pulled from his truck and beaten to within an inch of his life by a mob in South Central Los Angeles. Denny was white, the mob was black —there is no question that it was a hate crime. It was only by the intervention of black good Samaritans that Denny was not killed.

A list of fatalities published by the *Los Angeles Times* of Sunday, May 3, 1992 (Page A-10), includes the following:

> Wednesday:
> 8:15 PM: Louis Watson, 18, of West 43rd Place was fatally wounded by a gunshot to the head at a bus stop at Vernon and Vermont Avenues.

Moments later: Dwight Taylor, a 42-year-old black man, was fatally shot at 446 Martin Luther King Jr. Blvd.

9:00 PM: Arturo Miranda, 20, of West 120th Street was fatally shot in his car at 120th Street and Central Avenue.

9:26 PM: Edward Travens, a 15-year-old white youth, was killed in a drive-by shooting at San Fernando Road and Workman Street in the San Fernando Valley community of Mission Hills. Coroner's officials said they had reason to believe it was linked to racial unrest.

10:40 PM: Anthony Netherly, 21, a black man, was fatally shot at 78th and San Pedro Streets.

11:15 PM: Elbert Wilkins, 33, a black man, died at Martin Luther King Jr./Drew Medical Center after being shot in the back at 92nd Street and Western Avenue.

11:45 PM: Ernest Neal Jr., 27, a black man, died after being shot in the head in the same incident at 92nd Street and Western Avenue.

Thursday:

12:10 AM: Ira McMurry, 45, a white man, was fatally shot at 102nd Street and Avalon Boulevard. McMurry was shot in the head when he tried to stop looters from burning the liquor store next to his house.

12:30 AM: Deandre Harrison, a 17-year-old black youth, was shot at 114th Street and Slauson Avenue and later died at Martin Luther King Jr./Drew Medical Center.

12:30 PM: An unidentified black man died of gunshot wounds at Rosecrans and Chester Avenues in Compton.

1:30 PM: After flying to Los Angeles to inspect his machine shop, Howard Epstein of Orinda, Calif. was shot to death near 7th and Slauson Avenues and his car was ransacked by looters.

1:35 PM: Jose L. Garcia Jr., 15, died of gunshot wounds at Fresno Street and Atlantic Avenue.

5:00 PM: Patrick Bettan, 30, a white male, died of gunshot wounds suffered at 2740 W. Olympic Boulevard.

5:32 PM: A 49-year-old Latino male was gunned down at 3rd Street and Vermont Avenue.

About 6:30 PM: Matthew Haines fatally shot.

9:37 PM: Eduardo Vela, a 34-year-old Latino male, died of gunshot wounds, suffered at 5142 W. Slauson Avenue.

Time unknown: A man was found shot to death at Willowbrook Avenue and Alondra Boulevard.

Time unknown: A man was shot to death at Martin Luther King Jr. Boulevard and Rhea Street.

8:21 PM: A 32-year-old male Latino was stabbed to death at 2034 W. Pico Blvd.

Friday:

12:52 AM: A 25-year-old Latino male died of gunshot wounds suffered at Vermont Avenue and Santa Monica Boulevard.

1:10 AM: Kevin Evanahen, 24, died while trying to put out a fire at a check-cashing store at Braddock Drive and Inglewood Boulevard.

4:45 PM: Meeker Gibson, 35, a black male, was shot to death at Holt Street and Loranne Avenue in Pomona.

Time unknown: A 19-year-old Latino male was shot to death at 4028 Santa Monica Boulevard.

Time unknown: A black male was shot to death at 614 S. Locust St. in Compton.

Time unknown: A male Latino was brought dead on arrival to County-USC Medical Center with a gunshot wound. The location of the shooting was not known.

1:58 PM: Lucie Maronian, 51, a female Anglo, was stabbed to death on East New York Drive in Altadena. The coroner said sheriff's investigators considered the case to be riot-related.

Early evening: A 68-year-old white male was strangled at a looting scene at 11690 Gateway St. Coroner's officials said the man might have been a store proprietor trying to stop looting.

8:19 PM: A 32-year-old black man died of a gunshot wound at Daniel Freeman Memorial Hospital.

In Koreatown, merchants unable to get any police protection found themselves, and their firearms, the only thing standing between gangs of arsonists and looters and their stores.

Elsewhere in Los Angeles, citizens blocked off neighborhood streets and stood armed guard to prevent looters and arsonists from entering.

Clearly, the ordinary police force available to the City of Los Angeles to provide protection to the public is inadequate to extraordinary times ... and we are living in extraordinary times.

II. Board Discretion

I will now demonstrate that the Board's policy proceeds on a misunderstanding of the discretion regarding "good cause" that the Board is allowed under PC 12050, as that law must be interpreted according to the California Constitution.

Article 1, Section 1 of the California Constitution reads as follows: "All people are by nature free and independent, and have certain inalienable rights, among which are those of enjoying and defending life and liberty; acquiring, possessing, and protecting property; and pursuing and obtaining safety, happiness, and privacy." (as amended 7 November 1972.)

The California Constitution, itself, defines "good cause" for the purposes of PC 12050: good cause for carrying a firearm is defined as "defending life and liberty," "protecting property," and "pursuing and obtaining safety." The discretion mandated by PC 12050 to the Board is therefore on the question of "good moral character."

Further, not only do the people of California have these rights to defend and protect ourselves defined under the California Constitution, but the California Government Code specifically relieves all government entities and employees from any responsibility for protecting the public.

California Government Code, Section 845, states, "Neither a public entity nor a public employee is liable for failure to establish a police department or otherwise provide police protection service or, if police protection service is provided, for failure to provide sufficient police protection service."

Section 846 states, "Neither a public entity nor a public employee is liable for injury caused by the failure to make an arrest or by the failure to retain an arrested person in custody."

Section 845.8 states, "Neither a public entity nor a public employee is liable for (a) Any injury resulting from determining whether to parole or release a prisoner or from determining the terms and conditions of his parole or release or from determining whether to revoke his parole or release. (b) Any injury caused by (1) An escaping or escaped prisoner; (2) An escaping or escaped arrested person; or (3) A person resisting arrest."

Section 845.2 states, "Except as provided in Chapter 2 (commencing with Section 830), neither a public entity nor a public employee is liable for failure to provide a prison, jail or penal or correctional facility, or, if such facility is provided, for failure to provide sufficient equipment, personnel, or facilities therein.

Clearly, California law provides no responsibility for the police to provide protection to the public, nor any liability whatsoever for failure to do so and just as clearly, the California Constitution defines the people themselves as the holder of both that right and the resulting responsibility.

III. Alternative Methods Of Defense

My exploration of alternative methods of defense prove them completely inadequate to defense against violent hate crimes or vicious attack.

Here are some of the alternative methods of defense I have looked into:

1. *Martial Arts.* Martial arts training requires that an individual, to be successful, must be physically fit and trained to such a high degree that one is capable of taking on several opponents at once. Even Los Angeles Police Officers are not professionally trained to that degree, and the martial artist who can be so trained, and maintain such a skill level, is rare. Further, Dr. Keith Kato, a second *dan* Black Belt in karate with a doctorate in physics, who has written a thesis on the physics of martial arts, has concluded that martial arts are of virtually no use against an attacker armed with a firearm, since the firearm can be successfully fired before the martial artist can come within range to disarm the attacker.
2. *Chemical sprays.* A chemical spray requires a direct hit on the upper body of an attacker. It must be used at the range of several feet distance, and at that range, an attacker can frequently disarm the victim of the spray before it can be used. Further, even if the spray hits the attacker under optimal conditions, an attacker who is full of adrenaline, or stimulants such as crack cocaine or PCP, or depressants such as alcohol or heroin, may be largely immune to the effects.
3. *Stun Guns and Tasers.* Stun guns, requiring direct contact between the defender and the attacker, have all the problems of martial arts and chemical sprays. As we saw in the Rodney King beating videotape, even under conditions used by a trained professional such as Sergeant Stacey Koon, a Taser gun will not necessarily be effective in incapacitating the recipient of the

Taser darts, and a Taser is a more powerful stun gun than is available to the public.

4. *Knives.* Knife-fighting is a high art, like martial arts, and unless a knife-fighter is so trained, she or he is more likely to be disarmed or defeated by an attacker than be able to use a knife successfully in a self-defense. Knife-fighting is effective only in close-range hand-to-hand combat, and the outcome of such combat is highly dubious for anyone who is not both in top form and in top physical condition. Further, private citizens are restricted from carrying a knife as a defensive weapon.

IV. Conclusions

We have seen that there is a clear and present danger to the lives of the citizens of Los Angeles from both epidemic daily crime and the extraordinary dangers from criminal attacks in the aftermath of the Rodney King beating trial acquittal.

Further, we have seen that the citizenry cannot rely upon organized law enforcement for protection or defense against such crime; that by law the people have the right to defend themselves; that there is no responsibility under the California Government Code for any public entity to provide protection to the public, and no liability to any public entity or employee for failure to protect the public.

We have strong evidence — both statistical and from case studies — that firearms in the hands of private citizens provide a defense that is superior to available alternatives, and that firearms in the hands of those licensed to carry them after a background check and minimal training represent no statistically significant threat to public order or safety.

No other conclusion can be reached than that the Los Angeles Board of Police Commissioners' Policy Concerning Licenses to Carry Concealed Weapons is in error, and that the Chief of Police of the City of Los Angeles, as charged under PC 12050, must immediately resume issuing licenses to carry concealed weapons to citizens of Los Angeles County who can pass a background check showing good moral character.

As subsequent chapters will demonstrate, the Board of Police Commissioners was unable to refute the above arguments, and the Board Policy was revised within two years to ease the granting of licenses to carry concealed firearms by the City of Los Angeles. **— JNS**

Remarks to the Los Angeles Board of Police Commissioners

November 3, 1992

Mr. President and Members of the Commission.

On May 4th of this year, while Los Angeles was still smoldering from the Los Angeles riots, I made application to you for a license to carry a concealed firearm. In those riots we saw Reginald Denny pulled from his truck and beaten senseless by criminal gangsters. Matthew Haines was pulled off his motorcycle and murdered by thugs. Dozens of innocent Angelenos were murdered on the streets and thousands more seriously injured, and during the first days of rioting LAPD did virtually nothing to protect the public.

The 1992 Los Angeles riots were a wake-up call on the lawlessness of our streets, but the body count during *ordinary* times isn't all that much less than during the riots.

The theory under which the citizenry is expected to remain unarmed in the face of a well-armed criminal population is that professional law-enforcement can provide the public adequate protection. If this was ever true, it is not true now. Further, California law places the responsibility for protection against criminals on the people, not on the police.

Article 1, Section 1 of the California Constitution says, "All people are by nature free and independent, and have certain inalienable rights, among which are those of enjoying and defending life and liberty; acquiring, possessing, and protecting property; and pursuing and obtaining safety, happiness, and privacy."

California Government Code, Section 845, states, "Neither a public entity nor a public employee is liable for failure to establish a police department or otherwise provide police protection service or, if police protection service is provided, for failure to provide sufficient police protection service."

You have issued not one single license to carry a firearm to an ordinary citizen of this city since 1974. Yet Penal Code Section 12050 requires you to issue licenses to citizens of good moral character who provide you with good cause.

In the name of heaven, what more good cause is there for a citizen of good moral character to carry a firearm than the fact that for every armed policeman in LA there are dozens of armed criminals running around?

It is intolerable for you to deny the citizens of your city the means of defending themselves against armed and violent criminals, when it is blatantly obvious that your department is incapable of defending the public and hides behind legal immunity whenever its failure destroys lives.

For at least one of you, it is also hypocrisy. When Mr. Yamaki felt it necessary to obtain a license to carry a concealed firearm to protect himself, after uniformly denying these licenses to the citizens he is supposed to serve, why did he sneak off to another municipality so that this Commission could absolve itself of the responsibility? Why is Mr. Yamaki's safety worth more than those of the citizens of Los Angeles?

As it turns out, I no longer need to be subject to your decision. I have moved outside your jurisdiction, and I herewith notify you of that fact, as I agreed to do in my application. As such, I withdraw my application for a license to carry a concealed weapon.

My business here is ended. Yours, with the citizenry at whose pleasure you serve, is just beginning.

This second little address of mine to the Board of Police Commissioners got noticed, because of my having "outed" Commissioner Yamaki as a licensed gun carrier himself. I believe this was the political factor that caused the Board to decide to cut their political liabilities on the licensing question when a group of denied applicants filed suit against them. Here is how the *Los Angeles Times* — reluctantly, and in as minimal a fashion as possible — reported on what on any other issue would have been a major political scandal:

From the *Los Angeles Times,* Metro Section, November 4, 1992:

"In other action during the [Los Angeles Police] commission meeting, a speaker accused board member Michael R. Yamaki of hypocrisy for obtaining a concealed-firearm permit for himself from the Culver City Police Department while routinely voting against the granting of permits by the Los Angeles Police Department.

"J. Neil Schulman, a gun rights activist, noted that with the exception of a permit granted recently to Police Chief Willie L. Williams, the board has denied all concealed-gun permit requests since 1974.

"'When Mr. Yamaki felt it necessary to obtain a license to carry a concealed firearm to protect himself, after uniformly denying these licenses to the citizens he is supposed to serve, why did he sneak off to another municipality so that this commission could absolve itself of the responsibility?' Schulman asked.

"Schulman received no response from the board, and when asked after the meeting about Schulman's allegations, Yamaki ignored the questions.

"However, Culver City Police Chief Ted Cooke confirmed that Yamaki had obtained a permit this year."

Guns Are Still "Equalizers"

California State Senator Teresa Hughes (D-Inglewood) is so frightened about becoming a violent-crime victim, when she must travel in the Los Angeles area, that the Senate has agreed to hire an off-duty Los Angeles Police Department sergeant at $30-an-hour for Hughes' personal protection, paid for by the taxpayers.

One of those taxpayers, who could not afford a $30-an-hour bodyguard, was Sherri Foreman, who died, along with her unborn child, after being stabbed during a carjacking attempt at an automatic teller machine in Sherman Oaks on March 30th.

It's easy to focus on the aristocratic unfairness of a state government providing a police bodyguard to the people's elected representative while the California Government Code, Section 845, denies any responsibility for the government to protect the people whom she represents: "Neither a public entity nor a public employee is liable for failure to establish a police department or otherwise provide police protection service or, if police protection service is provided, for failure to provide sufficient police protection service."

But given that the dangers to both the Teresa Hughes's and Sherri Foreman's are tragically obvious, must one be a gun nut to suggest that handguns are still "equalizers," making it possible for individuals to rely on themselves for effective protection?

Sylvia Hauser wouldn't think so. She's not a member of the NRA and even favors some gun control. But in January, 1989, when she was working a midnight shift at a convenience store in West Virginia, a 16-year-old drug abuser, two weeks out of a detention center, kidnapped her with a .22 revolver and forced her to drive into the mountains, where he raped her.

When he told her he was going to kill her, she had nothing more to lose in going for the .45 pistol she had hidden in her pocketbook. After several exchanges of gunfire, Sylvia Hauser was unshot; her attacker lay mortally wounded.

Sylvia Hauser is not an Annie Oakley. Her only training in firearms was when her husband spent a day showing her how to use the gun, 18 months earlier. Her advice to Teresa Hughes is, "I think that anyone can learn to handle a gun, and if you handle it enough so that you're not afraid of it, you'll be able to take care of yourself."

Paxton Quigley, who has taught 3,500 women how to use a gun for self-defense, as well as having been a bodyguard to celebrities such as Yoko Ono, believes not only that Senator Hughes's ability to get police protection denied to her constituents places her "above the law," but also that her reliance on a bodyguard for protection is misguided. "Even though she might feel comfortable," Quigley says, "she should know in fact that if someone decides to attack her, they'll attack the bodyguard first then she'll be next. If Senator Hughes is an independent woman...I would urge her to learn how to fight for self-defense and use a handgun for self-defense."

Hauser's and Quigley's advice is confirmed by a 1979-1985 National Crime Survey from the U.S. Bureau of Justice Statistics, which shows that a robbery victim who resists attack with a firearm is half as likely to be injured as a victim who either offers no resistance or resists using any other weapon (17.4% injured as opposed to 33.2% injured). Further, an assault victim who resists with a firearm stands only a 40% as great chance of injury as a victim who either doesn't resist at all or resists using any other weapon (12.1% as opposed to 29.9% injured).

It's illegal in California for a private citizen to carry a gun without a concealed-carry-weapon's license, and licenses are all but impossible to get in the most-dangerous California cities — unless you have political pull. The Los Angeles Board of Police Commissioners has issued no CCW licenses to any ordinary Los Angeles resident since 1974. But Commissioner Michael Yamaki quietly obtained a license in 1992 from Police Chief Ted Cooke of Culver City. Evidently, Mr. Yamaki feels that firearms are useful for self-defense, but is fearful of extending that protection to the citizenry at large.

Such fears are groundless. Florida, which allows its citizens to carry firearms for protection after a background check and proof of competency, shows no danger to the public from licensed firearms carriers.

Teresa Hughes has precisely the same right to protection as every other California citizen. Article I, Section 1 of the California Constitution states: "All people are by nature free and independent. They have certain inalienable rights, among which are those of enjoying and defending life and liberty; acquiring, possessing, and protecting property; and pursuing and obtaining safety, happiness, and privacy."

If Senator Hughes is as concerned about her constituents' safety as she is about her own, then she should see that California adopts a concealed-carry weapons law modeled after Florida's. Otherwise, Sherri Foreman is just the latest in a long string of victims yet to come.

Los Angeles Revises Concealed-Weapons Policy

The Los Angeles Police Commission voted 4-0 last Tuesday, June 29, 1993 — two days before newly elected mayor Richard Riordan took office — to turn over the authority for issuing concealed-carry weapons licenses to the Chief of Police, and to adopt new CCW guidelines currently being written by LA City Attorney Byron Boeckman.

Okay, what's the big deal in that?

In 1974, when Tom Bradley was elected mayor of Los Angeles, he appointed a new police commission and told them he didn't want the City of Los Angeles issuing CCW licenses any more. The police commissioners, who serve at the pleasure of the mayor, complied by revoking the authority of the chief of police to issue CCW licenses, and took that authority upon itself. From 1974 until the present, the commission's board policy made obtaining CCW licenses all but impossible; for the 19 years this policy was in effect, the commissioners only once granted a license to carry — and that was in 1992, to their new Chief of Police, Willie Williams, who had not yet passed his qualifying exams as a California police officer, and was therefore not entitled to carry a gun.

But during that period, the Los Angeles Police Department gun detail accepted applications, forwarded them to an officer who always found insufficient reason to recommend that it be granted, and after a hearing before the police commissioners, they voted to turn the application down, regardless of how much danger there was to the applicant.

If there was someone the commissioners actually wanted to have a CCW license, they quietly called up Ted Cooke, Chief of Police of nearby Culver City — and so pro-gun he's part owner of the Beverly Hills Gun Club — and asked him to grant the license. Or they phoned LA County Sheriff Sherman Block who was sometimes willing to sign on the dotted line.

Adding insult to injury, Commissioner Michael Yamaki secretly slipped over to Culver City (he wasn't a resident) and got a CCW license for himself. So much for their official opinion that "concealed firearms carried for protection not only provide a false sense of security but further that the licensee is often a victim of his own weapon or the subject of a civil or criminal case stemming from an improper use of the weapon."

Meanwhile, a quarter of the gun owners polled by the *Los Angeles Times* just before the April, 1992 riots admitted to carrying illegally on occasion, and when Los Angeles gun owners got caught, were subjected to a misdemeanor conviction carrying a six-month sentence which deprived them of the right to own a gun entirely, as a condition of probation or parole.

After the LA riots, when thousands of Angelenos who'd been anti-gun changed their minds, it seemed a good time to try ending this impertinence. With firearms-activist, constitutional lawyer, and criminology professor Don Kates as attorney, and a prominent list of obviously-deserving plaintiffs, the Second Amendment Foundation and the Congress of Racial Equality — later joined by NRA — filed suit against the City of Los Angeles Board of Police Commissioners for violating the state laws which required them to use their discretion in issuing CCW licenses. Saying "no" to everybody doesn't qualify as discretion, in previous California legal decisions.

City Attorney Boeckman advised his clients, the Board of Police Commissioners, that they were going to lose the suit, which would have placed the issuance of CCW licenses under court supervision, aside from costing the city a bundle in legal costs defending the suit.

The June 29th vote was a vote to settle. The terms are that if Los Angeles brings itself into compliance with state law and begins issuing licenses to the satisfaction of the plaintiffs, the law suit will be dropped in six months' time.

The new guidelines — proposed by Don Kates, and now being reviewed by Boeckman and Chief Williams — should be in place by around the middle of July.

How I (and 4 Million Friends) Successfully Fought City Hall

A couple of years ago I tried to start a gun-rights organization called CESA, the Committee to Enforce the Second Amendment. It never grew very large because I soon found out that NRA and other organizations were starting to get into the very areas I wanted to focus on with a lot more vigor (particularly after the LA riots); but I started getting in touch with major gun rights theorists and activists regularly at that point.

I was particularly interested in the CCW (concealed-carry weapons) license issue, because California law says you can't carry a loaded gun without one, and it was almost impossible to get. (I stress "almost"; I found the way into one soon enough — but I had to move to do it.)

I called Don Kates, who's a well-known criminologist, professor of constitutional law, and a constitutional lawyer himself, and told him about the Board Policy of the Los Angeles Board of Police Commissioners, which, in essence, said that even though California Penal Code 12050 required them to consider issuing CCW licenses to county residents of good moral character who could show good cause for carrying a firearm, they didn't believe there *were* any good causes so they were going to make it as difficult as possible. They implemented this policy by denying all license applications for 19 years.

When I read that policy to Don and asked if it could be successfully overturned in court, he said, "Yes, but —" The "but" was the necessity of finding plaintiffs and getting money to pursue the lawsuit. I gave him a list of plaintiffs. He called Alan Gottlieb of the Second Amendment Foundation, expressed his opinion that he could overturn the policy, and Alan agreed to write the checks.

Here's how I described it in the press release I wrote:

Reversing an apparent national trend of ever-increasing firearms restrictions on private citizens, the Los Angeles Police Department has resumed issuing licenses to carry concealed weapons to private citizens for the first time since 1974. The 4-0 vote to return issuing authority to Police Chief Willie Williams, approved June 29, 1993 as one of the final acts by the Mayor-Bradley-appointed Los Angeles Board of Police Commissioners, was instituted in response to a lawsuit filed by the Second Amendment Foundation and the Congress of Racial Equality, and later joined by the National Rifle Association, on behalf of individuals who had unlawfully been denied such licenses by the police commission's policy.

Security Consultant D. Ray Hickman, one of the plaintiffs in this suit and a similar federal lawsuit, will be receiving his license at the Gun Detail office at LAPD's Parker Center at 1:00 PM on Tuesday, September 7, 1993. Ironically, because the LAPD's Gun Detail did not have the equipment necessary to physically produce the licenses, plaintiffs in the lawsuit dug into their own pockets and donated a typewriter, a Polaroid camera, and a laminating machine to LAPD.

California Penal Code Section 12050 requires a city's chief of police to issue CCW licenses to county residents of good moral character who can show good cause. The state's legislatively-mandated licensing procedure specifies a two-page application form, requires a fingerprint background check with both the state Department of Justice and the FBI, lists the firearms to be carried on the license, and requires the licensee to show proficiency with the weapon carried.

The California Department of Justice is unaware of any cases where a person issued a California CCW license has used it for criminal activities.

The "good cause" requirement for obtaining a CCW license includes both business reasons such as risk because of one's profession or providing protection services to others, and personal reasons, such as threats to one's self or family. The requirement that chiefs of police issue CCW licenses to qualified individuals is enactment of Article 1, Section 1 of the California Constitution, which states, "All people are by nature free and independent, and have certain inalienable rights, among which are those of enjoying and defending life and liberty; acquiring, possessing, and protecting property; and pursuing and obtaining safety, happiness, and privacy."

Contrary to popular opinion, neither state nor local government has any legal requirement to provide crime protection to a threatened individual, and no government entity or employee has any liability for failure to do so. (California Government Code Sections 845, 845.2, 845.8, and 846). Government entities and employees are also shielded from liability for issuing CCW licenses (California Government Code 818.4 and 821.2).

A quarter of the gun owners polled by the *Los Angeles Times* just before the April, 1992 riots admitted to carrying illegally on occasion.

If Police Chief Willie Williams issues CCW licenses in Los Angeles at a rate proportionate to the rate he issued them as Police Chief of Philadelphia — where he signed around 4000 CCW licenses — then Los Angeles should see approximately 10,000 licenses issued in the next few years.

Because of my involvement in this issue from the beginning, and several *LA Times* Op-Ed pieces I'd written demonstrating the usefulness of civilians carrying firearms by saving large groups of people, I got tapped to run the press conference in front of Parker Center at 1:00 PM on Tuesday, September 7, 1993. It turned out to be a media circus, with five TV crews, representatives from all the major radio stations in town, and the major Southern California newspapers. I had other people to shove in front of the TV cameras — Dan Gifford, a former ABC News and McNeill/Lehrer newsman who had got the first LAPD-issued CCW after Chief Williams, Elodie McKee, an actress and gun-rights activist, and Ray Hickman (referenced above), but I ended up being the person whom the radio and print media wanted to talk to, because Dan and Elodie were in front of the TV cameras, and Ray was upstairs at Parker Center getting his license.

So I got quoted a lot.

I had also just done an hour on Michael Jackson's talk show on KABC radio that morning, so it was a pretty busy day. I got the call from Jackson's producer at 9, was in studio an hour later, then after the show rushed home to field press inquiries and fax out more releases while I was trying to get into my suit to get downtown to Parker Center for the conference.

All in all, it's been a great victory for the gun-rights cause because we finally got some coverage of our point of view. My phone has been ringing constantly with inquiries by people who have good cause for carrying firearms and want to do whatever they can do to help. Three new local-area attorneys have signed into the cause — two from Beverly Hills. Yay!

I'll be working with a watchdog committee to track whether LAPD stays in compliance with the settlement terms. If they don't, the lawsuit will move forward in around six months or a year. But there's so much new pressure on them, I doubt they'll be effective at offering resistance, and they should be issuing a *lot* of licenses over the next few years.

Update, February, 1994: As of this writing, I am hearing reports that very few licenses have been issued; that the Los Angeles Police Department's Gun Detail telephone is busy all the time; and that applications are backed up at least six months without a response. I don't yet know if this is bureaucratic business-as-usual, or active resistance to issuing licenses from Chief Willie Williams's office. Either way, it seems that the City of Los Angeles is not in compliance with the terms of the settlement agreement, and further legal pressure will need to be brought to bear. **— JNS**

Update, February 1999: The City of Los Angeles is now under a court-enforced consent decree, and all rejected applications are now reviewed by a citizen's review board. It's still a discretionary process to get a license to carry from the City of Los Angeles, and the current Los Angeles, Chief of Police, Bernard Parks, is doing his best to avoid complying with the consent decree. I eagerly await discovering whether a court will put teeth into the enforcement of its decree or whether politics will prevail over the law. **—JNS**

The Thrill of My Life

Sunday, September 12, 1993

You know, being a writer is a lonely life. You work isolated at home, send out your work, and then, mostly, what you hear back is silence.

So when the value of one's work is recognized by the World Out There, it's a very big deal, and you note it down in the balance ledger of whether it's worthwhile to keep going or not.

I just had the thrill of my life. I was in front of my TV set, just about to go downstairs and remove my clothes from the dryer, when a commentary by KCBS Los Angeles anchorman Michael Tuck caught my eye.

Tuck started out by postulating a scenario in which other high school students would have been armed when one was shot and killed by a gang member a few days ago. He ranted, and raved, and foamed at the mouth against the "gun nuts" who would have armed the rest of the students, who would then have all pulled out their guns simultaneously, firing wildly in a cacophony not heard since Woodstock.

Mr. Tuck then talked about the lawsuit which I helped instigate, against the Los Angeles Police Department, which resulted in the LAPD once again obeying California law in its requirement that county residents of good moral character who can show good cause shall be issued licenses to carry concealed weapons. He ranted and raved, tossing around the phrase "gun nut" twice per sentence, then quoted me from Scott Harris's column in the September 6, 1993 *Los Angeles Times* — identifying me as a "ringleader" of those who filed the law suit — in which I stated, "It is a fundamental error in society to expect an elite group of professionals to provide public safety. In my view, public safety is everybody's job."

Then he called me a "gun nut" again, along with all the other gun nuts who think innocent people should be better armed than the criminals.

Wow.

I've had some thrills in my life, but this was the best.

It was thrilling when Anthony Burgess and Nobel laureate Milton Friedman lent their endorsements to my first novel.

It was thrilling when Robert Heinlein told me he laughed his ass off at the satirical parts of my second novel.

It was thrilling on two occasions when I twice received the Prometheus Award for my novels.

It was thrilling when the producer who gave Rod Serling his first job in television told me my 1985 *Twilight Zone* episode, "Profile in Silver," was in his opinion the only one which would have fit into the original show.

But to be called a ringleader of gun nuts by a news reader on a Sunday evening local broadcast, that has got to be the best.

Thank you, Michael Tuck. You made my day.

The Second Amendment and the Right to Keep and Bear Arms

This section contains my work on establishing that the text of the Second Amendment ("A well-regulated Militia being necessary to the security of a free State, the right of the people to keep and bear Arms shall not be infringed.") cannot be interpreted in any other way than as a constitutional protection of the right of the people to keep and bear arms. — **JNS**

Reply to the Executives of the ACLU of Southern California on the Meaning of the Second Amendment

Original ACLU materials are shown in *italics,* and the replies in standard typeface.

ACLU of Southern California Launches Educational Campaign on Gun Control and the Second Amendment

As the nation's oldest and most prominent defender of Constitutional Rights, the ACLU of Southern California today launched an educational campaign to eliminate popular myths about the Second Amendment to the U.S. Constitution.

"Governor Wilson's crime summit and other political posturing to 'get tough on crime' are not focusing on ways to limit violence in our communities," said Ramona Ripston, ACLU executive director. "We want to support one positive and obvious tool that will have a direct impact on thousands of lives. And, as an advocate of our freedoms under the U.S. Constitution, the ACLU wants to set the record straight on what our forefathers truly intended about our right to bear arms."

The Second Amendment was written shortly after the Revolutionary War when Bill of Rights author James Madison and other leaders were still suspicious of any centralized government. In that context, the phrase "a well regulated Militia, being necessary to the security of a free State" reflected a vital concern of that time: the ability of states to defend themselves against a possibly tyrannical federal government or outside threats to the Union. Equipment and ammunition were kept in the house of private citizens because the militia of 1792 consisted of part-time citizen-soldiers.

Correct as far as it goes, however it should be noted that the threat of abuse of power by the national government became significant during the Civil War, and has become incrementally greater ever since. The usurpations and abuses of government at all levels in this country has never been greater.

"In four cases in which the Supreme Court addressed the issue, it has consistently held that the Second Amendment does not grant a blanket right of individual gun ownership," said ACLU attorney Alan Friel. "Despite what is commonly believed, the Amendment does not prohibit rational and effective gun control."

Both statements are technically true, but misleading. First, the Second Amendment does not grant the right of individual gun ownership, because that right precedes the Bill of Rights; all the Second Amendment does is protect that preexisting right. Second, constitutional law has never been interpreted as granting a "blanket" right to do *anything* — and that applies to the First, Fourth, and Fifth Amendments as much as it applies to the Second. However, the ACLU has historically fought for the most extreme protections — and the harshest limitations on exceptions — to constitutional rights, and it is especially pernicious that the ACLU of Southern California is arguing against ACLU's traditional role of expanding, rather than contracting, the "blanket" protections of the Bill of Rights. As far as whether the Second Amendment prohibits rational and effective gun control, when some is proposed, we'll see. No gun control law has ever proven to be effective at producing the effects for which it was passed: the reduction of crimes committed with guns, or even the denial of guns to those who most misuse them.

As part of the campaign, the civil liberties group has published a new public education brochure and has placed a full-page advertisement in the West Coast edition of today's New York Times. *Public speaking and other educational activities are also planned.*

This is entirely contrary to the purposes of the ACLU, which is an organization devoted to the protection of individual civil liberties and rights. In effect, the ACLU of Southern California is becoming an advocate of greater restrictions on individuals and greater police authority in its place.

Brochure:

When the	*This*	*Illustration*
FOUNDERS	*is*	*of a*
of the	*not*	*handgun*
United States	*what*	*being*
of America	*they*	*pointed*
wrote the	*had*	*at*
SECOND	*in*	*the*
AMENDMENT ... ->	*mind.*	*reader*

This is grandstanding, an attempt to recruit the Framers of the Constitution to a point of view held by the modern authoritarians of the ACLU of Southern California, and entirely antithetical to the actual documented reasons and thoughts of those who wrote the Constitution, the Bill of Rights, and the Second Amendment in particular.

> *"A well-regulated Militia, being necessary to the security of a free State, the right of the people to keep and bear Arms shall not be infringed."*
>
> *The Second Amendment to the U.S. Constitution*

HAVE YOU ever heard someone say gun control is a fine idea — except that the Second Amendment prohibits it?

It's a popular sentiment. Fortunately, it's not true.

Get that? "*Fortunately*" indeed. The ACLU executives' agenda is exposed here: they wish greater gun control on the basis of personal opinions which have no grounds in ACLU doctrine, and are subverting the organization to their own personal ends. The fabrication of history begins here.

The Second Amendment was never intended as a gun license

for the entire American populace. As original drafted — and as consistently interpreted by the courts for more than a century — the Amendment does not grant any blanket right to own a gun nor does it stand in the way of rational, effective gun control.

The executives of the ACLU of Southern California betray their anti-libertarian, authoritarian stance when they equate the Second Amendment to a "license": they evidently cannot conceive of the Framers' premise that rights originate with the individual, instead of beginning as grants of privilege or immunity from the government, reducing us all again to subjects of a ruler. That was the purpose of the American Revolution: to free us from that view of the tyrannical relationship between the State and the individual. Again, the Second Amendment does not grant the right to keep and bear arms, nor does it claim to: it merely states that "the right of the people to keep and bear arms *shall not be infringed.*" The phrasing itself belies the possible interpretation that the Second Amendment is a *grant* of rights. The Framers understood that what they were doing was a limitation on the powers of the government they were forging. The ACLU executives are confounded by this thought.

The idea of gun ownership as an American birthright is nothing more than a popular myth.

Throwing the right to keep and bear arms into the memory hole portrayed in Orwell's *Nineteen-eighty-four* is worthy of the anti-Semites who claim that the Holocaust never happened. Seventy million Americans own firearms today. The sentiments to restrict the people's arms were as common at the time of the American Revolution as they are today, by those seeking a monopoly of force for the State. As James Madison, the chief author of the Bill of Rights put it in *Federalist Paper No. 26*, "The advantage of being armed...the Americans possess over the people of all other nations...Notwithstanding the military establishments in the several Kingdoms of Europe, which are carried as far as the public resources will bear, the governments are afraid to trust the people with arms."

The author of the Bill of Rights was aware that the American people being armed was an exception to the practice everywhere else on Earth (except Switzerland), and that the tendency would be for Americans to revert to the common condition of the rest of mankind if the right to keep and bear arms was not explicitly enshrined in our founding document. If the right to keep and bear arms is nothing more than a popular myth, with no basis in the history of our country, how is it that this right has survived for two centuries so that our civilian population is the best armed in the world?

This should be the first proof to the innocent that the executives of the ACLU of Southern California are attempting to deceive them about the actual history of the right to keep and bear arms, and the Second Amendment in particular.

Yet the controversy over gun control and the Second Amendment rages on.

Why, yes. Depriving an entire people of the right which is the practical defense of all their other rights is bound to cause controversy.

AS THE NATION'S oldest and most prominent defender of individual rights, the American Civil Liberties Union (ACLU) holds the U.S. Constitution and its Bill of Rights in the highest regard.

Indeed. I seriously doubt you could get ACLU's national executive director, Ira Glasser, or its president, Nadine Strossen, to dismiss the Second Amendment from the Bill of rights so cavalierly. They are more likely to understand that the weakening of any of the Bill of Rights is bound to weaken all the others.

To clear up many misconceptions, here are some questions and answers about the Second Amendment and gun control.

ACLU of Southern California
Questions and Answers
on the Second Amendment

Q Does the Second Amendment in any way guarantee gun rights to individuals?

A No. The weight of historical and legal scholarship clearly shows that the Second Amendment was intended to guarantee that states could maintain armed forces to resist the federal government.

According to Constitutional attorney Don B. Kates, Jr., you will not be able to find this position supported in *any* major law-review article, while the legal and historical scholarship regarding the Second Amendment's protection of an individual right to keep and bear private arms is so weighty as to be indisputable.

The historical and legal scholarship is most authoritative in a February, 1982 report issued by the United States Senate's Subcommittee on the Constitution, Committee on the Judiciary, titled "The Right to Keep and Bear Arms." To prove that, here are the two prefaces from that report, the first by the Committee Chairman, Senator Orrin G. Hatch (R., Utah) and the second by the Ranking Minority Member, Senator Dennis DeConcini (D., Arizona):

Senator Hatch:

In my studies as an attorney and as a United States Senator, I have constantly been amazed by the indifference or even hostility shown the Second Amendment by courts, legislatures, and commentators. James Madison would be startled to hear that his recognition of a right to keep and bear arms, which passed the House by a voice vote without objection and hardly a debate, has since been construed in but a single, and most ambiguous, Supreme Court decision, whereas his proposals for freedom of religion, which he made reluctantly out of fear that they would be rejected or narrowed beyond use, and those for freedom of assembly, which passed only after a lengthy and bitter debate, are the subject of scores of detailed and favorable decisions. Thomas Jefferson, who kept a veritable armory of pistols, rifles and shotguns at Monticello, and advised his nephew to forsake other sports in favor of hunting, would be astounded to hear supposed civil libertarians claim firearm ownership should be restricted. Samuel Adams, a handgun owner who pressed for an amendment stating that the "Constitution shall never be construed...to prevent the people of the United States who are peaceable citizens from keeping their own arms," would be shocked to hear that his native state today imposes a year's sentence, without probation or parole, for carrying a firearm without a police permit.

This is not to imply that courts have totally ignored the impact of the Second Amendment in the Bill of Rights. No fewer than twenty-one decisions by the courts of our states have recognized an individual right to keep and bear arms, and a majority of these have not only recognized the right but invalidated laws or regulations which abridged it. Yet in all too many instances, courts or commentators have sought, for reasons only tangentially related to constitutional history, to construe this right out of existence. They argue that the Second Amendment's words "right of the people" mean "a right of the state"—apparently overlooking the impact of those same words when used in the First and Fourth Amendments. The "right of the people" to assemble or to be free from unreasonable searches and seizures is not contested as an individual guarantee. Still they ignore consistency and claim that the right to "bear arms" relates only to military uses. This not only violates a consistent constitutional reading of "right of the people" but also ignores that the second amendment protects a right to "keep" arms. These commentators contend instead that the amendment's preamble regarding the necessity of a "well regulated militia...to a free state" means that the right to keep and bear arms applies only to a National Guard. Such a reading fails to note that the Framers used the term "militia" to relate to every citizen capable of bearing arms, and that Congress has established the present National Guard under its power to raise armies, expressly stating that it was not doing so under its power to organize and arm the militia.

When the first Congress convened for the purpose of drafting a Bill of Rights, it delegated the task to James Madison. Madison did not write upon a blank tablet. Instead, he obtained a pamphlet listing the State proposals for a bill of rights and sought to produce a briefer version incorporating all the vital proposals of these. His purpose was to incorporate, not distinguish by technical changes, proposals such as that of the Pennsylvania minority, Sam Adams, or the New Hampshire delegates. Madison proposed among other rights that "That right of the people to keep and bear arms shall not be infringed; a well armed and well regulated militia being the best security of a free country; but no person religiously scrupulous of bearing arms shall be compelled to render military service in person." In the House, this was initially modified so that the militia clause came before the proposal recognizing the right. The proposals for the Bill of Rights were then trimmed in the interests of brevity. The conscientious objector clause was removed following objections by Elbridge Gerry, who complained that future Congresses might abuse the exemption to excuse everyone from military service.

The proposal finally passed the House in its present form: "A well regulated militia, being necessary to the security of a free state, the right of the people to keep and bear arms, shall not be infringed." In this form it was submitted into the Senate, which passed it the following day. The Senate in the process indicated its intent that the right be an individual one, for private purposes, by rejecting an amendment which would have limited the keeping and bearing of arms to bearing "For the common defense".

The earliest American constitutional commentators concurred in giving this broad reading to the amendment. When St. George Tucker, later Chief Justice of the Virginia Supreme Court, in 1803 published an edition of Blackstone annotated to American law, he followed Blackstone's citation of the right of the subject "of having arms suitable to their condition and degree, and such as are allowed by law" with a citation to the Second Amendment, "And this without any qualification as to their condition or degree, as is the case in the British government." William Rawle's "View of the Constitution" published in Philadelphia in 1825 noted that under the Second Amendment: "The prohibition is general. No clause in the Constitution could by a rule of construction be conceived to give to Congress a power to disarm the people. Such a flagitious attempt could only be made under some general pretense by a state legislature. But if in blind pursuit of inordinate power, either should attempt it, this amendment may be appealed to as a restraint on both." The Jefferson papers in the Library of Congress show that both Tucker and Rawle were friends of, and corresponded with, Thomas Jefferson. Their views are those of contemporaries of Jefferson, Madison and others, and are entitled to special weight. A few years later, Joseph Story in his "Commentaries on the Constitution" considered the right to keep and bear arms as "the palladium of the liberties of the republic," which deterred tyranny and enabled the citizenry at large to overthrow it should it come to pass.

Subsequent legislation in the second Congress likewise supports the interpretation of the Second Amendment that creates an individual right. In the Militia Act of 1792, the second Congress defined "militia of the United States" to include almost every free adult male in the United States. These persons were obligated by law to possess a firearm and a minimum supply of ammunition and military equipment. This statute, incidentally, remained in effect into the early years of the present century as a legal requirement of gun ownership for most of the population of the United States. There can be little doubt from this that when the Congress and the people spoke of a "militia", they had reference to the traditional concept of the entire populace capable of bearing arms, and not to any formal group such as what is today called the National Guard. The purpose was to create an armed citizenry, which the political theorists at the time considered essential to ward off tyranny. From this militia, appropriate measures might create a "well regulated militia" of individuals trained in their duties and responsibilities as citizens and owners of firearms.

If gun laws in fact worked, the sponsors of this type of legislation should have no difficulty drawing upon long lists of examples of crime rates reduced by such legislation. That they cannot do so after a century and a half of trying—that they must sweep under the rug the southern attempts at gun control in the 1870-1910 period, the northeastern attempts in the 1920-1939 period, the attempts at both Federal and State levels in 1965-1976—establishes the repeated, complete and inevitable failure of gun laws to control serious crime.

Immediately upon assuming chairmanship of the Subcommittee on the Constitution, I sponsored the report which follows as an effort to study, rather than ignore, the history of the controversy over the right to keep and bear arms. Utilizing the research capabilities of the Subcommittee on the Constitution, the resources of the Library of Congress, and the assistance of constitutional scholars such as Mary Kaaren Jolly, Steven [*sic*] Halbrook, and David T. Hardy, the subcommittee has managed to uncover information on the right to keep and bear arms which documents quite clearly its status as a major individual right of American citizens. We did not guess at the purpose of the British 1689 Declaration of Rights; we located the Journals of the House of Commons and private notes of the Declaration's sponsors, now dead for two centuries. We did not make suppositions as to colonial interpretations of that Declaration's right to keep and bear arms; we examined colonial newspapers which discussed it. We did not speculate as to the intent of the framers of the second amendment; we examined James Madison's drafts for it, his handwritten outlines of speeches upon the Bill of Rights, and discussions of the second amendment by early scholars who were personal friends of Madison, Jefferson, and Washington and wrote while these still lived. What the Subcommittee on the Constitution uncovered was clear—and long-lost—proof that the second amendment to our Constitution was intended as an individual right of the American citizen to keep and carry arms in a peaceful manner, for protection of himself, his family, and his freedoms. The summary of our research and findings forms the first portion of this report.

In the interest of fairness and the presentation of a complete picture, we also invited groups which were likely to oppose this recognition of freedoms to submit their views. The statements of two associations who replied are reproduced here following the report of the Subcommittee. The Subcommittee also invited statements by Messr. Halbrook and Hardy, and by the National Rifle Association, whose statements likewise follow our report.

When I became chairman of the Subcommittee on the Constitution, I hoped that I would be able to assist in the protection of the constitutional rights of American citizens, rights which have too often been eroded in the belief that government could be relied upon for quick solutions to difficult problems.

Both as an American citizen and as a United States Senator I repudiate this view. I likewise repudiate the approach of those who believe to solve American problems you simple become something other than American. To my mind, the uniqueness of our free institutions, the fact that an American citizen can boast freedoms unknown in any other land, is all the more reason to resist any erosion of our individual rights. When our ancestors forged a land "conceived in liberty", they did so with musket and rifle. When they reacted to attempts to dissolve their free institutions, and established their identity as a free nation, they did so as a nation of armed freemen. When they sought to record forever a guarantee of their rights, they devoted one full amendment out of ten to nothing but the protection of their right to keep and bear arms against government interference. Under my chairmanship the Subcommittee on the Constitution will concern itself with a proper recognition of, and respect for, this right most valued by free men.

Orrin G. Hatch,
Chairman,
Subcommittee on the Constitution
January 20, 1982.

Senator DeConcini:

The right to bear arms is a tradition with deep roots in American society. Thomas Jefferson proposed that "no free man shall ever be debarred the use of arms," and Samuel Adams called for an amendment banning any law "to prevent the people of the United States who are peaceable citizens from keeping their own arms." The Constitution of the State of Arizona, for example, recognized the "right of an individual citizen to bear arms in defense of himself or the State."

Even though the tradition has deep roots, its application to modern America is the subject of intense controversy. Indeed, it is a controversy into which the Congress is beginning, once again, to immerse itself. I have personally been disappointed that so important an issue should have generally been so thinly researched and so minimally debated both in Congress and the courts. Our Supreme Court has but once touched on its meaning at the Federal level and that decision, now nearly a half-century old, is so ambiguous that any school of thought can find some support in it. All Supreme Court decisions on the second amendment's application to the States came in the last century, when constitutional law was far different that it is today. As ranking minority member of the Subcommittee on the Constitution, I, therefore, welcome the effort which led to this report—a report based not only upon the independent research of the subcommittee staff, but also upon full and fair presentation of the cases by all interested groups and individual scholars.

I personally believe that it is necessary for the Congress to amend the Gun Control Act of 1968. I welcome the opportunity to introduce this discussion of how best these amendments might be made.

The Constitution subcommittee staff has prepared this monograph bringing together proponents of both sides of the debate over the 1968 Act. I believe that the statements contained herein present the arguments fairly and thoroughly. I commend Senator Hatch, chairman of the subcommittee, for having this excellent reference work prepared. I am sure that it will be of great assistance to the Congress as it debates the second amendment and considers legislation to amend the Gun Control Act.

Dennis DeConcini,
Ranking Minority Member,
Subcommittee on the Constitution
January 20, 1982.

Senator DeConcini's recommendation that Congress needed to amend the Gun Control Act of 1968 was taken up only four years later, when the Democrats controlling the House of Representatives and again controlling the Senate, passed the 1986 Firearms Owners Protection Act, which recognizes "the rights of citizens to keep and bear arms under the second amendment to the United States Constitution."

You just barely might get away with dismissing the Senate Subcommittee's report as political opinion — but the 1986 Firearms Owners Protection Act's recognition of the Second Amendment is the law of the land passed by Congress and signed by the president.

The question is answered. The executives of the ACLU of Southern California are dead wrong.

Most scholars overwhelmingly concur that the Second Amendment was never intended to guarantee gun ownership rights for individual personal use. Small arms ownership was common when the Bill of Rights was adopted, with many people owning single-shot firearms for hunting in what was then an overwhelmingly rural nation.

What "scholars" concur that the Second Amendment was not intended to make such a guarantee would still have a hard time explaining away the clauses guaranteeing the right to keep and bear arms in 45 of the 50 state constitutions today. Why would state constitutions need to guarantee the right to keep and bear arms, if the only meaning of that phrase is to protect state governments from the federal government? And given that the right to keep and bear arms was — as the ACLU executives themselves admit — common at the time of the Bill of Rights' ratification, the individual right to keep and bear arms would be otherwise guaranteed by the *Ninth* amendment to the U.S. Constitution, which states, "The enumeration in the Constitution, of certain rights, shall not be construed to deny or disparage others retained by the people."

It should also be noted that the ACLU executives, in attempting to portray the right to keep and bear arms as something antiquated and outdated, focus on the technology of the time only having reached the stage of single-shot firearms.

Are they willing to apply that reasoning to the rest of the U.S. Constitution?

The first amendment's guarantee of free exercise of religion wouldn't apply to the Mormons or the Christian Scientists; there were no Mormons or Christian Scientists in 1791 when the Bill of Rights was added to the Constitution.

The first amendment's guarantee of freedom of the press wouldn't apply to anything printed using photography, or computer typesetting or offset printing, nor would the guarantees of freedom of speech apply to the broadcast media, or anything using telephones or telegraphs — none of which existed in the 1790's.

The fourth amendment's guarantees of freedom from unreasonable searches wouldn't apply to electronic wiretapping or the use of laser listening devices; nor satellite or infrared observation — the framers couldn't have possibly conceived of any of them.

Nor, I suppose, could the United States have an Air Force or spy satellites, since there is no authorization anywhere in the Constitution for anything other than land or naval armed forces.

Why is it that arguments such as this are never brought up with respect to any constitutional issue relating to progress, except when it is to destroy the people's right to keep and bear arms?

And how can it be that the American Civil Liberties Union of Southern California is controlled by persons who are so quick to divide the Bill of Rights so to allow authoritarians to conquer it?

Q Does the Second Amendment authorize Americans to possess and own any firearm they feel they may need?

A Clearly, no. The original intent of the Second Amendment was to protect the right of states to maintain state militias.

And who were the militia? According to George Mason, who refused to sign the U.S. Constitution because it did not yet have a Bill of Rights, the militia "consist now of the whole people."

Private gun ownership that is not necessary to the maintenance of militias is not protected by the Second Amendment.

That is just backwards. The arms that individual militia members own *are*, by definition, the militia arms.

Q Does the Second Amendment allow government to limit — even prohibit — ownership of guns by individuals?

A Yes. Federal, state and local governments can all regulate guns without violating the Second Amendment.

Repeating this assertion without proof does not change it from false to true. Such proof is impossible because of repeated court decisions over the last two centuries which state just the opposite. While it is true that the Supreme Court of the United States has never enforced the Second Amendment as clearly as gun-rights activists would hope, neither has it ever ruled against the Second Amendment as protecting an individual right to keep and bear arms. Specific citations will follow as the ACLU document brings them up.

State authorities have considerable powers to regulate guns. The federal government can also regulate firearm ownership, although some scholars believe that the federal power may not be as extensive as that of an individual state.

There is no disputing that the right to keep and bear arms is under attack both legislatively and in the courts, and there have, indeed, been some adverse lower-court decisions, allowing infringements on these rights of the people. This does not change either the historical facts of the establishment of the right to keep and bear arms in protections offered by the U.S. Constitution and state constitutions, or the malfeasance of judges who have falsified the precedents in order to advance their personal anti-firearms agendas.

California, for example, has limited the ability of local governments to regulate firearms. While the state has kept its broad regulatory power, cities and counties can only prohibit guns from being carried in public places.

Q How have the courts — particularly the U.S. Supreme Court — interpreted the Second Amendment?

A The Supreme Court has flatly held that the individual's right to keep and bear arms "is not a right granted by the Constitution."

The decision in which the Supreme Court "flatly held" this

was *U.S. v. Cruikshank*, referenced below, and the *complete* quotation from that decision which the ACLU executives deliberately leave out (because it would give away their game) is,

> The second and tenth counts are equally defective. The right there specified is that of bearing arms for a lawful purpose. This is not a right granted by the Constitution. Neither is it in any manner dependent upon that instrument for its existence.

What the Court meant is that the right to keep and bear arms preceded the constitution, and therefore was not a right granted by the constitution, such as, for example, the right to vote, which is not a natural right but is a created political right. The Court's reasoning was that only rights originating in the federal Constitution could be imposed on the states by federal courts. That decision by the Reconstruction-era Supreme Court ignored the intent of the authors of the Fourteenth Amendment to apply the protections of the Bill of Rights — including, explicitly, the Second Amendment — to what they saw as the jurisdiction of state courts. If the *Cruikshank* decision were applied today, it would strike down almost *all* federal intervention against state and local governments, because federal courts could not impose any of the Bill of Rights on state or local governments, or on private individuals. States could then revert to segregated schools and restaurants, there could have been no federal trial of the Los Angeles police officers who beat Rodney King, and states could allow the Lord's Prayer in public schools.

In the *Cruikshank* case, blacks who had been disarmed and terrorized by the Ku Klux Klan were arguing that the KKK had violated their rights; the Court was ruling that the federal courts had no jurisdiction to prevent the Klansmen from doing so. Is this what the ACLU of Southern California would like to see happen today?

Here are the Court's words:

> The third and eleventh counts are even more objectionable. They charge the intent to have been to deprive the citizens named, they being in Loui-

siana, "of their respective several lives and liberty of person without due process of law." This is nothing else than alleging a conspiracy to falsely imprison or murder citizens of the United States, being within the territorial jurisdiction of the State of Louisiana.

The rights of life and personal liberty are natural rights of man. "To secure these rights," says the Declaration of Independence, "governments are instituted among men, deriving their just powers from the consent of the governed." The very highest duty of the States, when they entered into the Union under the Constitution, was to protect all persons within their boundaries in the enjoyment of these "unalienable rights with which they were endowed by their Creator."

Sovereignty, for this purpose, rests alone with the States. It is no more the duty or within the power of the United States to punish for a conspiracy to falsely imprison or murder within a State, than it would be to punish for false imprisonment or murder itself.

In the four cases in which the high court has addressed the issue, it has consistently held that the Second Amendment does not confer a blanket right of individual gun ownership.

As I've demonstrated, in one of the four decisions, that is because the Court held the right existed previously and independently.

The most important Supreme Court Second Amendment case, U.S. v. Miller, *was decided in 1939. It involved two men who illegally shipped a sawed-off shotgun from Oklahoma to Arkansas, then claimed the Second Amendment prohibited the federal government from prosecuting them.*

The court emphatically disagreed, ruling that the Second Amendment has the "obvious intent" of creating state militias, not of authorizing individual gun ownership. In two earlier rulings in 1876 and 1886, the Supreme Court held that the Second Amendment affected only the federal government's power to regulate gun ownership and had no effect on state gun control powers. Those cases, Presser v. U.S. *and* U.S. v. Cruikshank, *formed the basis for the continuing legal decisions that the Second Amendment was not an impediment to rational gun control.*

The *Presser* case, if anything, destroys the "militia" premise the ACLU brochure is arguing; the Court was ruling against Presser that he and other members of a local self-organized militia didn't have the right to march armed as a group on city streets without a permit from local government. The question of whether the men had the right to carry arms as individuals was explicitly upheld as follows:

> It is undoubtedly true that all citizens capable of bearing arms constitute the reserved military force or reserve militia of the United States as well as of the States, and, in view of this prerogative of the general government, as well as of its general powers, the states cannot, even laying the Constitutional provision in question out of view, prohibit the people from keeping and bearing arms...

If anything, *Presser* contradicts *Cruikshank* in that it explicitly denies the states' ability to "prohibit the people from keeping and bearing arms."

The *Miller* case is odd in that the Supreme Court never heard arguments from the defense in overturning the lower-court ruling to dismiss charges on the basis of the defendants' Second-amendment rights; only a prosecution brief — and one which suffered from the same lack of historical veracity as the ACLU brochure's. Defendant Jack Miller had been murdered before the case reached the Supreme Court and the other defendant, Frank Layton, was in prison; no attorney argued their Second-amendment case to the Supreme Court.

Here is the meat of what the Supreme Court actually said in *U.S. v. Miller:*

> The Court can not take judicial notice that a shotgun having a barrel less than 18 inches long has today any reasonable relation to the preservation or efficiency of a well regulated militia; and therefore can not say that the Second Amendment guarantees to the citizen the right to keep and bear such a weapon.

The Supreme Court was stating that a weapon, to be protected by the Second Amendment, had to have a military application, specifically one that was useful to a citizen's militia. Weapons used only by gangsters, such as brass knuckles, would not, in their view, be promoting the framers' intent of a well-armed citizenry. In the absence of counsel for the defendants to provide evidence to the Court that a sawed-off shotgun had some military application — which would have been easy since shortbarreled shotguns were used in World War One — the court could "not take judicial notice" that a sawed-off shotgun was a "militia" weapon, and reversed the lower court's ruling on that basis and that basis alone.

In fact, by the Miller court's reasoning, full-auto M-16 assault rifles, full-auto AK-47's, and Uzis *would* be useful to militia, and therefore their ownership by civilians would be protected by the Second Amendment. Is this an argument that the ACLU of Southern California executives are ready to embrace?

In another case that the Supreme Court declined to review, a federal appeals court in Illinois ruled in 1983 that the Second Amendment could not prevent a municipal government from banning handgun possession. In the case Quilici v. Village of Morton Grove, *the appeals court held that contemporary handguns couldn't be considered as weapons relevant to a collective militia.*

The Supreme Court simply denied certiorari on the *Morton Grove* case, which gives it no precedential value outside of the federal district in which the case was resolved by the lower court. If the Supreme Court had actually wished to endorse the lower court's decision, and endorse the ACLU of Southern California executives' view of the irrelevancy of the Second Amendment, the Supreme Court could simply have issued a summary affirmation of the lower court's decision. It did not do so, leaving the question unresolved. Constitutional attorney Stephen Halbrook (mentioned earlier in Senator Hatch's preface) expressed to me privately in 1993 the thought that the Supreme Court had actually done Second-Amendment advocates a favor in denying cert on the *Morton Grove* case, since Quilici was both plaintiff and his own attorney, and refused to accept research and advice offered by renowned constitutional attorneys.

Q The National Rifle Association (NRA) says that the Second Amendment guarantees our right to keep and bear arms. Has the NRA got it wrong?

A Like any powerful special interest, the NRA works to secure its financial well-being. It insists on a view of the Second Amendment that defies virtually all court decisions and contradicts findings of most legal scholars. In so doing, the NRA actively perpetuates a seemingly endless cycle of gun-related fatalities.

Trust an ideologue to answer a question with an *ad hominem* attack on the motives of those who disagree with them, not only suggesting that the 3.4 million members of the National Rifle Association are motivated by financial well-being in their view of the purpose of the Second Amendment, but also scapegoating the law-abiding and well-trained NRA gun owners for the actions of the criminally insane few. This is a case of the pot calling the kettle black, since the ACLU of Southern California is financed by elite Hollywood jetsetters who undoubtedly feel firearms are a special privilege which they should enjoy as exclusively as their limousines and private spas, but also because the ACLU of Southern California is currently battling the public perception that its litigation on behalf of criminal defendants has created a judicial atmosphere in which no effective means remain for removing hardened criminals from society.

NRA intimidates politicians because it is very well financed and, like any wealthy single-issue special interest, can muster considerable pressure and tactics against legislators who oppose it. For decades, the NRA has aggressively promulgated its message.

This is likely envy speaking, since the National Rifle Association has 3.4 million members, while the total national membership of ACLU is reported to be 280,000. Which civil liberties organization is more likely to effectively lobby its views? One with almost 3-1/2 million members, or one slightly over a quarter million?

Other voices have begun to be heard, however, including the public health community, civil rights and civil liberties organizations, and groups committed to women's, children's, and family rights.

These voices are being heard because they play into the prejudices of the dominant media culture in this country. Meanwhile, none of the three major television networks will even *sell* commercial time to the NRA, while ostensibly news programs regularly air anti-gun propaganda as straight news.

The NRA implies that the Bill of Rights forces us to accept unlimited gun ownership and tolerate the human tragedies that guns cause in our society. That simply isn't true.

What isn't true is that unlimited gun ownership causes human tragedies. Where gun ownership and carrying is the most legally restricted and entangled in bureaucratic impediments — such as Washington D.C. — the crime rates are the highest. In places where gun ownership is free and easy — such as New Hampshire, Vermont, and Arizona — crime is substantially less. Still, the cause-and-effect relationship between gun ownership and crime is mutual, since high crime causes more gun ownership by potential victims at least as much as the reverse.

Q What are the Second Amendment positions of the American Civil Liberties Union and the ACLU of Southern California?

A For decades, both the national ACLU and its Southern California affiliate have agreed that the Second Amendment guarantees only the rights of states to maintain militias. The national ACLU has urged caution over gun control laws that, though well-intended, might infringe on other civil liberties.

The ACLU of Southern California believes effective gun control — especially of handguns and assault weapons — is essential to curbing the escalating violence in our society.

This irrelevant, quasi-religious belief by the executives of the ACLU of Southern California not only has nothing whatsoever to do with the purposes of the American Civil Liberties Union as a civil liberties organization, but it is also unfounded and contrary to the latest scientific evidence. The 1993 National Self Defense Survey conducted by professors Gary Kleck and Marc Gertz of the Department of Criminology and Criminal Justice at Florida State University found that there are 2.45 million genuine defensive civilian uses of firearms in a year, 1.9 million of them with handguns alone. That is a defensive use of a firearm once every 13 seconds.

Q The Second Amendment says "the right of the people to keep and bear arms shall not be infringed." Doesn't it mean just that?

A There is more to the Second Amendment than just the last 14 words.

Most of the debate on the Amendment has focused on its final phrase and entirely ignores its first phrase: "A well regulated Militia, being necessary to the Security of a free State ..." And to dissect the Amendment is to destroy its context.

Indeed. And that is precisely what the executives of the ACLU of Southern California are attempting to do. But if you wish a professional opinion on the textual meaning of the Second Amendment, see the analyses by A.C. Brocki and Roy Copperud, following this chapter.

While some scholars have suggested that the Amendment gives individuals the constitutional right to bear arms, still others have argued for discarding the Amendment as irrelevant and out of date.

Yes, and there is popular sentiment for repealing *all* of the Bill of Rights. Do the executives of the ACLU of Southern California wish to make the existence of all rights inferior to transient public opinion?

However, the vast majority of constitutional experts agree that the right to keep and bear arms was intended to apply only to members of state-run, citizen militias.

Yes? Precisely what experts are those? Certainly not those consulted by the United States Senate, when it issued its report on the question, or the Congress and President of the United States, when they enacted the 1986 Firearms Owners Protection Act.

Q If it doesn't guarantee the right to own a gun, why was the Second Amendment included in the Bill of Rights?

A When James Madison (pictured below Thomas Jefferson on the cover) proposed the Bill of Rights in the late 1780's, people were still suspicious of any centralized federal government. Just 10 years earlier, the British army had been an occupying force in Colonial America — enforcing arbitrary laws decreed from afar. After the Revolutionary War, the states insisted on the constitutional right to defend themselves in case the fledgling U.S. government became tyrannical like the British Crown. The states demanded the right to keep an armed "militia" as a form of insurance.

The executives of the ACLU of Southern California are guilty of something akin to blasphemy, by invoking Jefferson and Madison in support of their Orwellian reversal of history. In effect, we are hearing the sort of argument a spokesman for the Crown might have made to the American colonists that all's well with the world and there's no reason to keep firearms to prevent abuse of government power. The authoritarians of the ACLU of California masquerade as identifying with the now safely-entombed leaders of the American Revolution, but they are in fact counterrevolutionary Tories, who wish to restore this continent to European statism.

I've already quoted Madison about the value of civilian arms; here are a few choice quotes from Thomas Jefferson on the value of firearms:

> "A strong body makes the mind strong. As to the species of exercises, I advise the gun. While this gives moderate exercise to the body, it gives boldness, enterprise and independence to the mind. Games played with the ball and others of that nature, are too violent for the body and stamp no character on the mind. Let your gun therefore be the constant companion of your walk."
>
> — Thomas Jefferson, *Encyclopedia of T. Jefferson*,
> 318 (Foley, Ed., reissued 1967)

> "What country before ever existed a century and a half without a rebellion? ... The tree of liberty must be refreshed from time to time with the blood of patriots and tyrants. It is its natural manure."
>
> — Thomas Jefferson,
> Letter to William Stevens Smith,
> November 13, 1787.

> "What country can preserve its liberties if their rulers are not warned from time to time that their people preserve the spirit of resistance? Let them take arms."
>
> — Thomas Jefferson to James Madison,
> Dec. 20, 1787, quoted from
> "Papers of Jefferson" edited by Boyd et al.

And, most importantly, Jefferson writing in the Declaration of Independence:

> "We hold these truths to be self-evident, that all men are created equal, that they are endowed by their Creator with certain unalienable Rights, that among these are Life, Liberty and the pursuit of Happiness. That to secure these rights, Governments are instituted among Men, deriving their just powers from the consent of the governed, — That whenever any Form of Government becomes destructive of these ends, it is the Right of the People to alter or to abolish it, and to institute new Government, laying its foundation on such principles and organizing its powers in such form, as to them shall seem most likely to effect their Safety and Happiness."

Does it seem at all likely that Thomas Jefferson would have endorsed the notion that civilians are to be armed only after obtaining permission from government officials?

[Illustration. Caption: "A 1770 Paul Revere etching depicts British soldiers firing on a Boston Crowd." What *chutzpah*.]

Q What exactly is a "well regulated militia?"

A Militias in 1792 consisted of part-time citizen-soldiers organized by individual states. Its members were civilians who kept arms, ammunition and other military equipment in their houses and barns — there was no other way to muster a militia with sufficient speed.

Over time, however, the state militias failed to develop as originally anticipated. States found it difficult to organize and finance their militias, and, by the mid-1800's, they had effectively ceased to exist. Beginning in 1903, Congress began to pass legislation that would eventually transform state militias into what is now the National Guard.

Today, the National Guard — and Army Reserve — are scarcely recognizable as descendants of militias in the 1790's. The National Guard and Reserve forces, in fact, do not permit personnel to store military weapons at home. And many of today's weapons — tanks, armored personnel carriers, airplanes, and the like — hardly lend themselves to use by individuals.

As Senator Hatch pointed out, the current National Guards are not "descendants" of the militia at all; they were *not* organized under the militia clause of the constitution but under Congress's power to raise an army. The Supreme Court decision in *Perpich v. Department of Defense* — in which Governor Rudy Perpich of Minnesota was seeking to prevent use of the Minnesota National Guard troops outside of U.S. territory — established that as a legal issue.

Today, soldiers in the National Guards are dual-enlisted in their State Guards, subject to the military authority of the various state governors, and as reservists in the Armed Forces of the United States, subject to call up for active duty. They can be sent to train or even engage in overseas combat.

On the other hand, current United States law (10 USC, 311b) still defines most male adults in this country as members of the reserve militia.

Finally, the executives of the ACLU of Southern California's call for abandoning the Second Amendment is a prelude toward general restrictions on popular arms, the sort that might be used against ambitious politicians who seek to impose their elite policies on a recalcitrant public against its will. Considering how little popular support there is for many of the extremist positions taken by ultraliberal supporters of the ACLU of Southern California, it is not difficult to see that a well-armed and likely uncooperative citizenry is an impediment to utopian social engineering which requires docile submission by the public to government officials.

The national office of the ACLU is at least aware that armed police power in this country is dangerous to liberty: they have joined with the NRA and the Second Amendment Foundation in calling for a commission to investigate abuse of power by authorities in cases such as:

- The raid on the home of California millionaire Donald Scott, whose Malibu home was invaded — and Scott killed while sleepily trying to defend himself from what he thought was burglars — on a trumped up warrant alleging illegal drugs in an attempt to confiscate his estate under asset forfeiture laws;
- The entrapment of backwoodsman Randy Weaver of Ruby Ridge, Idaho by federal Alcohol, Tobacco, and Firearms agents attempting to blackmail him into spying for them on fellow white supremacists; they tricked him into sawing off a shotgun past the legal limit. His continued refusal led to an FBI sniper murdering his wife (while she held their infant child) and Weaver's older son. Weaver was tried and acquitted for shooting back in spite of attempts (established by civil-liberties attorney Gerry Spence in Weaver's trial) by federal officials to falsify evidence. No charges have yet been filed against any federal officials;

- The invasion and opening of initial gunfire on the law-abiding Branch Davidians in Waco, Texas by ATF agents attempting to draw attention away from a sexual harassment scandal at the agency, and the subsequent burning down of the Branch Davidian complex by FBI-driven tanks collapsing the structure and causing combustion; 81 men, women, and children died in that fire.

With government out of control, is this the time for a civil liberties organization to advocate disempowering the civilian population by disarming them?

Guns in America:
The Statistics:

- *Firearms were used to kill more than 60,000 people in the last two years. Handguns kill 22,000 per year, 60 each day, including 12 children.*

And, according to the National Self Defense Survey, firearms *saved* five million people from criminals in those same two years. That's 6,849 lives defended by privately owned firearms per day.

- *U.S. civilians own 211 million guns, including 66.7 million handguns.*

- *A new handgun is produced every 20 seconds and is used to shoot someone every two minutes.*

Yes, and a handgun prevents a criminal attack every 16 seconds.

- *Every day, handguns are used in 33 rapes, 575 robberies, and 1,116 assaults.*

According to data from the National Self Defense Survey, of the 1.9 million handgun defenses in one year, about 8 percent of the defensive uses involved a sexual crime such as an attempted sexual assault — 416 handgun defenses per day, or a dozen handgun defenses for each time a handgun is used by a rapist. Twenty-two percent involved robbery — 1145 handgun defenses per day, or twice as many handgun defenses for each time a handgun is used in a robbery. About 29 percent involved some sort of assault other than sexual assault — 1510 per day, or one-and-a-half times as often as handguns are used in non-sexual assaults. It seems the executives of the ACLU of Southern California, if they got their way and succeeded in further restricting handgun availability to the general public, would be making it easier for rapists than the perpetrators of any other crime.

- *In late 1993, a Time Magazine/CNN poll found that 92% of Americans supported the recently passed Brady Bill, which requires a five-day waiting period to buy a handgun.*

And reverts to an NRA-backed instant background check after five years.

- *The same poll found that 60% favor even stronger gun-control laws.*

Which is meaningless, since most people polled have no idea what the *current* gun control laws are. If you were to poll most Californians (especially those who don't own a firearm) whether they favor imposing the Brady Law's five-day waiting period on California, you'd probably get an overwhelming "yes" — from people who aren't even aware that there has been a *fifteen*-day waiting period in California since 1975.

- *More than 600,000 guns are sold each year in California alone.*

Obviously being purchased by people who think they have the right to keep and bear firearms. Or should only the opinions of elitist executives of the ACLU of Southern California carry political weight?

- *A Seattle-based study concluded that for each example of a gun used in self-defense to kill an intruder, there were 43.9 other gun fatalities. That includes 2.3 incidents of accidental gun deaths, 4.6 criminal homicides, and 37 suicides.*

If one compares the National Self Defense Survey's estimated 1,728,000 gun defenses in or around a home in one year with a conservatively high estimate of gun-related homicides and fatal gun accidents in the home in a year — at most about 8,000 — one can compute that a gun kept in the home for protection is about 216 times as likely to be used in a defense against a criminal than it is to cause the death of an innocent victim in that household.

- *In 1989, 178 justifiable homicides were reported nationwide, but 1600 accidental killings involving guns.*

In fact, the number of justifiable homicides in a year are, according to Gary Kleck, closer to 2,800, since FBI crime reports used by statisticians exclude any justifiable or excusable homicide which isn't labelled that in the initial police report. But even this is likely also an underestimate, since police are reluctant to classify any homicide as "justifiable," preferring to classify them as either unsolved or accidental.

As far as firearms accidents are concerned, they are down 40% from ten years ago, and down 80% from 50 years ago.

- *Shooting is the leading cause of death among African-American males ages 15 to 24.*

No one questions that African-Americans are the worst victims of crime of all kinds — and even the Reverends Jesse Jackson or Louis Farrakhan could not deny that these crimes are being done by young black males. But is this surprising in a culture whose family structure was destroyed by utopian government programs which created a generation of fatherless boys and inner-city government schools that taught a philosophy of dependency on big government rather than self-reliance? Who is historically more responsible for this state of affairs: the more-conservative NRA or the more-liberal ACLU?

- *The Los Angeles County Sheriff's department recovers 30,000 guns a year during routine criminal investigations of which 6,000 have been legally purchased then stolen.*

Are we also going to blame automobile owners when their cars are stolen or carjacked for use in a robbery? Talk about blaming the innocent for the actions of the guilty!

- *Gunshot wounds to children nearly doubled between 1987 and 1990. Firearm murders of young people age 19 and under went up 125% between 1984 and 1990.*

This is an odd definition of "children," which includes 18 and 19 year-old individuals who can serve in the military and on police forces. We must also seriously doubt whether it is firearms that are at fault in the deaths of children who are recruited into criminal gangs even before puberty.

- *Every six hours, a teenager or preteen commits suicide with a gun.*

And almost all studies of suicide show no correlation between the availability of any particular means of suicide and the suicide rate. Japan has few guns, yet has twice the U.S. suicide rate. *The American Journal of Psychiatry* from March, 1990 reported in a study by Rich, Young, Fowler, Wagner, and Black that all gun-suicides which were statistically reduced in the five years following Canada's handgun restrictions beginning 1976 were substituted 100% by suicides using other methods, mostly jumping off bridges. Therefore, eliminating firearms does not eliminate suicide: it merely shifts the suicide to other causes, and no rational public policy can conclude that the availability of firearms is a causative factor.

- *An estimated 1.2 million elementary school-age latchkey children have access to guns when they are home alone.*

Parents who leave their children home alone are morally and legally responsible for what ill befalls their children, whether it is from firearms, or from poison under the sink, or from a box of matches.

- *Most Los Angeles high school students say they could buy a gun on the street in an hour or less if they needed it.*

Perhaps they need it. School authorities and police seem singularly unable to protect them from the well-armed gangsters among them.[1]

- *When firearm suicide and homicide rates in Los Angeles County are combined, the total rate is higher than that for motor vehicle crashes.*

And when the suicide and homicide rate in Japan is compared to the United States, it is higher than the combined U.S. rate. Yet Japan has few guns.

[ILLUSTRATION of a shadowy figure holding a handgun menacingly. Are the executives of the ACLU of Southern California trying to sell civil liberties, or *Argosy Magazine*?]

- *At least four federal safety standards regulate the manufacture of teddy bears. No federal safety standards apply to the manufacture of guns.*

Are they seriously suggesting that guns are inadequately designed to perform their function effectively — which is to fire energy-laden bullets at those who attack the innocent? Firearms are dangerous by necessity. The object is to make them dangerous only to those who need to be, and deserve to be, stopped by them. That is the purpose of firearms safety training — which the NRA was doing fifty years before the ACLU was even formed. I am constantly amazed that people who are afraid to be in the same room with a gun think they know how to tell firearms designers, instructors, and experienced shooters how to make guns safe. The elitist arrogance of those who would run our country seems to be unlimited.

- *In 1993, handguns were used to kill 82 people in Japan, 76 people in Canada, 33 people in great Britain, and 40,000 people in the United States.*

End of ACLU materials

Yet, we observe that in the absence of firearms, the Japanese still manage to die at their own hands as often as Americans. As do the Scots and the Northern Irish, according to data from Interpol, which show national homicide rates for these British countries greater than that of the United States. As for Canada, its homicide rate compares to that of demographically similar areas of the United States.

The last paragraph from the ACLU brochure is, incidentally, copied from the literature of Handgun Control, Inc. Are liberal pocketbooks getting so tight that the ACLU of Southern California must compete for contributions against Sarah Brady?

— J.Neil Schulman

Footnote:

1. The *Los Angeles Times* of February 20, 1994 reports in a story titled "Violence on School Campus Eludes Solutions," "[The Los Angeles Unified School District] has expelled a record number of students for bringing guns and knives on campus and has begun using metal detectors to search students for weapons. But students continue to bring weapons to school in large numbers. Supt. Sid Thompson acknowledges that school officials remain unable to ensure the safety of the district's 640,000 students. ... The problem has escalated so high that many students believe they must arm themselves for protection and there is little shock at seeing a weapon on campus, said school district police chief Wes Mitchell. 'It has become an informal social norm that kids need to protect themselves, so why not carry the tools to protect themselves?' said Mitchell, who added that the district should provide more education about guns and violence."

The following article appeared in the September, 1991 issue of *California Libertarian News*, official newsletter of the California Libertarian Party.

English Usage Expert Interprets 2nd Amendment

I just had a conversation with Mr. A.C. Brocki, Editorial Coordinator for the Office of Instruction of the Los Angeles Unified School District. Mr. Brocki taught Advanced Placement English for several years at Van Nuys High School, as well as having been a senior editor for Houghton Mifflin. I was referred to Mr. Brocki by Sherryl Broyles of the Office of Instruction of the LA Unified School District, who described Mr. Brocki as the foremost expert in grammar in the Los Angeles Unified School District — the person she and others go to when they need a definitive answer on English grammar.

I gave Mr. Brocki my name, told him Sherryl Broyles referred me, then asked him to parse the following sentence:

"A well-schooled electorate, being necessary to the security of a free State, the right of the people to keep and read Books, shall not be infringed."

Mr. Brocki informed me that the sentence was overpunctuated, but that the meaning could be extracted anyway.

"A well-schooled electorate" is a nominative absolute.

"[B]eing necessary to the security of a free State" is a participial phrase modifying "electorate."

The subject (a compound subject) of the sentence is "the right of the people."

"[S]hall not be infringed" is a verb phrase, with "not" as an adverb modifying the verb phrase "shall be infringed."

"[T]o keep and read books" is an infinitive phrase modifying "right."

I then asked him if he could rephrase the sentence to make it clearer. Mr. Brocki said, "Because a well-schooled electorate is necessary to the security of a free state, the right of the people to keep and read books shall not be infringed."

I asked: can the sentence be interpreted to restrict the right to keep and read books to a well-schooled electorate — say, registered voters with a high-school diploma?" He said, "No."

I then identified my purpose in calling him, and read him the Second Amendment in full:

"A well-regulated Militia, being necessary to the security of a free State, the right of the people to keep and bear Arms, shall not be infringed."

He said he thought the sentence had sounded familiar, but that he hadn't recognized it.

I asked, "Is the structure and meaning of this sentence the same as the sentence I first quoted you?" He said, "yes." I asked him to rephrase this sentence to make it clearer. He transformed it the same way as the first sentence: "Because a well-regulated militia is necessary to the security of a free state, the right of the people to keep and bear arms shall not be infringed."

I asked him whether the meaning could have changed in two hundred years. He said, "No."

I asked him whether this sentence could be interpreted to restrict the right to keep and bear arms to "a well-regulated militia." He said, "no." According to Mr. Brocki, the sentence means that the people *are* the militia, and that the people have the right which is mentioned.

I asked him again to make sure:

Schulman: "Can the sentence be interpreted to mean that the right can be restricted to "a well-regulated militia?"

Brocki: "No, I can't see that."

Schulman: "Could another professional in English grammar or linguistics interpret the sentence to mean otherwise?"

Brocki: "I can't see any grounds for another interpretation."

I asked Mr. Brocki if he would be willing to stake his professional reputation on this opinion, and be quoted on this. He said, "Yes."

At no point in the conversation did I ask Mr. Brocki his opinion on the Second Amendment, gun control, or the right to keep and bear arms.

— July 17, 1991

The following is reprinted from the September 13, 1991 issue of *Gun Week*, and also appears under the title "The Text of The Second Amendment" in *The Journal on Firearms and Public Policy*, Summer 1992, Volume 4, Number 1.

The Unabridged Second Amendment

If you wanted to know all about the Big Bang, you'd ring up Carl Sagan, right? And if you wanted to know about desert warfare, the man to call would be Norman Schwarzkopf, no question about it. But who would you call if you wanted the top expert on American usage, to tell you the meaning of the Second Amendment to the United States Constitution?

That was the question I asked A.C. Brocki, Editorial Coordinator of the Los Angeles Unified School District and formerly senior editor at Houghton Mifflin Publishers — who himself had been recommended to me as the foremost expert on English usage in the Los Angeles school system. Mr. Brocki told me to get in touch with Roy Copperud, a retired professor of journalism at the University of Southern California and the author of *American Usage and Style: The Consensus.*

A little research lent support to Brocki's opinion of Professor Copperud's expertise.

Roy Copperud was a newspaper writer on major dailies for over three decades before embarking on a distinguished seventeen-year career teaching journalism at USC. Since 1952, Copperud has been writing a column dealing with the professional aspects of journalism for *Editor and Publisher*, a weekly magazine focusing on the journalism field.

He's on the usage panel of the *American Heritage Dictionary*, and *Merriam Webster's Usage Dictionary* frequently cites him as an expert. Copperud's fifth book on usage, *American Usage and Style: The Consensus*, has been in continuous print from Van Nostrand Reinhold since 1981, and is the winner of the Association of American Publishers' Humanities Award.

That sounds like an expert to me.

After a brief telephone call to Professor Copperud in which I introduced myself but did *not* give him any indication of why I was interested, I sent the following letter on July 26, 1991:

I am writing you to ask you for your professional opinion as an expert in English usage, to analyze the text of the Second Amendment to the United States Constitution, and extract the intent from the text.

The text of the Second Amendment is, "A well-regulated Militia, being necessary to the security of a free State, the right of the people to keep and bear Arms, shall not be infringed."

The debate over this amendment has been whether the first part of the sentence, "A well-regulated Militia, being necessary to the security of a free State," is a restrictive clause or a subordinate clause, with respect to the independent clause containing the subject of the sentence, "the right of the people to keep and bear Arms, shall not be infringed."

I would request that your analysis of this sentence not take into consideration issues of political impact or public policy, but be restricted entirely to a linguistic analysis of its meaning and intent. Further, since your professional analysis will likely become part of litigation regarding the consequences of the Second Amendment, I ask that whatever analysis you make be a professional opinion that you would be willing to stand behind with your reputation, and even be willing to testify under oath to support, if necessary.

My letter framed several questions about the text of the Second Amendment, then concluded:

I realize that I am asking you to take on a major responsibility and task with this letter. I am doing so because, as a citizen, I believe it is vitally important to extract the actual meaning of the Second Amendment. While I ask that your analysis not be affected by the political importance of its results, I ask that you do this because of that importance.

After several more letters and phone calls, in which we discussed terms for his doing such an analysis, but in which we never discussed either of our opinions regarding the Second Amendment, gun control, or any other political subject, Professor Copperud sent me the following analysis (into which I've inserted my questions for the sake of clarity):

[Copperud:] The words "A well-regulated militia, being necessary to the security of a free state," contrary to the interpretation cited in your letter of July 26, 1991, constitute a present participle, rather than a clause. It is used as an adjective, modifying "militia," which is followed by the main clause of the sentence (subject "the right," verb "shall"). The right to keep and bear arms is asserted as essential for maintaining a militia.

In reply to your numbered questions:

[Schulman: (1) Can the sentence be interpreted to grant the right to keep and bear arms *solely* to "a well-regulated militia"?;]

[Copperud:] (1) The sentence does not restrict the right to keep and bear arms, nor does it state or imply possession of the right elsewhere or by others than the people; it simply makes a positive statement with respect to a right of the people.

[Schulman: (2) Is "the right of the people to keep and bear arms" *granted* by the words of the Second Amendment, or does the Second Amendment assume a preexisting right of the people to keep and bear arms, and merely state that such right "shall not be infringed"?;]

[Copperud:] (2) The right is not granted by the amendment; its existence is assumed. The thrust of the sentence is that the right shall be preserved inviolate for the sake of ensuring a militia.

[Schulman: (3) Is the right of the people to keep and bear arms conditioned upon whether or not a well-regulated militia is, in fact, necessary to the security of a free State, and if that condition is not existing, is the statement "the right of the people to keep and bear Arms, shall not be infringed" null and void?;]

[Copperud:] (3) No such condition is expressed or implied. The right to keep and bear arms is not said by the amendment to depend on the existence of a militia. No condition is stated or implied as to the relation of the right to keep and bear arms and to the necessity of a well-regulated militia as requisite to the security of a free state. The right to keep and bear arms is deemed unconditional by the entire sentence.

[Schulman: (4) Does the clause "A well-regulated Militia, being necessary to the security of a free State," grant a right to the government to place conditions on the "right of the people to keep and bear arms," or is such right deemed unconditional by the meaning of the entire sentence?;]

[Copperud:] (4) The right is assumed to exist and to be unconditional, as previously stated. It is invoked here specifically for the sake of the militia.

[Schulman: (5) Which of the following does the phrase "well-regulated militia" mean: "well-equipped," "well-organized," "well-drilled," "well-educated," or "subject to regulations of a superior authority"?]

[Copperud:] (5) The phrase means "subject to regulations of a superior authority"; this accords with the desire of the writers for civilian control over the military.

[Schulman: If at all possible, I would ask you to take into account the changed meanings of words, or usage, since that sentence was written two-hundred years ago, but not to take into account historical interpretations of the intents of the authors, unless those issues can be clearly separated.]

[Copperud:] To the best of my knowledge, there has been no change in the meaning of words or in usage that would affect the meaning of the amendment. If it were written today, it might be put: "Since a well-regulated militia is necessary to the security of a free state, the right of the people to keep and bear arms shall not be abridged."

[Schulman:] As a "scientific control" on this analysis, I would also appreciate it if you could compare your analysis of the text of the Second Amendment to the following sentence,

"A well-schooled electorate, being necessary to the security of a free State, the right of the people to keep and read Books, shall not be infringed."

My questions for the usage analysis of this sentence would be,

(1) Is the grammatical structure and usage of this sentence, and the way the words modify each other, identical to the Second Amendment's sentence?; and

(2) Could this sentence be interpreted to restrict "the right of the people to keep and read Books" *only* to "a well-educated electorate" — for example, registered voters with a high-school diploma?]

[Copperud:] (1) Your "scientific control" sentence precisely parallels the amendment in grammatical structure.

(2) There is nothing in your sentence that either indicates or implies the possibility of a restricted interpretation.

Professor Copperud had only one additional comment, which he placed in his cover letter: "With well-known human curiosity, I made some speculative efforts to decide how the material might be used, but was unable to reach any conclusion."

So now we have been told by one of the top experts on American usage what many knew all along: the Constitution of the United States unconditionally protects the people's right to keep and bear arms, forbidding all government formed under the Constitution from abridging that right.

As I write this, the attempted coup against constitutional government in the Soviet Union has failed, apparently because the will of the people in that part of the world to be free from capricious tyranny is stronger than the old guard's desire to maintain a monopoly on dictatorial power.

And here in the United States, elected lawmakers, judges, and appointed officials who are pledged to defend the Constitution of the United States ignore, marginalize, or prevaricate about the Second Amendment routinely. American citizens are put in American prisons for carrying arms, owning arms of forbidden sorts, or failing to satisfy bureaucratic requirements regarding the owning and carrying of firearms — all of which is an abridgement of the unconditional right of the people to keep and bear arms, guaranteed by the Constitution.

And even the ACLU, staunch defender of the rest of the Bill of Rights, stands by and does nothing.

It seems it is up to those who believe in the right to keep and bear arms to preserve that right. No one else will. No one else can. Will we beg our elected representatives not to take away our rights, and continue regarding them as representing us if they do? Will we continue obeying judges who decide that the Second Amendment doesn't mean what it says but means whatever they say it means in their Orwellian doublespeak?

Or will we simply keep and bear the arms of our choice, as the Constitution of the United States promises us we can, and pledge that we will defend that promise with our lives, our fortunes, and our sacred honor?

I was looking at the "View" section of the *LA Times* from December 18, 1991 — an article on James Michener which my ex-wife Kate had saved for me to read — when the beginning of Jack Smith's column caught my eye: "Roy Copperud had no sooner died the other day than I had occasion to consult his excellent book, 'American Usage and Style: The Consensus.'"

Thus I learned of the death of Roy Copperud, the retired USC professor whom I had commissioned to do a grammatical analysis of the Second Amendment. It seems to have been one of the last projects he worked on. It is certainly one of the most important.

Roy Copperud told me afterwards that he, personally, favored gun control, but his analysis of the Second Amendment made clear that its protections of the right of the people to keep and bear arms were unaffected by its reference to militia. This sort of intellectual and professional honesty is sorely lacking in public discourse today.

In my several letters and phone conversations with Professor Copperud, I found him to be a gentleman of the old school.

The planet is a little poorer without him. **—JNS**

Some Notes and Discussion on the Second Amendment

The Meaning of the "Well-Regulated Militia"

"A well-regulated militia" in the preamble to the Second Amendment means "civilians who are trained how to use arms," as opposed to army regulars. In essence, the Second Amendment means, "Since it is necessary for the security of a free society that civilians know how to use arms, the right of the people to own and carry arms shall not be abridged." While Professor Copperud was technically correct that the meanings of the words haven't changed in 200 years — the definition of "militia" in the dictionary and on the law books hasn't changed — the public understanding of the word "militia" has been corrupted so most people today believe that the "militia" is a military unit rather than a civilian concept. This is precisely the "war is peace and freedom is slavery" corruption of language that George Orwell warned us against in *Nineteen eighty four.*

As far as the legal standing of the right to keep and bear arms in this country, it's mixed. The Supreme Court has never made a ruling on the second amendment *per se* and given the current makeup of the Court, it must make Handgun Control, Inc., very nervous to contemplate what would happen if a Second Amendment case *does* reach the Supreme Court.

From a Discussion on the GEnie Computer Network

Barry, Message 126: There is *no* "limiting prefix" in the Second Amendment. Two prominent, impartial linguistic experts — one considered the tops in his field — analyzed the text of the Second Amendment and came to this conclusion. Read Messages

72 and 73 in this topic for the full text of their analyses. On the interpretation of the Constitution. Article 9 of the amendments reads, "The enumeration in the Constitution, of certain rights, shall not be construed to deny or disparage others retained by the people."

That is instruction from the framers on how the constitution is to be "construed" — that is, "constructed."

The *Oxford English Dictionary* does not give a definition of "well-regulated" but instead gives citations for its use. Here are its citations, which bracket the writing of the Second Amendment:

1709: "If a liberal Education has formed in us well-regulated Appetites and worthy Inclinations."

1714: "The practice of all well-regulated courts of justice in the world."

1812: "The equation of time .. is the adjustment of the difference of time as shown by a well-regulated clock and a true sun dial."

1848: "A remissness for which I am sure every well-regulated person will blame the Major."

1862: "It appeared to her well-regulated mind, like a clandestine proceeding."

1894: "The newspaper, a never wanting adjunct to every well-regulated American embryo city."

Find me "regulation" by an outside authority in any of these uses.

Neil

A Note on the Punctuation of the Second Amendment

I just received the following courtesy of Francis Warin of Oak Harbor, Ohio, in response to my article in *Gun Week*, "The Unabridged Second Amendment." Mr. Warin has apparently been distributing this letter since 1978.

THE LIBRARY OF CONGRESS
Congressional Research Service
Washington, D.C. 20540

To: Honorable Paul Findley
Attention: Miss Evans
From: American Law Division
Subject: Punctuation of the Second Amendment to the Constitution of the United States

This will refer to your request of July 5, 1972 on behalf of Mr. James H. Macklin for information relative to the captioned subject. Mr. Macklin had noted that the punctuation of this amendment varied with the different sources which have reproduced it.

By resolution in 1789, Congress proposed twelve articles to the legislatures of the several states as amendments to the Constitution of the United States. Ten of these articles were ratified by the legislatures of three-fourths of the states by 1791, including the amendment in question which was adopted in this form: "A well regulated militia being necessary to the security of a free state, the right of the people to keep and bear arms shall not be infringed." 1 *United States Statutes at Large* 21, 97.

Information pertaining to the debate on this amendment in the state and Federal legislatures may be found in: Schwartz, Bernard, *The Bill of Rights: A Documentary History*, 2 volumes, Chelsea House, New York, 1971. This work retains the original spelling, grammar and style of all documentary material.

[signature]
Paul L. Morgan
Legislative Attorney

In other words, according to the Congressional Research Service of the Library of Congress, the text of the Second Amendment ratified by the legislatures contained only *one* comma, and the comma between "arms" and "shall" which some cite as changing the meaning of the amendment is not in the original text.

— September 18, 1991

Reserve Militia Training and Regulation Act: a Proposal

Constitution of the United States of America

Article I, Sect. 8:

The Congress shall have Power

To provide for calling forth the Militia to execute the Laws of the Union, suppress Insurrections and repel Invasions.;

To provide for organizing, arming, and disciplining, the Militia, and for governing such Part of them as may be employed in the Service of the United States, reserving to the States respectively, the Appointment of the Officers, and the Authority of training the Militia according to the discipline prescribed by Congress;

Amendment II:

A well-regulated Militia being necessary to the security of a free State, the right of the people to keep and bear Arms shall not be infringed.

The purpose of this proposal is to draft "The Reserve Militia Training and Regulation Act," and get it enough support from both reasonable gun-control advocates and gun-rights advocates to get it in front of Congress.

This is not a discussion of the National Guard. At this point, the National Guard serves a defined function as a military organization that can be called out by the individual states in event of statewide emergency, and as a reserve military force which the president can call up, even for fighting overseas. Whatever the merits of this treatment of the National Guard, it is not militia as the term was originally conceived by the authors of the Second Amendment.

The Second Amendment regards the militia as the people themselves, able-bodied and armed for defense against dangers to the civic safety and liberty from enemies both foreign and domestic. The original constitution, before amendment, has a militia clause which grants Congress the power "To provide for calling forth the Militia to execute the Laws of the Union, suppress Insurrections and repel Invasions; to provide for organizing, arming, and disciplining the Militia, and for governing such part of them as may be employed in the Service of the United States, reserving to the States, respectively, the appointment of the Officers, and the authority of training the Militia according to the discipline prescribed by Congress." The Constitution also provides that, "The President shall be Commander in Chief of...the Militia of the several States, when called into the actual Service of the United States..."

A bill for training and regulation of the militia is, therefore, not only constitutional, but constitutionally mandated.

The "militia" as defined by U.S. Code is every able bodied male between 17 and 45 who is a citizen of the United States or has declared an intention to become one, as well as female members of the National Guard and former members of the regular armed forces under age 64. U.S. Code further goes on to divide the militia into two classes — the organized militia which consists of the National Guard and Naval Militia, and the reserve or unorganized militia which consists of the members of the militia who are not members of the National Guard or the Naval Militia (10 USC, 311 b).

In *Presser v. Illinois* (1886), the Supreme Court stated "It is undoubtedly true that all citizens capable of bearing arms constitute the reserved military force or reserve militia of the United States as well as of the States, and, in view of this prerogative of the general government, as well as of its general powers, the states cannot, even laying the Constitutional provision in question out of view, prohibit the people from keeping and bearing arms..."

U.S. v Miller (1939) recognized that the "militia comprised all males physically capable of acting in concert for the common defense" and that when called to service these men are expected to appear "bearing arms supplied by themselves and of the kind in common use at the time."

In the last month, as I write this, we have seen on television news reports of massacres of innocent people by deranged, armed individuals. George Hennard, in Killeen, Texas, killed 23 and wounded 19 on October 16th, in a lunchtime cafeteria, using a couple of 9 millimeter semi-auto pistols. Dr. Gang Lu, a Chinese post-graduate student at the University of Iowa's physics department, killed five and wounded one with a .38 revolver, on November 1st. Thomas McIlvane, a fired postal worker, killed four and wounded eight others with a sawed-off .22 rifle, on November 14th, in Royal Oak, Michigan.

All three gunmen made themselves their final victims, shooting themselves, fatally, as their last act. Retributive justice can have no deterrence on individuals who intend to kill themselves after committing murder. And police, even with excellent response times, can't be everywhere at once.

According to the FBI, the United States is experiencing three such massacres — defined as one gunman and four or more fatalities — *every month.*

Combine this with the rates for street crime — drive-by shootings, gang-related shootings, muggings, "wildings," rapes, purse-snatchings, etc. — and we have a society where the streets are a literal war-zone.

Advocates of gun-control believe crime can be stemmed by the passage and enforcement of laws restricting ownership, possession, and carrying firearms. Their thesis looks attractive in the abstract; but when you consider the over 200 million firearms that already exist in this country, no one can make a reasonable case that gun-restriction affects other than the extremely law-abiding — the least likely class to pose a threat to public safety.

However, the media is almost universally in favor of gun control, regardless of its practicality. It is obvious that any political change in this situation in the direction of increasing the ability of the public to defend itself, must come under the heading of "regulation."

Which is precisely what the militia is supposed to be: well-regulated. Armed, trained, and ready at all times to defend the country from all enemies, foreign and *domestic*.

If three massacres a month isn't a reason enough to make better use of the militia, then what is?

The purpose of "The Reserve Militia Training and Regulation Act" is to provide training *on demand* for any sane, adult, able-bodied American who is not a criminal, in the use of firearms, with the mandate that once trained, such people can be expected to maintain weapons at home, keep themselves able to use them safely and effectively, and be expected to carry arms, for the defense not only of themselves, but in defense of their loved ones, neighbors, and co-workers.

The reserve militia is not to be maintained as a standing army or "select" militia; it is not to be called up, as the National Guard is, for service, military or otherwise.

The militia must be civilian, not military or paramilitary, and its methods and functioning should be as narrowly focused to the purposes of *individual* defense as humanly possible.

The militia should be governed by civilian laws, rather than the Universal Code of Military Justice.

No uniforms, no dress or hair codes. No militaristic trappings, such as saluting, marching, dress parades, etc.

No discrimination, whether based on gender, sexual preference, age (beyond excluding juveniles), and the usual race, creed, religion, national origin, color, etc.

"Able-bodied" should be defined as broadly as possible. If a paraplegic wishes to participate, and is capable of wielding an effective weapon, it should be permitted. Likewise, obesity shouldn't be a factor, so long as it doesn't interfere with the ability to utilize weapons properly. Likewise, if you're 75 and still have good eyes and a steady hand.

Militia training should be designed to be as unobtrusive to civilian life as possible. No "boot camps." No rigorous physical training. No requirements to leave home for training; training schedules should be evenings and weekends, and allow for flexible schedules as much as possible.

No use of militia for propaganda, even in the "best" of causes. No pamphleteering, picketing, or marching while armed. No organization of private or political paramilitary units by militia. No vigilantism.

Everything above is designed to distinguish the militia from military and police organizations, which presumably can continue functioning as usual.

Here is a preliminary overview of what the Reserve Militia Training and Regulation Act might accomplish:

1) United States Code Title 10 Section 311 would be amended to redefine militia from its current definition to that of any able-bodied person 17 or older, not a convicted felon (unless pardoned) or a person who has been found not guilty of a felony by reason of insanity (unless legally declared restored to sanity), who is a citizen of the United States, or has declared intent to become a citizen of the United States. Able-bodied would be defined so as not to exclude paraplegics capable of using weapons, or those who are otherwise physically imperfect, so long as the imperfections do not make it impossible to train in or use weapons.

2) A provision would be inserted forbidding involuntary call-ups of reserve militia for military service.

3)a) United States Code Title 32 Section 109 would require every State to provide training and qualification in firearms to any member of the reserve militia upon request. Standards of qualification would be comparable to that of NRA qualification, and training programs would continue to be under the jurisdiction of the Director of Civilian Marksmanship.

b) Once qualified with a weapon, a member of the reserve militia would be immune from all local, state, and federal laws which restrict or delay purchase of that weapon, purchase of ammunition for that weapon, and ownership of that weapon and, except for fully automatic weapons, bearing of that weapon in a condition loaded and ready for use, in all places, public and private, except that courts and legislative bodies may set restrictions for trials and legislative sessions. Militia members who have qualified with fully-automatic weapons would in addition be immune from laws against transporting them, unloaded, for purposes of training, practice, repair, display, or during purchase or sale.

4) Provision would be made for making available weapons and ammunition, and providing places for regular marksmanship practice, to militia members who could not otherwise afford to do so. Provision would also be made for the storing of ammunition, reserved specifically for the defense of the United States, in private homes.

5) This legislation would in no way act as a restriction upon the keeping and bearing of arms by those who do not participate in militia training. It would merely have the affirmative effect of *enabling* the keeping and bearing of arms to those who are currently restricted from doing so by local, state, and federal legislation.

"With Liberty and Justice For All"

The arguments for firearms rights don't exist in a vacuum. They touch issues of general political history, theories of crime and punishment, social rights and regulations, and what it means to grow up. Most of what I wrote in this section began in arguments via computer conferencing systems, as disagreements about firearms issues spilled over into arguments about everything from abortion to TV violence.

This is the section of the book where I'm most likely to get cheers and jeers from traditional NRA members. They'll like what I have to say about firearms rights. They're not as likely to like what I have to say about much of anything else. **— JNS**

Open Messages to Judge Glen Ashman

The following messages, posted in the Gun Control topic in the "Legacy" Legal RoundTable on GEnie, were to Judge Glen Ashman, who at the time of the exchange sat on the City Court in East Point, Georgia, and was running for Superior Court in Clayton County, Georgia. Judge Ashman argued in previous messages that "the second amendment is not absolute" and allows some federal regulation on firearms, and that "unlike the other bill of rights [the second amendment] has never been made applicable to the states, so state bans on guns are constitutional."

Judge Ashman's personal opinion, from a message posted in the Gun Control Topic on March 6, 1992, was as follows: "We need a ban on handguns, and on most other guns not used for hunting. We need a safety course requirement before you can buy a gun. ... We need waiting periods to buy and background checks too."

It was in this context that I opened a discussion with him. For copyright reasons, I include only my messages. **— JNS**

Mon Mar 16, 1992 at 22:48 EST:

Judge Ashman, since I am not in your court and you can't cite me for contempt, let me explain to you why I will never surrender my arms to any government official, nor will I let any legislature, court, or other official disarm me or tell me the time or manner in which I may carry my arms.

The question on arms is: who is sovereign in a free society — the people or the State? The question of keeping and bearing arms is the question of where power is ultimately to reside: in the hands of the people, or in the hands of government officials, whether they style themselves "representatives" of the people, judges, or police.

The power to disarm is the power to conquer. If some government official has the power to say that a private person does not have the right to be armed, then that government official has sovereign power, and the private person being denied that right is merely a subject.

It is right and proper to discuss tests for whether a government official or employee may or may not be armed. But for a private, sovereign citizen to be so questioned *in any way* is an affront to the concept that the people are sovereign.

The position that there must be government-administered tests to keep and bear arms is no different than the position that there must be government-administered tests for a citizen to vote, or for a citizen to own property, or for a citizen to speak freely. They are all of a piece. They are all attempting to replace the sovereignty of the people with the sovereignty of the official, who will use this sovereign power to grant privileges and favors.

This is what the American Revolution was fought to overthrow. That we have it back is a grand scandal on this continent, and a tragedy for a country that was once a beacon of liberty to the human race.

Free human beings — free *men* in the gender-free sense of the word — do not ask permission to bear arms. They bear arms because they are *free*. Their arms are their empowerment as sovereigns. Their arms are a warning to all criminals, invaders, and kings that they will not have their liberties trifled with.

The Declaration of Independence states the question clearly. It says, "that all men are created equal, that they are endowed by their Creator with certain unalienable Rights, that among these are Life, Liberty and the pursuit of Happiness. That to secure these rights, Governments are instituted among Men, deriving their just powers from the consent of the governed."

At the point where a government declares itself sovereign, and me its subject — which any attempt to disarm me does — then I withdraw my consent to be governed and further hold, as did the Declaration of Independence, "That whenever any Form of Government becomes destructive of these ends, it is the Right of the

People to alter or to abolish it, and to institute new Government, laying its foundation on such principles and organizing its powers in such form, as to them shall seem most likely to effect their Safety and Happiness."

I do not delegate my fundamental rights to a representative to decide whether or not they shall be taken from me. I do not grant any court the moral right to decide this question. I am a free man and intend to remain so. I may be conquered by villains with more guns on their side. But I will never concede that they have any right to do so.

I do not think judges hear warnings like this very often. Judges tend to get into the habit of thinking that they have power. They issue an order for someone to be carried to jail, and armed officers enforce it.

There are not enough bailiffs, police, marshals, or soldiers to disarm the American people. There are seventy million of us armed, and we will not tolerate it.

If you deprive the people of our rights, we hold the right — and the final power — to take from you the authority to rule on *our* laws. Our highest law of the land says, in plain language, "the right of the people to keep and bear arms shall not be infringed."

You have a choice. You can enforce that law — and to hell with the precedents of cowards, liars, and poltroons who sat on benches before you and corrupted its meaning — or you can begin to contemplate the manner that the American people will use to bring down that court into rubble, and replace it with a judge who *will* enforce it.

Perhaps you think there are not many who will agree with me passionately enough to back this position with our lives, our fortunes, and our sacred honor.

King George the Third didn't think so, either.

Respectfully submitted,

J. Neil Schulman,

Sovereign Citizen

Tue Mar 17, 1992 at 23:57 EST:

Judge Ashman, I didn't come by my opinion lightly. First of all, the warning against "anarchy" doesn't work with me, since I've probably called myself an anarchist as much as any other label for the last two decades. Not that I believe in nihilism or terrorism; I merely believe that social institutions — whether they're joint stock companies or condo associations or even "governments" — can't make third party contracts without the consent of the third parties. A legislature or court can't deprive me of my rights, because *I* don't grant them jurisdiction to do so. I grant jurisdiction for dispute settlement, and to reduce criminal invasions against life, liberty, and property. But there is a natural and logical limit to that jurisdiction: when it ceases to work to those ends, I call a halt.

I've called a halt. I won't have my right to bear arms infringed. My consent is publicly withdrawn from any institution that attempts to do so, and I will use any effective and *moral* means at my disposal to see that my rights — and those of my fellow countrymen — are not abridged.

You are right. The Supreme Court, if they wish to avoid a civil war in this country, had better come out with a decision that enforces the Second Amendment. If they do, lower courts and politicians better obey. If the Supreme Court abdicates its duty to enforce the Constitution, then it's time to impeach the Justices by any moral means necessary, and replace them with Justices who take the Framers seriously.

I had the late Roy Copperud, the definitive expert on American Usage and Style, analyze the text of the Second Amendment. I can email you (or post here) a copy of the article I wrote based on his analysis of the text. What Copperud said is that the words "A well-regulated militia being necessary to a free state" are grammatically *incapable* of acting as a restriction on the only clause in that sentence, which is, "the right of the people to keep and bear arms shall not be infringed." The reference to a well-regulated militia (aside from being redundant; it's another way of saying "the people as a whole, armed and ready") is a present participial phrase. It is not a subordinate clause; it is not a restrictive clause;

it is not a clause at all. It is an *explanation* of why this right is being mentioned in the Constitution, rather than being taken for granted, with all the rights preserved but not enumerated in the Ninth Amendment.

Let's talk about some of the "limits" on freedom you mention.

Speed limits: limited by contract, when you agree to drive on state highways. A libertarian can argue that the state should not be building roads or operating them — and an anarchist can argue that they should be liberated from state control — but nonetheless there is an explicit agreement when one applies for a license to abide by the state's rules of the road.

Perhaps the battle over roads was more important than our ancestors thought. The principle of state control over our right of passage seems to have eroded all sorts of other rights as well.

Libel laws do not limit freedom of speech. They limit freedom of lying. They say in essence that the passage of provably toxic information — false and damaging — is action, rather than symbolism. There is a clear epistemological difference.

DUI laws — same argument as speed limits. On a private road, with everyone signing waivers of risk and liability, I would have no possible objection to drunk driving. A sign at the on ramp should probably say something like, "*ABANDON HOPE ALL YE WHO ENTER.*"

Zoning laws are another example of private rights being violated by the state. There are contractual alternatives which are acceptable — land-use covenants, condo agreements, etc. But the idea that a government should be able to condemn or restrict the use of someone else's property is another major violation of private sovereignty.

As for criminal laws — well, if by that you mean the invasion of another's right to life, liberty, or property — then that is the one alienation of rights I observe as valid. A person who invades another has entered into what one theorist[1] has called an "anti-contract": a contract for *past* performance. By their actions, they have already agreed to the cost of their invasive acts.

That current legal statutes don't rest on such logic don't bother me at all. I am not a lawyer. I'm a sovereign citizen fighting for my rights.

What bothers me is that you hold authority granted you by sovereign citizens, and your personal opinions, if enacted by you on the bench, would violate that sovereignty. By doing so, you violate your orders. You are told to uphold their rights. You would infringe them.

I appreciate your being in this discussion to listen to the opinions of people, such as me, who are not lawyers, and do not care for precedents. As a matter of fact, I don't even care much for law itself. I only care about rights and justice, equity and fairness. To the extent that the written statutes bring about that result, they should be observed. When they cease to do so, the law is destructive, and must be disobeyed as strictly as obedience to a just law.

You may very well end up sitting on a gun case some day, in which the fate of some citizen is in your hands. On that day, you will have a choice. You will either break with the precedent of bad law and enforce the sovereign rights of the citizen "in the dock," or you will bend to tradition and rob him of his rights.

I hope you find the truth of this before that day is again before you.

Neil

Wed Mar 18, 1992 at 23:10 EST:

Judge Ashman, if quoting the Declaration of Independence on the right to overthrow despotic government is treason in the United States, that is proof the despots are in charge and the revolution is overdue. One would have to be pretty cowardly — in a country which is heir to Patrick Henry, Sam Adams, and Thomas Jefferson, just to name a few — to worry about that for a split second.

As a matter of fact, the Constitution defines treason in Article 3, Section. 3. as: "Treason against the United States shall consist only in levying War against them, or in adhering to their enemies, giving them Aid and Comfort. No Person shall be convicted of Treason unless on the testimony of two witnesses to the same overt Act, or on Confession in open Court."

There isn't a word in the Constitution about *sedition*, or overthrowing the government.

In fact, I prefer ballots to bullets. In the last 24 hours we have seen a referendum in South Africa abolish apartheid. Last year we saw the world's most evil empire collapse with virtually no bloodshed. Good for the despots! They may finally have learned something from history if they realize that guns won't save their lives if the people say "enough."

But I don't count on despots or ruling classes to give up their power without a fight. Much blood was shed in South Africa before this referendum was possible. The people in the former Soviet Union had flexed their muscles enough to let the coup-plotters know they were finished.

I believe in keeping my powder dry.

Let me go back to your other points, in order. You say there is a problem with "misuse." Well, that is precisely the non sequitur that statutes in this country perpetrate:

Premise: a thing can be *misused*;

Conclusion: that thing, and its proper use, must therefore be regulated.

This logical mistake is the justification for *endless* tyranny because there is *nothing* that *can not* be misused.

Water can quench thirst; it can also be used to drown a person.

A baseball bat can hit a home run; it can also fracture a skull.

A kitchen knife can carve Thanksgiving turkey; it can also carve Grandma.

A chain saw can make a clearing to build a house in the woods. It's also Jamie Lee Curtis's old nightmare.

We are a tool-using race. Everything we touch becomes our tool. Our legends tell us that God created a perfect world. A few years later, Cain found the tool to murder his brother Abel.

Firearms are a tool, an "anti-personnel" weapon. If the person using it is wicked, the tool will be used for evil. If the person using it is good, the tool will be used to stop evil.

For most of the Cold War, Great Britain and France had nuclear capability. Why is it we were worried about nuclear attack by the

Soviet Union and not France or Britain? The answer is simple and telling: we did not think the people of France or Britain were evil, so we did not fear their weapons.[2]

Good people should be armed against evil people. Bad people, when they use their weapons to commit evil, should be stopped.

If guns are the number one cause of death for young black males, then good young black males need to be heavily armed, and the faster the better. Evidently their murderers are armed already.

As far as background checks, I have no objection to background checking criminals who have already forfeited their sovereignty. In my novel *The Rainbow Cadenza* I postulated implanting radio transponders into criminals to mark them. (Mind you, the society that did this in my novel used this technology badly because innocent people, by our standards, were declared criminal; there is no tool that can't be misused.) Nevertheless, if you feel the need to hunt down criminals to disarm them, feel free to suggest this. It's already being used on livestock.

As far as discussing the "law" on gun control, it is far too narrow to discuss statutes and legal precedents without a prior discussion of philosophy of law and natural rights. That is what is missing from gun-control debates today. Everyone wants to discuss social utility — whether law (a) will produce effect (b). Well, it's possible to discuss the social utility of slavery, also. It's wonderful for the masters, isn't it? The masters have dirt-cheap labor — and kinky sex on the side. One can easily define the slaves as animals, rather than humans; that avoids the problem of discussing rights, doesn't it?

Funny how this argument strikes us as hollow now.

Rights must be discussed first. Only *then* can you discuss social usefulness.

In my previous message I stood on my right as a sovereign citizen to either consent, or not consent, to being governed, according to whether the government protected my rights or violated them. I don't care what the legislators decide on the subject; I don't give a damn what the courts have decided. *These are my rights we are discussing.* Respect them or else. I stand in the tradition of Jefferson, Adams, and Henry: and our public *servants* had better get the hell out of the armory — the master just got home to take charge.

As far as your oath to support the Constitution as amended, that is an oath to the Constitution, not to precedents. If those precedents defy the Second Amendment, it is your duty to the Constitution, and to the people of the United States, to rule that way. If you are overruled, you will have done *your* duty, and it will be the judge who has overruled you who will have to deal with the people's just wrath for that act of sedition.

Footnotes:

1. Samuel Edward Konkin III.
2. Thanks to KABC Talk Radio host Dennis Prager for this analogy.

A Rather One-Sided Debate on Gun Rights

The following is a selection of messages I wrote between July 21, 1992 and February 7, 1993, posted in the Gun Control topic in the Public Forum * Non-Profit Connection Bulletin Board on GEnie. Again, for copyright reasons, I'm posting only my own writings and have removed the last names and log-on addresses of the other participants in the discussion. I've also edited the messages for clarity and to remove irrelevancies and redundancies.

— JNS

Sun Jan 17, 1993 at 21:44 EST:

Gun police, Bob?

Back when the federal constitution was being debated, James Madison wrote Federalist Paper #46 (under the pen name Publius), discussing the respective powers of the federal government, the states governments, and the people. Madison's premise was that the federal government could safely be given militaristic powers without fear of becoming a tyranny, because the natural loyalties of the people would be to their states rather than the federal government; and any attempts at tyranny by the federal government would be quickly dealt with by the state legislatures, working in concert if necessary.

Madison didn't foresee the outcome of the Civil War, though, less than a century later, and the subsequent winnowing away of the sovereignty of the states as compared to the federal government.

Here's an excerpt from what Madison had to say in Federalist 46:

> The only refuge left for those who prophesy the downfall of the State governments is the visionary supposition that the federal government may previously accumulate a military force for the projects of ambition. The reasonings contained in these papers must have been employed to

little purpose indeed, if it could be necessary now to disprove the reality of this danger. That the people and the States should, for a sufficient period of time, elect an uninterrupted succession of men ready to betray both; that the traitors should, throughout this period, uniformly and systematically pursue some fixed plan for the extension of the military establishment; that the governments and the people of the States should silently and patiently behold the gathering storm, and continue to supply the materials, until it should be prepared to burst on their own heads, must appear to every one more like the incoherent dreams of a delirious jealousy, or the misjudged exaggerations of a counterfeit zeal, than like the sober apprehensions of genuine patriotism. Extravagant as the supposition is, let it however be made. Let a regular army, fully equal to the resources of the country, be formed; and let it be entirely at the devotion of the federal government; still it would not be going too far to say, that the State governments, with the people on their side, would be able to repel the danger. The highest number to which, according to the best computation, a standing army can be carried in any country, does not exceed one hundredth part of the whole number of souls; or one twenty-fifth part of the number able to bear arms. This proportion would not yield, in the United States, an army of more than twenty-five or thirty thousand men. To these would be opposed a militia amounting to near half a million of citizens with arms in their hands, officered by men chosen from among themselves, fighting for their common liberties, and united and conducted by governments possessing their affections and confidence. It may well be doubted, whether a militia thus circumstanced could ever be conquered by such a proportion of regular troops. Those who are best acquainted with the last successful resistance of this country against the British arms, will be most inclined to deny the possibility of it. Besides the advantage of being armed, which the Americans possess over the people of almost every other nation, the existence of subordinate governments, to which the people are attached, and by which the militia officers are appointed, forms a barrier against the enterprises of ambition, more insurmountable than any which a simple government of any form can admit of. Notwithstanding the military establishments in the several kingdoms of Europe, which are carried as far as the public resources will bear, the governments are afraid to trust the people with arms. And it is not certain, that with this aid alone they would not be able to shake off their yokes. But were the people to possess the additional advantages of local governments chosen by themselves, who could collect the national will and direct the national force, and of officers appointed out of the militia, by these governments, and attached both to them and to the militia, it may be affirmed with the greatest assurance, that the throne of every tyranny in Europe would be speedily overturned in spite of the legions which surround it. Let us not insult the free and gallant citizens of America with the suspicion, that they would be less

> able to defend the rights of which they would be in actual possession, than the debased subjects of arbitrary power would be to rescue theirs from the hands of their oppressors. Let us rather no longer insult them with the supposition that they can ever reduce themselves to the necessity of making the experiment, by a blind and tame submission to the long train of insidious measures which must precede and produce it. The argument under the present head may be put into a very concise form, which appears altogether conclusive. Either the mode in which the federal government is to be constructed will render it sufficiently dependent on the people, or it will not. On the first supposition, it will be restrained by that dependence from forming schemes obnoxious to their constituents. On the other supposition, it will not possess the confidence of the people, and its schemes of usurpation will be easily defeated by the State governments, who will be supported by the people. On summing up the considerations stated in this and the last paper, they seem to amount to the most convincing evidence, that the powers proposed to be lodged in the federal government are as little formidable to those reserved to the individual States, as they are indispensably necessary to accomplish the purposes of the Union; and that all those alarms which have been sounded, of a meditated and consequential annihilation of the State governments, must, on the most favorable interpretation, be ascribed to the chimerical fears of the authors of them.

Much as I respect Madison, his vision of the future was fatally flawed. The usurpations of the federal government over both the states and the people is virtually unlimited. A state can't set speed limits on its own highways without being blackmailed by the federal government about the age at which it legalizes drinking alcoholic beverages. The federal government, with powers of taxation and central banking which would have been unthinkably evil to Madison, has built up a federal debt which threatens to bankrupt our economy — and still the people can't muster the power to rein in its servants.

And with the institutional barriers which the Founding Fathers imagined would protect us from tyranny eaten away, one by one, over the last two centuries — protections against seizure of property, protections against indictments without grand-jury approval, protections of the rights of the people to be secure in their persons and homes from unreasonable searches — you would take from us our final line of defense against total victory of the forces of statism. For a chimerical vision of public safety — in the name of "gun control" that has never proven substantially effective in reducing crime — you would take the people's sovereignty over their rebellious, spendthrift, and maniacal public servants — and make our possession and carrying of arms subject to our servants' approval.

Neil

Mon Jan 18, 1993 at 04:25 EST:

Rich, it's not so much that an aroused and armed public would make an attack on the army or the government, but rather that an armed public is capable of withstanding an aggressive attack by a government/army which is out of control. As we saw in the collapse of the Soviet Union, revolutions happen when governments attempt to seize power and don't have the force necessary to do it. (If they successfully have the force to do it, they get to write the history books and it's called putting down a rebellion.)

Madison and the other Founding Fathers saw an armed public, organized into state militias or not, as a repository of the people's liberty — as the practical implementation of the people's sovereignty. Certainly the object is not to foment armed rebellion against Congress, but to attempt to tame Congress by electoral and other institutional means.

But the logic of power has its own moments of truth. If things go the way trends say they might, we could have an economy bankrupted by the federal debt in our lifetimes. My first novel, *Alongside Night* (Crown 1979; Avon 1987) explored this scenario. When money calculated in dollars — bills marked legal tender — aren't accepted anymore, when the phrase "the full faith and credit of the United States government" is no longer accepted by foreign banks or foreign governments, we face a crisis in which the ability of the American people to rely on themselves for their own security against criminals, men-on-horseback, and foreign interlopers becomes real and pressing. You can't count on the U.S. army when the government doesn't have anything to pay the army with any more. This has happened in history time and time again.

There's another issue. The logic by which the federal government was given the power to pass laws directly affecting individuals through courts and punishments — as opposed to merely imposing rules on sovereign states as was done under the Articles of Confederation — equally applies in the modern day to the United Nations. Sooner or later the logic of empire is going to demand that individual countries submit their citizens to the direct courts and punishments of the United Nations.

Speaking for myself, I observe the rest of the world being considerably less free — less concerned with individual liberty — than the United States, even in its current degraded condition. And I think the relinquishing of our national independence is to be resisted. We are the only nation on earth with a Second Amendment — the only nation that in its founding accords the rights of sovereignty to its people, rather than to an aristocracy, a technocracy, or a theocracy.

As we go on this issue, so goes the world.

It's rather important that we stand fast.

Neil

Tue Jan 19, 1993 at 04:53 EST:

Bob, whether the enforcement of laws denying sovereign individuals their rights to the means of force is local, state, or federal, it still works to the benefit of those whose ultimate goal is the destruction of citizen sovereignty and the replacement of it with a more powerful ruling class.

You have supported *my* point unwittingly, when you concede that the federal government can blackmail lesser governmental entities. It doesn't matter that the gun police would be state rather than federal. The policies would be set by political groups with a nationwide or international agenda.

You try to shrug off this point with a witticism about, "Today the Brady Bill, tomorrow the world." You bet, son. That ain't a joke; it's exactly right. Today the agenda is to use whatever political means can undercut the *right* to keep and bear arms, and diminish it to a mere privilege under police control. Once that is accomplished, all institutional protections of the rights of the people are merely subjects for political debate — and rights are no longer the basis for making those determinations: power is.

The destruction of rights is incremental. Those who would enslave us are patient. It's done one step at a time. The targets are always the weakest links: those who abuse the rights that others need for lawful and moral purposes.

The strategy is to focus on short-term practical concerns, and try to wipe from people's minds the thought that there are any larger or longer term issues.

No. I do not accept your context. Street violence is not the only important issue. As a matter of fact, street violence is a consequence of the general breakdown of social customs and mores into anomie — and anomie is precisely the situation in which decent people most need the physical force necessary to defend themselves from those would attack their lives, liberties, and property.

The issue here is not merely guns. Guns are merely the ultimate means by which these issues are discussed. The issue is power. The issue is whether ultimate political power is to be reserved to politicians and police, or to the people.

And that, my friend, is the basis that we will defeat this attempt to destroy the people's liberty, which comes among us dressed as crime control.

Neil

Thu Jan 21, 1993 at 23:57 EST:
Kate:

I was not arguing that guns can't kill. You have shifted the argument to different grounds. I was arguing against your point that this is the *only* purpose to which they can be put. Guns, as inanimate objects, have no purposes of their own. To impute a purpose to them implies that they were engineered to perform a certain function by purposeful beings.

This is not an academic or trivial point. The rhetoric of "guns have only one purpose: to kill" is a misstatement with political purpose: to deny that guns have moral or otherwise lawful functions, particularly by others than police or armies.

So, when I point out that guns can sometimes just threaten instead of kill, I am both describing a function to which they can be put and a lawful and moral purpose for which a person might wish to obtain them.

In fact, your army instructors are incorrect. The purpose of modern military small arms is not to kill the enemy. If that were the purpose, NATO would not have mandated full-metal jacket rounds, which are less lethal than expanding rounds. The purpose of modern military small arms is to wound the enemy, in order to require the enemy to require units to divert resources from attack or defense into transporting casualties to the rear instead.

The problem with the gun control movement is that it keeps on missing the target. Its proper aim should be to disarm criminals. Instead, it attempts to disarm everyone. And because of this, it sours the idea of even reasonable measures aimed at disarming criminals, because of long historical experience with demagogues who use incremental regulatory measures in order to eliminate entire fields of human action.

First the government says that it just wants to tax firearms. Then it must have enforcement agents to collect that tax, right? Next thing you know, interstate commerce is being used as an excuse for federal BATF agents to raid the homes of honest gun owners, wantonly destroying their property, looking for (and often not finding) certain classes of firearms which don't have the right excise tax stamps.

Then gun control advocates wonder why the NRA goes ballistic whenever they propose handing more regulatory power over firearms into the hands of the government.

Neil

Fri Jan 22, 1993 at 08:40 EST:
Kate:

Look, there are two different arguments we could have at this point. I can try to convince you that liberty is an important enough value that, even granting that guns make society more violent or dangerous, it's still worth it. Or I can try to convince you that firearms widely dispersed in the hands of the citizenry actually make society safer and less violent, because criminals outgunned have fewer potential occasions to attack. I believe both, and have facts and history to bring up in defense of my position.

If you value safety above freedom, we don't have a lot in common to talk about anyway. All I could say to you is to quote Ben Franklin: "They that can give up essential liberty to obtain a little temporary safety deserve neither liberty nor safety."

My response is Patrick Henry's: "I know not what course others may take, but as for me, give me liberty or give me death."

This may not be an adequate response to a Canadian. But then again, judging from history, Americans have always been testier about our individual freedoms than Canadians.

As for the practical response, your per capita murder rate is comparable to our lower density states, many of which have little gun control. Canada just doesn't have areas as densely populated as New York City or New Jersey, for example which have both heavy gun control and high murder rates. If you've been taught that there is a causal relationship between high murder rates and high density of guns in the United States, then you need to understand that statistical correlations don't tell you cause and effect. It's just as likely that there are more guns where the murder rate is high because frightened people go out and buy more guns for defense against crime. This happened in Los Angeles, where I live, right after our riots last spring.

One thing you might be interested in: Canadians suffer a higher rate of home burglary with the family present than Americans do. American burglars know they might get shot, and tend to limit their burglaries to houses they case out to make sure they're empty. It's also why our armed robbers love robbing 7-11 convenience stores. The Southland Corporation, which owns 7-11, has made it a policy to forbid their clerks to be armed. Of course some robbers kill the unarmed clerks anyway, because 7-11 also requires the clerks to make frequent cash deposits into a safe they can't open.

You ask if your VCR is worth killing over. No. But the forcible invasion of your home is. A person who would do that is capable of anything, including rape, kidnaping, mutilation, torture, or murder. Do you want to take that chance? Feel free. I won't. That's the reason to keep firearms. If the burglars haven't cut the phone lines to begin with (as many do), then the time it takes the police to get to you after you call will be the longest of your life. That's assuming that they even answer the emergency call right away. It could be busy. They could put you on hold because they are overloaded. There could be a general emergency — such as an earthquake, hurricane, or rioting — in which the entire emergency phone system is overloaded and goes down — as happened here in Los Angeles during the riots.[1]

Then again, you might live in a poor black neighborhood where the police take their sweet time responding, if they come at all. Sorry. I don't believe in either Santa Claus or police protection. But then again, you're closer to the North Pole, and maybe you know better.

As for firearms training, I say the more the better. I myself have taken police reserve training in addition to NRA courses.

Bob:

Guns are not the most lethal weapon currently available to criminals. Not by a long shot. The most lethal weapon currently available to criminals is gasoline. Dirty syringes are also right up there.

As for the Constitution being a living document, and times requiring change, I agree. The protections against government power which the Founding Fathers expected would protect us from tyranny haven't worked. We are on the brink of economic and social collapse because the government has invaded all spheres of society, destroying productive enterprise, breeding crime, and destroying social cohesion. The solution is to expand liberty and to restrict political power.

And on the off-chance that the politicians might not like this to happen, I think keeping the people armed and ready is of overriding importance. If I have to choose between your opinion and that of Jefferson or Madison, guess which one I'll go with?

Neil

Sat Jan 23, 1993 at 03:51 EST:

Kate,

1) Your point about my ignorance of Canada is well-taken. My knowledge of Canada's bill of rights was the 1960 version, which could be changed by parliament alone; I was unaware that Canada had adopted a charter of rights and freedoms into its constitution in 1982. I stand corrected.

Nevertheless, I still maintain that the U.S. is freer than Canada. A constitutional guarantee of rights on paper is not self-enforcing — as your constitutional crisis is demonstrating. Scissors cut paper — and so do guns, as I have proved every time I shoot paper targets at the range.

2) You say that power isn't in the hands of the people in the U.S. either, because we still have an aristocracy, despite our constitutional rights. Which misses my point. What power we haven't been deprived of by our "aristocracy" is *because* they haven't been able to disarm us. Of course we have a privileged class, and of course many of them try to disempower others to their benefit. Which it is harder for them to do if the others are armed and unwilling to be so abused. That is my point.

3) Finally, you ask if our constitution is so strong and our rights so enshrined, why we need arms to defend them. Precisely because words on paper don't enforce themselves: when words fail, it takes arms to do that.

4) U.S. cities of 4 million where it's safe to walk the streets: there aren't any. All U.S. cities of that size have both severe restrictions on gun ownership and high crime rates.

Sat Jan 23, 1993 at 05:17 EST:

The following chart integrates a comparison of per capita homicide and robbery rates of various American cities, divided between those with restrictive guns laws/enforcement and lenient gun laws/enforcement.

Cities: Restrictive Gun Laws/Enforcement

Rates per 100,000 (1990)	Homicide	Robbery
Newark, NJ population: 275,221 (1990 census)	41	2188
Detroit, MI population: 1,027,974 (metropolitan area: 4,382,297) (1990 census)	57	1266
New York City, NY population: 7,322,564 (1990 census)	31	1370
Baltimore, MD population: 736,014 (metropolitan area: 2,382,172) (1990 census)	41	1288
Chicago, IL population: 2,783,726 (1990 census)	31	1335
Washington, D.C. population: 606,900 (metropolitan area, 3,923,574) (1990 census)	78	1274
Boston, MA population: 574,283 (1990 census)	25	1049

Cities: Lenient Gun Laws/Enforcement

Rates per 100,000 (1990)

	Homicide	Robbery
Austin, TX population: 465,622 (metropolitan area: 781,572) (1990 census)	10	314
El Paso, TX population: 515,342 (1990 census)	7	268
Wichita, KS population: 304,011 (metropolitan area: 485,270) (1990 census)	6	355
Tucson, AZ population: 405,390 (metropolitan area: 666,880) (1990 census)	7	223
Corpus Christi, TX population: 257,453 (1990 census	11	173
Omaha, NE population: 335,795 (metropolitan area: 618,262) (1990 census)	3	180
Colorado Springs, CO population: 281,140 (metropolitan area: 397,014) (1990 census)	3	92

Sat Jan 23, 1993 at 17:34 EST:

Bob:

Ah, yes. Transfer the liability for the criminal misuse of firearms to the manufacturer. This means that the manufacturer of a device is liable when that device, which has no defects, is intentionally misused by a consumer.

Would you like to see this as a precedent for transferring liabilities on other devices to the manufacturer, when they are misused? Let's say, make swimming pool manufacturers responsible when people drown in their pools. Let's make Ma Bell responsible when people make harassing phone calls. Let's make Ford responsible when a bank robber's getaway car runs over a pedestrian.

What's that, Bob? You say that you *don't* work for the Trial Lawyers Association?

Bob, let's talk for a moment about the public opinion polls which show that Americans want more gun controls. What is it that public opinion polls measure? Public opinions! And what are public opinions based on? What the public knows, or think they know. Where do they get these "facts"? Largely, from evaluating what they see on television, hear on radio, and occasionally what they read in newspapers and magazines. And what do we see on TV, hear on radio, and read in mass-market magazines? We see the same illogical arguments about blaming inanimate objects for what criminals and morons do with them, as we have been seeing in this discussion topic.

When writers like me break through into the media, pointing out that guns are frequently used by the good guys to stop the bad guys, we see public opinion changing.

When there are riots in Los Angeles and people see armed homeowners setting up barricades to keep out carloads of armed rioters, people change their minds, and in a matter of a couple of weeks, the *Los Angeles Times* pollsters register a 9% increase in the number of non-gun-owners who decide to become gun owners.

Bob, you ask me for a case where a country with an armed citizenry has had to fight off tyranny. That's like asking me to find a country which regularly uses pesticides where pesticides have fought off locusts. If you have the pesticides, you don't have locusts. If you have an armed citizenry, tyranny is inhibited at the git go. In World War II, which citizenry was better armed: Switzerland or France? And which one was invaded and occupied by Nazi Germany?

Okay, Bob. Let's say I agree with you. Criminals go into areas with little gun control and buy guns, which they then use in areas with more restrictive gun control. Does that tell us anything? You bet. It tells us that criminals like to take their guns into areas where they know they have easier pickings: a disarmed public to prey upon. They damn well don't want to stick around the areas where they bought their guns — too many of the good guys might have guns and shoot back. Have you just made my case for me, or what?

Bob, your history of the 2nd amendment is flawed. The entire issue of keeping and bearing arms was written into the Constitution precisely because the British governor of Boston, General Gage, had required the colonists to keep their arms at an armory — then the colonists couldn't get them back when they needed them to fight off the British. The attempts by Gage to send troops to collect the arms of British subjects at Lexington and Concord wasn't forgotten, either.

The *right* to keep and bear arms means: keeping arms *where* you can get them *when* you need them, and carrying them where you need them, without having to get permission from others.

Neil

Sun Jan 24, 1993 at 11:37 EST:

Bob:

I disagree with the justice of transferring liability to manufacturers whose products are not defective, regardless of whether the product is crop-dusting equipment, firearms, or chemicals. Life can't be made risk-free; to the best of my knowledge, we all die sooner or later anyway, and just because bad things happen doesn't mean that someone else is at fault and lawyers need to write bad laws to find a scapegoat for everything that goes wrong in life.

Seriously, are you so intent on crippling firearms manufacture that you are really want to saddle this country with such an extreme precedent of liability?

Look, Bob. First you complain that gun control doesn't work because it isn't everywhere. Then you try to claim the success of gun control in some places. Well, which is it? Either gun control works at reducing the supply of guns or it doesn't. Either gun control can keep guns out of the hands of criminals, or the rest of us need to be armed to fight back. Make up your mind.

Finally, on rights. Are you maintaining that we have them or that we don't? If you're saying that rights are merely political agreements, then I assume you see nothing wrong with slavery, so long as it was constitutional? If you think otherwise, I'd like to know on what basis, if it isn't that rights precede politics.

As for chimps and whales — when they ask me to recognize their rights, I'll take it seriously.

Neil

Mon Jan 25, 1993 at 01:40 EST:

Bob,

As I said in a previous message, guns and gun control aren't ultimately the issue we're debating. As we can see from following the threads, the issues are all sorts of other things: conceptions of rights versus governmental restrictions; differences about risks and liabilities; basic differences in political philosophy.

There is room for disagreement about individual risk assessment versus the dangers to others.

When reasonable people can disagree, who decides? Do we sue each other in court and let judges decide? Do we let legislators come up with a decision that is binding on both those who agree and those who don't? Or do we let individuals decide for themselves?

The same problem that we are discussing here arises in the social conflict between those who believe abortion is murder and those who believe it's no one's business but a woman's to decide whether or not to have one.

The bottom line is: my position on private ownership and carrying of firearms is akin to the pro-choicers who believe the moral choice should be made by the individual, and you — like the anti-abortion groups — believe that laws should be passed which impose their moral judgments on everyone.

You see, even if the anti-abortion group has a morally superior argument — and remember, this is a hypothetical "even if" — so long as there is a large sector of society who believes differently, it is politically impractical to impose their view on the whole of society.

The same is true of firearms. Even if you were right — and remember, this is a hypothetical "even if" — so long as millions of Americans believe they have the right to own and carry firearms, it is politically impractical to impose your view on the whole of society.

You can't escape the fact that there are two hundred million privately owned firearms in this country, in around sixty million households. Even if regulations are passed restricting ownership of "assault weapons," the failures of such laws in California and New Jersey to cause more than a small minority of owners to register their guns shows the distrust and indifference gun owners have for such laws.

And given the failures in prohibiting popularly desired commodities — everything from liquor to pornography — there is no historical basis for anyone to take seriously the idea that gun restrictions of the sort you propose would have any significant effect at reducing the firearms available to the irresponsible, the psychologically unstable, and the criminal.

What your proposals and those of Handgun Control, Inc., do accomplish however — what the constant attacks on gun owners and the 3 million member NRA by establishment media and institutions accomplishes — is to convince us that we are being devalued and trivialized by people who think they have the standing and the power to decide what's best for us, even though we think they're dead wrong. And under such circumstances, we will fight tooth and nail against even the most moderate and otherwise reasonable restrictions on firearms availability, because we believe them to be merely baby steps towards the destruction of our long-established political right to keep and bear arms.

I don't expect you to give up.

But understand why we won't, either.

Neil

Mon Jan 25, 1993 at 23:43 EST:

Bob,

When Florida changed its law six years ago, CBS's *60 Minutes* declared that allowing anyone who wanted to carry a gun to do so would turn Florida into the "Gunshine State." They've never gone back to look at what actually happened, nor have they retracted their prediction of shootouts at every traffic accident.

Out of 101,009 people who have been issued a Florida license to carry a concealed firearm — and this includes Miami, a city with a metropolitan area population of 3,192,582 (1990 census) — only 15 have afterwards committed a crime with a firearm — and only one of those is a homicide.

That means that 100,994 out of 101,009 have not misused their firearm since being licensed. It also means that the rate of criminal misuse is 1 out of 6734.

The homicide rate in Florida is down 20% since 1987. This is the only reliable measure of crime, since there's a body to count. All other crime rates — burglary, robbery, rape — are estimates based on crime reports and surveys; and most criminologists consider the homicide rate the only one that tells us anything useful about crime trends.

Meanwhile, the national homicide rate is up 15% during that same period.

The success of Florida clearly demonstrates that it is possible to implement a program for honest, decent people to carry arms, without arming criminals in any statistically significant number. And, even with such a small a number as 80,891 additional citizens on the street carrying guns, the deterrent effect on crime is noticeable.

Neil

Tue Jan 26, 1993 at 02:59 EST:

Bob,

Here's how I see the cases of abortion and gun-control as equivalent.

1) Those who oppose legal abortion think legal abortion fosters the criminal killing of human beings, and therefore they wish to outlaw it for everyone, regardless of whether they agree. Those who oppose legal ownership and carrying of guns think legal guns foster the criminal killing of human beings, and therefore they wish to outlaw it for everyone, regardless of whether they agree.

2) Those who favor legal abortion think the question of whether legal abortion fosters the criminal killing of human beings is a question that must be answered by individuals for themselves, rather than the government forcibly imposing the views of those who think legal abortion fosters the criminal killing of human beings on those who disagree. Those who favor legal ownership and carrying of guns think the question of whether legal ownership and carrying of guns fosters the criminal killing of human beings is a question that must be answered by individuals for themselves, rather than the government forcibly imposing the views of those who think legal ownership and carrying of guns fosters the criminal killing of human beings on those who disagree.

3) In both the case of abortion rights and gun rights, there are millions of Americans who think it should be legal. Those who wish to restrict either abortions or guns wish to impose their opinions by force of government arms on those who disagree with them. Further, to the extent they succeed in restricting or prohibiting an activity which millions of people favor, they foment disrespect for the law, encourage civil disobedience and political strife, and destroy the social harmony necessary for a free society.

This said, let me answer your question, for myself only. My response is not binding on anyone else in the firearms rights movement. I believe that the quality of life is more important than mere elimination of risk. We all die sooner or later anyway, so we stand a 0% chance of avoiding the risks to our lives anyway. To me, individual liberty and justice are more important than mere reduction of risk of dying from gunfire.

Now, undoubtedly, you agree. You advocate gun control because you believe it would improve the quality of life. The difference is that you are taking a utilitarian view — trying to arrive at a political solution which benefits "the greatest good for the greatest number" — where I believe that such decisions are value judgments that must be made by individuals for themselves, and that we do not have a free society if uniform value judgments are imposed on all individuals.

That's why I say it comes down to pro-choice or anti-choice.

Neil

Thu Jan 28, 1993 at 02:56 EST:

Bob,

Bob, you misunderstood what I said. I have no doubt that you, for one, do not believe that the basic moral question is one of liberty. Nor do we disagree that most people in this society don't divide the issues that way, either, which is the reason that there isn't a pro-liberty party and an anti-liberty party.

Most people are not persuaded that there are *any* fundamental principles defining good and bad, just or unjust, workable or non-workable. I don't know whether you believe in consistency to a set of principles or what principles *you* might have — but you and I both agree that liberty is not their basis.

Now, about the shooting in Tampa, Florida today. You have been arguing that we need more gun control laws, that such laws will have an impact on reducing crimes of violence. Here we have Florida, which makes carrying a gun without a license a felony. It's already against the law. The police can arrest you for it. What more do you want? Police are not supermen, and just because a law is passed doesn't mean it can always be enforced effectively. I don't know what magic you expect your elite gun police and elite gun courts can bring to reducing the criminal use of guns. They'll be just people, too. On the other hand, elite gun police and elite gun courts would likely be used to deny guns to people who would use guns for self-defense.

Obviously, there aren't enough people carrying guns to the office in Tampa, Florida, so that when a madman with a gun comes in and starts shooting up the place, there's somebody ready to shoot back.

However, Florida law allows people to carry guns for self-protection from crazy people with guns — and I expect the number of Tampa workers carrying guns to work for self-defense will be increasing dramatically in the next few months.

Neil

Sat Jan 30, 1993 at 05:42 EST:

Bob,

The Ten Commandments (the ten "blessings" in original titling) are not principles — they are orders. One can possibly *derive* principles from them — such as that murder of a fellow countryman is evil — but the principles themselves are not contained in the text itself.

Not only are principles not just arbitrary orders, they must be self-consistent. For example, suppose I said, "Even to illustrate a point, it is never allowable to use the word 'mudgumple.'" My principle of never using 'mudgumple' to illustrate a point has been violated by the very sentence which uses it to illustrate that point. It is self-contradictory — self-refuting — and thus does not stand up to the test of logic.

Now, when I said, "Most people are not persuaded that there are *any* fundamental principles defining good and bad, just or unjust, workable or non-workable," I suppose, to be perfectly truthful, I'd have to exclude people who believe in the Ten Commandments. Their fundamental principle is, "The Ten Commandments defines right and wrong." If the Ten Commandments say you shouldn't do something, then their principle is, "If the Ten Commandments forbids that, then it must be wrong to do it." They require no further argument, no demonstration of the truth of that premise.

But there are several prior premises that go deeper even than that. One of them is, "I don't know what right and wrong is unless someone else tells me." Another is, "I know that the Bible is written (or authorized) by God, and God knows right from wrong, therefore I can believe what the Bible says." Still another is, "I know that the translation of the Bible I am reading is accurate to what God wrote (or authorized)." Still another is, "I know that what God told the Israelite nation to do four millennia ago applies to me today as well."

You see how a simple thing like taking the Ten Commandments as final, unquestioned, literal truth bites its own tail? At any point you can come back with, "Well, how do you know that?" "How do you know that the Bible was written by God, rather than men?" "How do you know that the translation is accurate — are you a scholar in ancient Aramaic and Greek who has read the originals, or do you rely on the opinions of scholars? If the latter, why do you trust them?" And finally, "How do you know that the rules God made for the Israelite nation weren't specific to those people at that time? How do you know that God doesn't intend us to live by different standards or rules?"

Even a person who wants to forego the necessity of thought about discovering principles of right and wrong finds that it can't be done without giving the matter some thought. No matter how much you want to abdicate the responsibility for figuring out right and wrong for yourself, sooner or later you have to, if for no other necessity than discovering for yourself which authority in interpreting the text you are going to believe.

Here, then, is a solid principle we can begin with: "It is impossible to know rules about right from wrong without learning the premises on which those rules are based."

Now, let's go to some of your statements about principles.

What I understand you to be saying is: Most people who hold to moral principles believe in being faithful to them until they are convinced otherwise. But because moral principles are learned, such faithfulness to principle is spotty.

If this *is* what you're saying, then I would tend to agree with you. But it misses my point. My point is that most people have never thought it through, don't care to think it through, and because they have no basic philosophy of their own — no worldview — to base their actions on, they tend to go with the flow and do what everybody else around them is doing. In other words, for most people, "right" is what most other people around them *say* is right — even if they don't do it themselves — or "what Billy Graham, my teacher, Carl Sagan, and Dan Rather tell me is right." If you want to know what's right, turn on TV and see what people are saying. Or listen to a call-in show. Once you know the answers other people give, you can pick one or two and be done with the question, without the necessity of difficult thinking.

What I was attempting to do in my question to you was to elicit your own worldview — the basic premises or principles you are using to judge principles of government and social order. More fundamental to that, since many of my messages have expressed my philosophical worldview — the basic premises I'm arguing from — I was trying to find out if you have a philosophically consistent worldview as well. Once I knew that, I could discover where we part, and focus on the different premises themselves. That would enable me to attempt criticizing any contradictions I found in your statements of principles, and possibly, at least between us, discover a closure on the many issues we've been discussing, so we don't have to go back over the same tiring arguments again and again.

In the absence of a worldview to argue against, let me just go after one principle I can divine from your message. You said that while you don't believe in "absolute liberty," you do believe in some "qualified freedoms."

Let's define our terms. By absolute liberty, I mean that each individual in a society holds the right to take action regarding the furtherance of his/her goals and value-judgments, limited only by the borders beyond which such actions deprive others of the exact same right. Historically, by the way, this is known as "the law of equal liberty."

Now, this is already a rather big "qualification" on freedom. It forbids action that deprives others of their freedom of action, or that deprives anyone of anything which is rightfully theirs without their consent. We can spend a good deal of time arguing how such rights can be derived — and what are their natural limits — but that goes far beyond the scope of the immediate question, even though what gun-control versus gun rights ultimately is addressing is the question of where those borders are.

For the sake of this discussion, I just want to emphasize that I don't believe that just because a group of people get together in large numbers and become powerful, it gives them greater rights over individuals or groups who are not as powerful. I believe that principles of right and wrong are independent of, and prior to, questions of political decision-making and the implementations of those decisions by force.

Okay, let's get to some specifics. I asked you, "Here we have Florida, which makes carrying a gun without a license a felony. It's already against the law. The police can arrest you for it. What more do you want?"

To which you replied, "I want it to work! And if it doesn't work, if criminals still get guns and shoot wives or former supervisors, then the law should be changed."

Bob, you are making an assumption that I have to challenge as utopian. You are assuming that no matter what a problem is, legislation can be drafted that will fix it. Further, you are assuming that even properly drafted legislation will be able to be enforced to an extent able to make an effective impact on that problem.

Or, to boil this down to an aphorism: "If wishes were horses, beggars would ride."

Bob, will you not even concede the *possibility* that it may not be possible to keep guns out of the hands of criminals to any significant extent? We are living in a country which has spent billions and billions of dollars trying to eliminate poverty with government programs. Poverty is still with us. The government spends money on research to cure diseases: AIDS is not yet cured, nor is cancer or heart disease. Laws are passed to require seat belts in cars, then — when many people choose not to use them — laws are passed requiring people to wear seat belts. Yet, tens of thousands of people die every year in car accidents because they aren't wearing seat belts.

We could, of course, pass a law that every car have a video camera in it, transmitting to roadside police receivers, to ensure that every one wears their seat belt. And we can have elite seat-belt police and elite seat-belt courts, who do nothing but enforce this law.

But at what cost? Some lives would be saved, certainly, but privacy would be lost in cars, the quality of life reduced thereby, and the death rate would be unchanged: one person, one death — sooner or later.

Your suggestion that requiring a reference from a neighbor, before you're allowed to buy a gun, would have changed the outcome in Tampa, Florida, is such a suggestion. Suppose you ride a motorcycle and have long hair, and your next- door neighbor is a Jehovah's Witness. Do you think they're going to give you a good reference? Or suppose your dog uses their tree for a toilet. Or suppose you're white, and your wife is black, and they're bigots. The possibilities of abuse are endless.

Yet, you are so dubious that an armed citizen in that Tampa cafeteria would have been able to stop the gun attack that this tyranny-by-the-next-door-neighbor seems preferable to you.

Obviously I believe otherwise. I've written two Op-Ed pieces for the *LA Times* about individuals in restaurants who were able to put up an effective defense because they were armed — and I also believe Kleck's estimates about the high number of gun defenses. But my point is, I think society has less to fear from the occasional armed psycho than it does from giving next-door neighbors the ability to veto each other's rights. That violates the principle of liberty — the law of equal liberty — as I defined it earlier in this message. And I believe such violations corrupt and destroy the social bonds which make peaceful and productive coexistence possible.

Neil

Thu Feb 04, 1993 at 07:29 EST:

Bob,

You say it's immoral to kill other human beings unless such killing saves innocent lives.

If your definition of "saving innocent lives" concedes that other criminal activities such as robbery, rape, burglary, and mayhem threaten innocent lives — and that it is therefore rightful to use lethal force against someone doing these — then I agree with this. Otherwise, I'd need a more detailed list of justifications and excuses for the use of lethal force.

You also say it's proper for society to regulate human conduct so as to effectuate saving innocent lives.

If by "regulate" you mean pass laws which impose sanctions on people who kill other human beings other than to save innocent lives as discussed above, then I agree. If you mean restricting the freedom of people who have *not* killed other people, or otherwise threaten them with theft, injury, or other invasion, then I don't agree that it's proper. That would contradict your first premise by failing to make a clear distinction between "innocent" and "not innocent" and treats the innocent the same as the guilty; and without such a distinction between innocent and guilty, your first premise which relies on such a distinction logically self-destructs on its own internal contradiction.

Neil

Sun Feb 07, 1993 at 19:30 EST:

Bob,

There is a moral argument to be made here as well as a tactical argument. If you are arguing that a store owner who risks his life attempting to kill an armed robber is morally inferior to the store owner who allows the robber to take the cash box (which "isn't worth dying for"), then you must be an Ayn Rand Objectivist. Only the Objectivist's belief that sacrificing yourself for others is evil could find fault with a hero who risks his life to rid his neighbors of a clear-and-present danger to their lives.

By being armed, a robber is threatening to take a life if you don't give him what he wants. His claim of being armed, and the demand for any sort of compliance under threat of force, justifies use of lethal force to prevail against his threat. There is *no* situation, short of the armed robber's throwing down his weapons, and offering unquestionable and unconditional surrender — where it is not acceptable to use lethal force against him.

What is also hard for me to understand is why you would consider for a split second that a kidnaper who has just come in, after you have untied and armed yourself, deserves to live any longer than it takes for you to pull the trigger.

As a moral proposition, those who use lethal force to deprive others of their lives, liberty, and property have given up their right to life. Whether or not you ask for their surrender is entirely a tactical question, not a moral one. Does the kidnaper have information — perhaps about other hostages — which you need? Will confederates execute other hostages if they hear gunshots?

Bob, this is why it's important that you not base your moral arguments on the mistranslation "Thou shalt not kill." That mistranslation of the original Hebrew "You shall not murder" leads to moral imbecility.

Bob, in our constitutional system, government has not a single right which is not delegated to it by sovereign individuals. Moreover, the calculus that government may regulate a thing because that thing is used more for immoral purposes than moral purposes legitimizes totalitarian tyranny.

Are there more Danielle Steele soft-core porn books sold than C.S. Lewis's Christian apologetics? The government may then regulate what books may be sold, and which ones you may buy.

Do high-fat foods promote heart disease more than they provide nutrition? The government may then limit you to buying no more than one package of hot dogs per month.[2]

Can any justification be found for allowing alcoholic beverages to be legally sold, when alcohol demonstrably has more negative impact on society — and promotes more immoral behavior — than any other single factor in society?

Obviously not. And it was tried. The law met with massive

non-compliance, and gave birth to organized crime in America for the first time — organized crime which found other commodities to switch to when Prohibition was repealed, so as to remain in business even today.

The principle and legal precedent that is applied today to the dangers of firearms will be some fanatic's legal argument tomorrow for fatty foods and books.

That is why an attack on the Second Amendment is an attack on the rest of the Bill of Rights. You can't isolate this single issue from the rest of society. People argue by analogy in order to arrive at principles which may be applied to other problems.

Bob, there's no such thing as a principle or conclusion that applies specifically to firearms that does not equally apply to other objects, defined by use, operation, and purpose.

If your conclusions are generally indefensible, then your conclusions about guns are specifically indefensible, and demonstrating this to you — if you are intellectually honest — must lead to you abandon any argument that does not stand up to the criticisms of fact, logic, and principle.

You can either be consistent to a set of correctly formulated, and reality-checked, principles, or you can slide into contradiction, absurdity, and hypocrisy.

Those are the only alternatives reality allows us.

You say it will be a lot easier to limit gun smuggling than drug smuggling. I find this belief naive. Just what is going to make these forces more incorruptible than other police forces, which are corrupted all the time? Entire narcotics squads in New York City have been discovered to be on the take from drug dealers, and police property rooms used as a storefront. Do you think that putting on a badge and swearing an oath relieves a person of being human? Your elite gun police will have power, and not only do we all know Lord Acton's dictum that power tends to corrupt, but if — in fact — the elite gun police are the only thing standing in the way of a criminal getting a gun, the elite gun police will be offered bribes seductive enough to corrupt a monk.

As for your contention that gun smuggling will be easier to

limit than drug smuggling, this is an unproved assumption which on the face of it is absurd. Don Kates's article "Points of Comparison Between Banning the Handgun and Prohibition of Liquor" provides an effective rebuttal. Further, I don't believe you could find any law enforcement officer who would take your contention seriously.

Bob, are you saying that if someone is attacking my sister and I shoot the attacker to incapacitate him and stop the attack, without firing a warning shot first, then I am acting immorally?

If you believe this, then you don't understand the first thing about how firearms are supposed to be used defensively. I do not know of a single instructor of combat handgunning — in law enforcement or outside it — who teaches shooting to warn, or to wound, as opposed to shooting at the center of body mass to incapacitate.

I would not draw a firearm unless I believed it was a life-or-death case. But in my police reserve training I learned that an attacker armed only with fists — much less a broken bottle, a chair, or a knife — can represent a lethal threat. A below-the-belt punch can kill. A blow to the head can kill. Further, lethal force is justified if a reasonable person can conclude that a successful attack could cause bodily mayhem, such as injury to a vital organ, or permanent damage such as being blinded.

Neil

Footnotes:

1. It doesn't even take a riot. On March 15, 1994, a fire in a Pacific Bell switching station knocked out 911 service for most of Los Angeles.

2. I thought I was arguing to absurdity here. But in the February 19, 1994 *Los Angeles Times*, a letter from Sidney Gold, MD, of Granada Hills, California, one-ups President Clinton's proposed hike in the cigarette tax to pay for health-care reform. Dr. Gold seriously suggests a one-cent per gram tax on "the fat, cholesterol, and sodium contained in the foods we eat."

The following article appeared in the Sunday *Orange County Register*, Commentary section, May 16, 1993.

Was Waco Warranted?

Whoever said that difficult cases make for bad law must have been thinking of the gun-control proposals that are already being discussed in the wake of Waco.

The February 25, 1993 warrant that the federal Bureau of Alcohol, Tobacco, and Firearms (ATF) obtained was for David Koresh's arrest and the search of the Mount Carmel facility. Once one gets past padding and irrelevancies, the warrant alleges reasonable suspicion that Koresh was buying up parts to convert two semi-auto AR-15 rifles into full-auto AR-15's functionally similar to the full-auto M-16 assault rifles used by the military. Buying such parts is of itself legal, but conversion of semi-auto to full-auto without first acquiring an occupational license from ATF and paying a $200 federal excise tax has been prohibited since the National Firearms Act of 1934.

This 1934 law is convoluted and ambiguous, made even more so by the 1968 Gun Control Act and the 1986 McClure-Volkmer Act. Congress passed these laws under its authority to levy excise taxes and regulate interstate commerce, but the federal statutes make mere possession of legal parts which could be used to convert a semi-auto rifle to full-auto illegal unless you *first* get a manufacturing license from the ATF. In other words, you have to pay the tax *before* you have possession of that which is being taxed — a unique interpretation of how excise taxes are supposed to work.

Since 1986, when Congress passed the McClure-Volkmer Act, no licenses to manufacture full-auto weapons with parts manufactured after 1986 will be issued at all. This is not a legally permissible form of federal gun control, since the Constitution grants Congress no authority to regulate the manufacture or possession of firearms, for their own use, by private citizens. The 1968 Gun Control Act and the 1986 McClure-Volkmer Act — which regulate interstate commerce in firearms — are constitutionally inapplicable to the manufacture, possession, or peaceful use of firearms on one's own property — which is all the original warrant alleges Koresh did. The tenth amendment to the U.S. Constitution states, "The Powers not delegated to the United States by the Constitution, nor prohibited by it to the States, are reserved to the States respectively, or to the people." Texas does not prohibit, nor does it require licenses, for manufacturing or owning fully automatic firearms.

The 1939 Supreme Court decision *US v. Miller* — the latest applicable precedent — affirmed the Second-amendment-right of a private citizen to own military small arms, requiring that a weapon, to be protected by the Second Amendment, must be "part of the ordinary military equipment or that its use could contribute to the common defense." In other words, the federal government would only have authority to restrict arms that *don't* have military application.

Now we get to Koresh. The affidavit attached to the ATF's February 25th search warrant includes the following, written by ATF Special Agent Davy Aguilera:

> On February 22, 1993 ATF Special Agent Robert Rodriguez told me that on February 21, 1993, while acting in an undercover capacity, he was contacted by David Koresh and was invited to the Mount Carmel Compound. Special Agent Rodriguez accepted the invitation and met with David Koresh inside the compound. ... David Koresh told Special Agent Rodriguez that he believed in the right to bear arms but that the U.S. Government was going to take away that right. David Koresh asked Special Agent Rodriguez if he knew that if he (Rodriguez) purchased a drop-in-sear for an AR-15 rifle it would not be illegal, but if he (Rodriguez) had an AR-15 rifle with the sear that it would be against the law. David Koresh stated that the sear could be purchased legally. David Koresh stated that the Bible gave him the right to bear arms.
>
> David Koresh then advised Special Agent Rodriguez that he had something he wanted Special Agent Rodriguez to see. At that point he showed Special Agent Rodriguez a video tape of ATF which was made by the Gun Owners Association (G.O.A.)[1] This film portrayed ATF as an agency who violated the rights of Gun Owners by threats and lies.

Clearly, David Koresh believed that the federal gun-control laws were unconstitutional, and that ATF was acting illegally. If the serving of the ATF warrant had gone off peacefully —as was previously the case even when Koresh was arrested for attempted murder several years earlier (he was exonerated) — then the issues raised under the federal firearms laws probably would have been litigated. Now, even though the federal firearms laws need even more pressingly to be litigated, the emotions surrounding anything having to do with the Davidians' fiery death are bound to make for bad precedents.

As it stands now, we have what is supposed to be a federal tax law being used for constitutionally questionable purposes — and the warrant which was issued, based on David Koresh having failed to pay excise taxes, resulted in an army of federal agents being used to serve a warrant in a maximally violent manner on the unproven allegations that David Koresh had an immoral lifestyle and was somehow, therefore, unworthy of possessing dangerous weapons. Not only had allegations regarding child abuse at the Davidian residence been previously investigated by Texas authorities and found to be groundless — again, with local authorities gaining access to the Davidian residence without problem — these charges are not within federal jurisdiction in the first place.

All of this finally comes down to prudential considerations. What do we as a society have to fear more — a David Koresh, or an Adolf Hitler? The 1938 Nazi Weapons Law — functionally similar to our current federal gun-control laws — disarmed Germany's Jewish citizens and made it possible for the democratically-elected German government to murder millions of innocent people. Even if we were to concede that David Koresh had the lifestyle of Idi Amin, Koresh did not represent anywhere near as lethal a threat as a government gone feral. Clearly, if we make our gun-control laws aggressive enough to be effective in disarming extremists, we also disarm the bulk of the peaceful citizenry which could deter political murders a hundred thousand times as large as anything a minor cult could accomplish.

The same arguments which demand that a balanced ecology requires not eliminating species of toads can be used for a political ecology. Political ecology demands that the citizenry remained armed to counterbalance weapons held by potentially predatory governments. You have to decide whom you fear more: a citizenry which outguns police or police which outgun the citizenry. The former may tend towards anomie — as advocates of gun-restrictions claim — but the latter has historically proved genocidal time and time again.

If anything has come clearly out of this tragedy, it's that the ideological conflict between those who believe public security can be achieved by an armed government and a disarmed populace, and those like me who believe that an armed citizenry is the bulwark of a free society, needs to be discussed dispassionately and publicly. The hyperemotionalism resulting from using Waco as an example of what needs to be done, one way or the other, is bound to make for bad law.

The Bureau of Alcohol, Tobacco, and Firearms found plenty of excuses in existing gun-control laws to serve an arrest warrant on David Koresh. That they failed to do so in a reasonable manner is surely no reason to burden sane and civil gun-owners with laws that will make them even more vulnerable to the predations of the demagogues who roam this planet — whether they enchant eighty followers or eighty million.

After writing this article, shortly after the final holocaust at the Branch Davidians' Mount Carmel Center in Waco on April 19, 1993, I became one of a number of journalists who looked into misconduct by the ATF and FBI agents in charge of the raid, stand-off, and final assault. I've concluded several things.

The first is that when it comes to opposing what they perceive as "gun nuts" and "cultists," the major media in this country are willing to allow government officials unchallenged credibility in their claims about the Branch Davidians criminality, regardless of evidence to the contrary. It's a sad day when one gets a more balanced account of a major federal law-enforcement operation from *Soldier of Fortune* magazine than *any* major-city newspaper, national magazine, or television network.

It's my current personal belief that the initial ATF raid on Waco was conducted as a public-relations stunt before Congressional budget hearings, where ATF officials were otherwise going to have to explain a sexual-harrassment scandal at the agency which CBS's *60 Minutes* had uncovered a few weeks earlier.

Experts in law-enforcement have told me the affidavit used to obtain the warrant failed to provide any reasonable cause to believe the Branch Davidians were engaging in illegal activities.

Further, the warrant did not authorize a no-knock raid, nor the violence which the ATF agents used in serving what was *only* supposed to be a search warrant against a group of people who had never resisted authorities before. And, there is much evidence that the ATF agents fired first, and that it was only after the Branch Davidians called 911 twice to get the agents to stop shooting that they unpacked firearms which were supposed to be sold at a gun show, to defend themselves and their children.

During the 51 days when the FBI cut off the Branch Davidians from all communication with the outside world, the only source the American people had about the events in Waco were the daily news briefings by FBI agent Bob Ricks. The press were kept three miles away and did nothing to protest getting only the official, censored story. During that period, and on the final day, the FBI employed methods of psychological and chemical warfare, on a house containing children, that would have been called war crimes if presented in testimony at Nuremberg.

And, the best evidence I've been able to obtain as of this writing is that the FBI, not the Branch Davidians, started the final fire by knocking against the house with their combat engineering vehicles, which resulted in the deaths of 81 men, women, and children, who seem to have done nothing more dangerous than buy and sell legal guns for profit, engage in unorthodox religious and sexual practices, and believe that the Book of Revelation applied to them.

In this belief, David Koresh was certainly correct.

The final irony of Waco is the date of the final assault, April 19, 1993: the anniversary both of the rout of British soldiers on a gun-confiscation detail by intransigent gun owners at the Old North Bridge, Concord Massachusetts, on April 19, 1775; and the fiftieth anniversary of the uprising against the Nazis by the Jews of the Warsaw Ghetto, on April 19, 1943.

As of this writing, the only persons tried for the deaths at Waco were those who were living peacefully in their bible center before the government troops showed up. All the eleven Branch Davidians charged with murder and conspiracy to murder the ATF agents who invaded their home were acquitted of those charges; the only convictions were for voluntary manslaughter and firearms violations.

So tell me. What are you supposed to do when it looks as if the federal government can cover up war crimes on its own citizens with a Soviet-style show trial of the victims, and nobody with a nationally respected voice seems to care?— **JNS, 1994**

[Note: Since the original publication of *Stopping Power,* the Academy-Award-nominated documentary film, *Waco: The Rules of Engagement,* has played at the Sundance Film Festival, theatrically in major cities, on HBO, and on home video. What was at the time I wrote the above article a fringe position has now entered the mainstream, with rave reviews and serious consideration given by (the late) Gene Siskel and Roger Ebert, *The New York Times,* the *Washington Post,* and other major newspapers. Apparently, I was too mild in my accusations against the federal government at Waco. There is evidence that not only did they start the fire, but they released hydrogen cyanide gas which killed the children and machine-gunned anyone trying to escape. **—JNS, 1999]**

Footnote:

1. Like much else in the affidavit, this was incorrect. The organization is Gun Owners of America.

The following article appeared in the Commentary section of the Sunday, June 21, 1993 *Orange County Register*, under the title, "Tube Shocks."

Does Hugging on TV Cause Real Violence?

What does watching TV make you do?

Since we live in a violent society, we're constantly hearing arguments that seeing TV violence, particularly as kids, desensitizes us so we accept real violence more offhandedly — maybe it even triggers real violence.

But TV also shows lots of hugging. The standard plot for most family sitcoms is (1) Problem causes family members to get mad at one another; (2) Family members abuse each other in cute ways; (3) All is forgiven by end of show and everybody hugs.

So television gives us a conflicting set of images: violence and hugging.

Every popular medium has undergone the charge that it corrupts youth. The novel was attacked, then movies, radio, comics, rock and roll, and now TV, music videos, and rap. The theory behind the attacks is always the same: if Johnny commits a crime, he's not responsible and his parents are not responsible: Something Else is responsible.

The problem in this society isn't the easy availability of drugs, or guns, or pornography, or television, although all are scapegoated. All are mere inanimate things: they do only what we have them do.

All supposedly scientific studies on the subject of TV violence "causing" real violence are based on a theory of cause-and-effect that is contrary to humans having the capability of making responsible, moral choices.

But we are volitional beings by nature: we choose what we do and what we make ourselves. You take two brothers from an identical lousy environment — missing father, overworked mother, no money, rotten inner city neighborhood. One brother joins a gang and has committed his first murder within a couple of years. The other brother hides out from the gangs at the public library and learns to read out of boredom. Because of reading, he manages to stay in school and takes a fast-food job while attending night college.

Even if you postulate a deterministic model of human behavior, comparing two specific phenomena in isolation tells us nothing useful. How can you isolate one specific set of television images from the effects of the other available images? Further, how do you go inside the skulls of the people doing acts of violence and find out the actual causes, when even asking won't give you a sure answer?

Serial killer Ted Bundy claimed in a final death-row interview that reading pornography made him do it. But how did that screwed up psyche *know* what was cause and what was effect? It's just as likely that the same impulses that attracted him to pornography attracted him to violent acts, and there was a third (prior) cause.

Studies linking TV violence with real violence try to reduce human behavior to stimulus and effect. It may work with rat psychology, but it doesn't work with human psychology. We aren't robots which are programmed. We learn, choose what we focus upon, change our minds, ignore what we don't like or believe, focus on what we like and believe. If someone is prone to violence, then they will probably seek out and obtain violent images — and if it isn't broadcast on TV, it will be sought and obtained otherwise.

A mere statistical link between two phenomena — TV and violence — supposes a causal link which is unproven. It's just as likely that TV violence, by providing a catharsis to those who would otherwise commit real violence, prevents real violence.

Furthermore, TV violence is almost always part of a morality play. When criminals initiate violence on TV, cops use violence to make sure they don't get away with it. If TV drives home any lesson, it's that using violence for criminal purposes will bring you to a violent end.

It's even more probable — given that TV is demand-driven — that the increase in real violence is the cause of the increase of violence on TV. The more violence there is in real life, the more reason there is to portray it on news and other "non-fiction" programs, and the more demand there is from violence-interested individuals to see it portrayed.

Showing that real violence causes TV violence is simple. But statistical correlations between any two particular phenomena, in the absence of a valid theory of human nature, prove so little that one could just as easily come up with a plausible-sounding theory of how hugging on TV sitcoms causes real violence.

Try this on for size.

Johnny is a latch-key kid whose father beat him every night before the age of five, then abandoned him and Johnny's mother. Johnny is left at home alone for hour upon hour, and watches TV. Johnny is fascinated by the TV sitcoms which show functional families. He watches them all: *Family Ties*, *The Cosby Show*, *Roseanne*, *Who's the Boss?*. Over and over again, young Johnny sees these families hugging each other.

He watches these scenes of family hugging for years, and they have a cumulative effect. When Johnny is eleven-years-old, he's in a sporting goods store at a mall, when he sees a son hug his father, who has just bought the son a new baseball bat.

Johnny goes over to the baseball bats, picks out a nice heavy one, then goes over to the son and smashes the bat into his head, fracturing his skull and instantly killing him.

Now, what conclusions do we want to draw from this incident?

1) Hugging on TV causes senseless violence, and the networks should be subject to greater regulation by the FCC.

2) Baseball bats are dangerous and should require a fifteen-day waiting period and background check before they are sold, and they should never be allowed to be sold to minors.

3) Johnny committed the act of violence because he was jealous that another boy had a father who loved him, which Johnny never had. The trigger for the incident of violence, and the par-

ticular tool Johnny used to commit it, are more or less random.

This is the sort of question that might appear on your average test in verbal logic to get a job.

But I wonder how many members of Congress, or sociologists, or journalists — or lobbyists against pornography, rock videos, guns and TV violence — could pass such a test?

If there is any valid criticism of TV, it's the same one that can be brought against drugs: both can be distractions designed to dull the pain of living in a stupid, brutal, and hope-destroying society. TV, not religion, is today's opiate of the masses.

If you want to change TV, change the desire of the viewing public from distraction to intellectual stimulation.

Or you can just change the channel.

Old Enough to Die, Old Enough to Live?

Should it be legal for kids to carry guns to school? Ask almost anyone, the answer will be, "Of course not."

That was easy; let's try a harder one.

Should a 14-year-old who kills a schoolmate for his CD-player be tried as an adult for murder — and if convicted be executed alongside the 25-year-old murderer?

That one, you'll get answers on both sides.

Here's one more: why is it junior-high kids are old enough to be given condoms to prevent pregnancy and AIDS, but they aren't old enough to have monogamous sexual partners in a legally recognized marriage?

All these questions hinge on the definitions of what is a child and what is an adult.

Biology divides mammals between childhood and adulthood at the point when an animal is capable of sexual reproduction. In the primates, this is the onset of menses in the female, and the onset of spermatogenesis in the male.

Through most of human history, the biological line between childhood and adulthood — puberty — was the cultural and legal dividing line also. English common law allowed marriage at twelve for females and at fourteen for males. The Jewish *bar mitzvah*, in which a 13-year-old Jewish male takes on the responsibility to God for his own sins — provided another clear dividing line. In much of the Third World today, economics requires recognition of a post-pubescent individual as an adult.

In the modern United States, we ignore both biology and tradition by raising the age of legal adulthood. Military eligibility is set at 17 with parental consent. At 18 we require draft registration, allow voting and, in many states, legalize marriage and the ability to make binding contracts in one's own name. The remaining rights of legal adulthood — such as drinking alcohol — start at 21.

The major reasons for extending the age of legal majority past biological maturity are both political and cultural. They include compulsory education in government-approved curricula to the age of 16 in most states, and cultural expectations of higher education for the affluent, which extend economic dependency on one's parents often into one's mid-twenties.

The words "adolescent" and "teenager" have no biological existence; they refer to legal definitions and social expectations.

Recognized adults find it difficult to regard today's post-pubescent, pre-majority individual as a peer. We see today's average teenager as subliterate or barely literate. They have no opinions that aren't designed to fit into their peer group. They have little self-esteem and even less self-control. They're sexually obsessed and don't know how to deal with the emotional turmoil this brings on. They're obsessed with trivia and frivolity; are financially and emotionally dependent on parents who are resented for being needed; are incapable of thinking independently and in abstract, time-conditional terms; and are constantly finding new ways to test their survival. In today's relativistic climate, they are often completely amoral.

Given such a wretched subculture, we're not surprised that teen suicide is high, that teen murderers are increasingly common, and that youth gangs don't even have the decency to rumble; they just do drive-by shootings.

It's also not surprising that thoughtful people express concerns about allowing such a class to have firearms.

Such concerns, however, were also made about the freed slaves in the postbellum South. White Southerners looked upon them as immature, dependent, illiterate, and unsuited for full citizenship. The first gun-control laws in this country were passed to require black freedmen permission from white officials to own or carry arms.

The question of "kids and guns" is at the forefront of the gun-control debate today. Handgun Control, Inc., in its literature, defines a "child" as a person nineteen or under, in order to obtain statistics that show that "children" are dying from gunfire out of proportion to the rest of society. If an 18-year-old "gangsta" Crip shoots a 17-year-old Blood from a moving car, Handgun Control would classify that as a child shooting a child.

When 13-year-old gang members must "make their bones" — commit a murder — in order to be given a share of the proceeds from lucrative drug sales ... when "teenage" pregnancy, AIDS, and junior-high-campus distribution of condoms are political issues ... when courts are lowering the age when a "child" may be held answerable as an adult for a felony to as low as twelve, the discrepancy between our culture's picture of childhood and reality is highlighted.

The question of how to turn the irresponsible child into the responsible adult is likewise dependent on whether even a grown-up in our social order is to be treated as an adult. Our society is increasingly paternalistic in its politics. Our drug laws presume that we cannot make rational decisions about what chemicals we may ingest; government assumes the parental role of both prescribing and proscribing.

Our consumer-protection and business-regulatory laws presume that we as individuals, or even in private groups, are incompetent to prevent ourselves from being swindled; government assumes the parental role of deciding for us who is trustworthy to do business with.

Isn't it obvious that the object of the Nanny State is to breed a culture of permanent juveniles? And isn't it equally obvious that the extension of legal and cultural childhood to years past puberty is the main mechanism for accomplishing the disempowerment and trivialization of the adult population?

Today we have public schools where armed 14-year-old gangsters run protection shakedowns on their fellow students. The shakedowns are enforced with lessons in schoolyard shootings of those who resist. If non-gang student victims decide that their lives are threatened and choose to arm themselves in defense, our modern defender of the children would disarm them and leave them at the mercy of their criminal peers.

It is, perhaps, too much to expect our society to allow its young adults their citizenship rights, when even their parents are denied many of theirs. But is it too much to ask for simple consistency?

Whatever age society says is old enough to be held answerable for a crime must be the same age society calls the age of legal majority. If one is old enough to be tried for murder, one is old enough to defend one's life from murderers. If one is old enough to see one's comrades die on a battlefield, fighting for one's country, one is old enough to buy a drink to drown out the memory. If one is old enough to be handed a condom in the school entranceway, it is old enough to decide to marry.

And while it's no certainty, human history suggests that a biological adult, when granted both adult rights and responsibilities, just might start acting like one.

Instead of Crime and Punishment

Is there any relation between crimes and arrests, or crime and punishment, for that matter? On this second question, we know there is not: according to the Department of Justice, 75%–80% of violent crimes in this country are committed by repeat offenders. Further, a chart in the Los *Angeles Times* provides good evidence there is little relationship between crimes committed and arrests made, as well.

As a sidebar to an article in the February 27, 1992 *Los Angeles Times* on the brutality of the Japanese criminal justice system, the *Times* provided a chart of Violations of Criminal Law per 100K of population in various countries, and another chart comparing the Arrest Rates in those countries.

The Violations chart shows Britain leading the pack with 7,355 criminal law violations per 100K, West Germany with 7,031 (the stats are from 1989, pre-German-unification), France with 5,831, the U.S. with 5,741, Japan with 1,358, and South Korea with 912.

The Arrest Rate chart (also 1989) shows South Korea with 78.8%, West Germany with 47.2%, Japan with 46.2%, France with 38.8%, Britain with 33.6%, and the U.S. with 21.1%

Since every country on this list aside from the U.S. has a virtual prohibition of private ownership of firearms, gun control doesn't lead to a less-criminal society. Obviously that is a blind alley for those seeking a reduction of crime.

Further, a comparison of the West German crime rate with its arrest rates also seems to blow out of the water the argument made by American law & order advocates that a greater certainty of arrest and punishment will necessarily lead to less crime: West Germany has both the second highest crime rate and the second highest arrest rate — possibly the first highest arrest rate, since the South Korean arrest claims, requiring superhuman powers worthy of Sherlock Holmes, strain any sensible person's credulity.

Indicting The Criminal Justice System

Libertarian critics of the policy of crime and punishment have long argued that crime is a necessary product of the very nature of the State, created by it, along with provoking foreign threats to justify a military-industrial complex, as a way of manipulating the public into submission to political control. It is a sweeping charge and one which is likely to be dismissed as crackpot by anyone who can't conceive of an alternative way of thinking about the subject.

But if we were to indict the criminal justice system as a criminal conspiracy might be so indicted, and look for evidence to support the charge, what do we find as the system's "modus operandi"?

First, the State creates a set of laws which mix the concept of crime as an attack upon an individual's life or property with the idea that a crime is anything the State says it is — and thus crimes without victims — or with "the State" as the sole "victim" — are created wholesale. Thus "possession" of a prohibited substance or object, even if such possession has inflicted no actual damage upon another person, in many cases receives as much punishment from the State as a robbery or murder. Additionally, the State sets itself up as the judge of what is an offense against itself, the judge which decides whether someone is guilty of an offense against itself, and the judge which decides what pains and costs to inflict upon a transgressor against itself. Then it sends out armed agents to enforce its decisions. Thus does the State treat itself as a God or Sovereign, whose will is to be feared and obeyed, and everyone else treated as one of its subjects.

Second, the "protection" of the "public" from crime, defined however the State decides, is turned over to the State which taxes the public on the basis that they "need" protection from crime, then hires police to "enforce the law" — but police have no legal obligation to protect the public which is being taxed to pay them from criminals, and suffer no liability from failure to do so.

Third, a "criminal justice" system is set up in which the guilt or innocence of a suspect bears only passing resemblance to the sentences imposed on them after plea bargains which trade ease of conviction for reduced sentences — regardless of whether the person charged is guilty or innocent. No compensation is given to those who are charged but found innocent, and often have their lives ruined by the accusation; compensation of the victim of a crime exists only as an occasional sideshow: the center ring is reserved for imprisonment of the criminal at taxpayer's expense, imposing additional costs upon the victim.

When the system is supposedly "working," those who are found guilty are sent into prisons which ensure that a prisoner will learn the craft of crime as a permanent lifestyle, creating a revolving-door criminal class which provides permanent employment for police, lawyers, prison-guards, and "crime-fighting" governors and legislators — while everything these officials do, regardless of their rhetoric, *increases* the number of attacks by criminals on the innocent.

When the system is supposedly "not working," this massive prison bureaucracy is so clogged that convicted criminals are sent back out the street in short order, to attack more innocent victims and provide more grist for the criminal-justice mill.

Meanwhile, the same system which creates crime and does little to protect the public from it also demands that the public disarm and rely on the government for protection against criminals.

Is the libertarian indictment fantasy? Or is it a stripping away of the Emperor's New Clothes? It seems hard to avoid the conclusion that if you put all this together, Criminal Justice is the protection shakedown of the public by professional organized criminals in control of an entire society: a system set up to terrorize the public into a condition where it will abide any amount of legalized theft and police control in order to be liberated from constant criminal invasions engineered to justify the system itself.

In a precise metaphor: the disease is being spread by the very doctors the public relies on for the cure.

A New Theory of Crime Management

The alternative to the game of Cops and Robbers by which the criminal justice system encourages criminals to prey upon the public so there is an excuse for the State to catch and imprison them, is to eliminate the State from the system as much as possible.

The public must come to realize that the first line of defense against criminal invasion of their lives and property is themselves. No one cares about protecting you, your loved ones, and your neighbors as much as you do — and no one aside from the potential victim is more likely to be able to provide effective counter-measures against invasion. The defense against criminal invasion requires vigilance, planning, and a willingness to fight back. The best and surest way to reduce crime is to make it unprofitable and dangerous for the criminal. The likelihood that a criminal attack will result in the criminal's being injured or dying during the attack is, both logically and practically, the surest way to achieve a low-crime society. The example of Switzerland, a society organized along the lines of universal defense by all citizens, and where criminal attacks are virtually non-existent, comes to mind immediately.

Further, there are three "criminal justice" systems already at work in our country, and the system of police, criminal indictments, trial, and punishment is the least effective of the three. The other two are the system of civil laws by which individuals who cause damage to another can be sued and compensation collected, and the insurance industry, by which victims can measure the statistical likelihood of victimization against the costs of potential attack, and calculate proper "compensation" for themselves in advance.

The criminal justice system promotes crime and protects criminals rather than fighting it. You don't have to be a radical libertarian to agree with that view. But the American people still need to ask themselves whether the problems are due to an unwillingness of the system to enforce its own criminal code, or whether the theory of crime and punishment on which that code is based does precisely what it is functionally structured to do: victimize the public at all turns.

To implement the new paradigm, the concept of "crime" must be completely severed from its statutory definitions and replaced with a simple test: If a crime has been committed, (a) Who committed it, (b) Who is the victim, and (c) What costs has the criminal invasion imposed upon the victim? If these three questions cannot be answered clearly and firmly, there will have been no crime committed.

The solution of what to do with a criminal who is not killed in process of the crime — a criminal who is captured alive or manages to escape, or must be hunted down — must be made as much as possible contingent on the accountable costs the criminal has imposed upon the victim. Instead of "rehabilitating" a criminal or "punishing" a criminal, the object must be to calculate as much as is humanly possible the costs that a criminal has imposed upon a victim (and the costs of apprehension and conviction as well), and extract as much value as possible from that criminal so that it may be used in compensation to the victim.

The object of "criminal justice" must be restricted to (a) augmenting the public's first-line self-defense with additional lines of response, such as armed response to burglar alarms; (b) detective work to locate, identify, and capture those who have committed criminal invasions or thefts; and (c) a trial system to assure that those charged with an invasion or theft actually committed it, and upon proof beyond a reasonable doubt, to calculate the costs of that invasion and extract that cost from the criminal so that it may be used to compensate the victim. In the case where a criminal invasion has produced irreparable harm such as the death of a victim or victims, the murderer must be regarded as the property of the victim's heirs, to dispose of as they wish, limited only by such mitigations that the precepts of society deem humane.

There can be no doubt that the current criminal justice system has failed. A proof of this failure is that each year the increased crime rate is used as an excuse to ask for more money and wider powers. This sort of reward for failure occurs only in the public sector; in the private sector, where competition is allowed, merchants who operate on this basis are driven out of business by customers going elsewhere and, if the failure is deliberate policy, the merchant indicted for fraud. They are not given more money and told to keep trying.

The question remains: do the American people have the courage and clarity of thought to identify the cause of the failure of the criminal justice system as its very design, and redesign the system so that it makes sense?

The following article appeared, in edited form, in the September, 1992 issue of *Liberty*.

If Execution Is Just, What Is Justice?

Democracy has no more sensitive gauge than the public opinion poll, and the recent *Los Angeles Times* poll which shows that four out of five Californians favored the execution of murderer Robert Alton Harris tells us everything we need to know about the political will of the people on this subject.

But while the voice of the people may be the final word regarding our political decisions, few could argue that it disposes of moral questions, or even that such a political will is unchanging. At various times in human history, the voice of the people has favored slavery, the execution of blasphemers, and the Divine Right of Kings. Obviously, both a public moral sense, and the political will which follow from such feelings, are subject to revision.

The largest single reason, given by those who supported the decision to execute Harris, was "Justice/Eye for An Eye." I find it both refreshing and comforting that moral, rather than merely utilitarian, considerations are at the forefront of most people's consciousness.

Still, the question remains to be asked: on what basis does one believe that retribution — "an eye for an eye" — is a valid principle of moral justice?

Is it primarily an emotional, rather than an intellectual, reaction based on empathy to the victims? What, then of the revulsion felt by others to the premeditated killing of a hogtied man?

Is it a sense that something which was codified four millennia ago in the Code of Hammurabi must be right because of its age? What, then, of that code's literal call for retaliations including putting out eyes and cutting off hands?

Is it because the Old Testament tells us that God told Moses that He was ordering us to execute murderers? First, how do we know that early authors didn't do some rewriting, or even that

Moses — a politician — wasn't lying when he said the code was written by God? Second, if we are using the Book of Exodus as our legal code, why are we not executing people who curse their parents, or witches, or those who commit bestiality, or those who make sacrifices to any other deity? Third, if we take the New Testament as updated orders, do we obey Jesus when he says he who lives by the sword dies by the sword, or when he tells us that he who is without sin shall cast the first stone? And fourth, what business does a secular state have enforcing a *religious* code in the first place?

If we answer that we do not decide what is moral or just based on emotions, or tradition, or ancient religious writings, then there remain only two other ways to derive moral premises: direct revelation or human reason. Either our moral premises are personally dictated to us by a Superior Power — and that claim must be backed with incontrovertible proof or it has no merit — or we must use our own powers of reason to figure out morality for ourselves.

Perhaps such a rational inquiry can begin by asking why it is right for the State — a secular organization acting as agent for ordinary individuals — to do that which is universally despised when done by any of those individuals? Does the State act from practical, utilitarian considerations alone — in which case such utility must first be subjected to moral limitations — or can it justify its killings on the basis of moral premises which can be derived without reference to sectarian religious documents?

The State of California finds it fairly straightforward to define justifiable homicide for the private individual. According to the California Department of Justice's booklet *California Firearms Laws 1991*, "The killing of one person by another may be justifiable when necessary to resist the attempt to commit a forcible and life-threatening crime, *provided* that a reasonable person in the same situation would believe that: a) the person killed intended to commit a forcible and life-threatening crime; b) there was imminent danger of such crime being accomplished; and, c) the person acted under the belief that such force was necessary to save himself or herself or another from death or a forcible and life-threatening crime. Murder, mayhem, rape, and robbery are examples of forcible and life-threatening crimes."

For the private person — or even the police officer — the instant the threat ends, the grounds for justifiable homicide end.

Strictly speaking, the State is no more than a group of individuals acting for common purpose. It is hard to imagine how it may rightly do more than the sum of the rights of the individuals comprising that group. How, then, does this transformation — whereby homicide is justified long after the threat has ended — occur? Does mere group procedure sanctify killing? If so, how many individuals must be in a group before it earns a license to kill? What *moral* premise distinguishes the state criminal justice system from the lynch mob?

The obvious answer is that in the absence of a Divine Ruler anointed by God, there is no moral basis for the State to do anything which it is not right for the private individual or group to do. Logic dictates that if it is morally justifiable for the State to kill in just retribution, then it must likewise be morally justifiable for other individuals or groups to do so as well — the Mafia, the Crips, and the Bloods included.

If it seems obviously wrong to you that private individuals have a right to retaliate — if California's definition of justifiable homicide seems to you to be based on a valid moral premise — then you must come up with a *moral* justification for the State to do that which none of its principals may do.

For me, I answer that it is wrong to punish murderers with death, because it far exceeds the scope of human justice. Human justice is based on the concept of seeking repair rather than further destruction. The religious concept of just retribution — punishment, by another name — is mere tit for tat, not derivable from principles of reparative equity and therefore thoroughly irrelevant to justice or moral behavior as it may be enforced by a legal system. The allure of legal punishment is to adrenaline rather than reason.

Consequently, I see no possible justification for the State, as an agent of the people, to claim a moral right to do that which none of its principals may do. If we have learned anything in four millennia of limiting the role of government, it is that if civil justice is to exist in a secular society, it means limiting equity among individuals to reparation of wrongful harms.

If one believes, as I do, that killing a murderer has no moral basis, it does not logically follow that one is advocating that murderers should continue to enjoy a pleasant life at the expense of their victims. The principle of reparation derives the object that murderers should labor hard until the end of their days, and all that they produce beyond their mere subsistence should be paid to the heirs of their victims. There is no reasonable moral basis for the practice of murderers spending their days being supported as privileged wards of a welfare state. Such false humanitarianism is gravely offensive to those who remember the murderer's victims, and such offense is possibly the basis for much of the emotion behind calls for state executions.

To those of religious precepts, I must argue that it is quite enough for the institutions of a non-theocratic society to place immovable walls between murderers and the rest of us, and extract what value can be obtained for their victims' benefit. That is all safety and equity calls for. That is all that we — as individuals or as a group — are entitled to. Beyond that imperfect human institutions should not go, and what perfect vengeance is required must be left to God, who in His own good time disposes of all lives as He sees fit anyway.

A Note to Freedom Activists

The following was a message to libertarians and Second Amendment absolutists explaining why I was proposing compromise language for the Brady Bill. — **JNS**

I am a libertarian anarchist who believes not only in the absolute right to self-defense, and the right to keep and bear arms that derives from that, but also in other absolute human rights derived from "the right to life, liberty, and the pursuit of happiness" (or "life, liberty, and property," if you prefer; property rights logically derive from the rights to life and liberty anyway).

But what most defenders of rights don't understand is that rights are inherent and natural, not political. States do not grant rights. Legislation and court decisions therefore can neither grant rights nor deprive people of them. Only the "end-users," so to speak, of legislation and court rulings — that is, the "law enforcement" end of the state, whether it be individuals labeled police or tax collectors, or DEA, ATF, FBI, HUD, etc. — can violate rights. Their reasons for violating rights are irrelevant at the point when they commit those violations.

What the institutional structure of the State does is grant privileges and immunities. Legislation and court rulings — used as the decision-making basis and "authority" of the "law-enforcers" — either create a rationale for someone to hassle or arrest you for violating a statute or court decision, or it doesn't.

That's why — in seeking to influence the passage of legislation or decision-making of judges, or even the enforcement policies of "law enforcers" — one is making no statement, for or against, rights held by the people. One is merely trying to prevent the State from violating rights by verbal, rather than forcible, means — a wise strategy when one is conquered and outgunned.

That is also why, with no contradiction whatsoever, I participate in the political system by voting, and would serve on a jury if my time permitted it. (Personal circumstances currently don't.) I could conceivably even serve in legislative office, attempting to use my vote to make legislation achieve a closer approximation of privileges and immunities to natural human rights.

A gun permit is an immunity granted by the government, telling its law-enforcers not to arrest you. It would be nice if the personnel involved in interpreting the State's primary document — the Constitution — were honest enough to admit that their rules don't allow them to interfere with the people's right to keep and bear arms, but since these personnel don't have the integrity to do that, there is certainly nothing wrong with seeking as little interference with our rights as is realistically possible at this time and place, since the ideology of those in power isn't going to recognize our rights and they have better-organized methods of enforcing their will than we have of preventing them from doing so.

If you can convince enough of the people to resist infringements on their rights, terrific. We will be free. But I do not see that as a realistic possibility anytime soon.

The State has controlled public education for most of this century, and has used public education to instill an unthinking support for its policies and personnel in the majority of people. Most people are incapable of reading with logical comprehension and analysis at all, and those who can are usually pushed into colleges and universities controlled by the most radically pro-statist ideologues in our society.

The radical statists spread out from the universities and control all the other intellectual professions: news media, law, and medicine. Judges are appointed from their ranks and legislators are elected from their ranks. They gain control of unions, guilds, professional organizations. They control both the Republican and Democratic parties, and gerrymander the electoral process so that the balance of power does not radically shift between the two parties. This tends to homogenize both parties, eliminating other-than-centrist ideologues from positions of power or effectiveness.

Third party movements are marginalized by a refusal of the media to take them seriously or even count their vote totals on election days. Independents are taken seriously only when they are ideologically within their parameters of centrist political philosophy.

We are currently living in occupied territory. The enemy has the primary and secondary schools, the universities, the mass-media (print and broadcast), and the control of virtually all membership organizations from the American Association of Retired Persons (AARP) to the American Medical Association (AMA) and the American Bar Association (ABA — the lawyers).

We have computer bulletin boards, radio talk shows, Rush Limbaugh, Ross Perot (occasionally), a few conservative and libertarian educational institutions and publications, and a few hundred thousand libertarians and patriots who have managed to cut their way through the bullshit to think for themselves.

We also have a bunch of people with a neanderthal sense of strategy and a consequent habit of alienating their potential converts with inappropriate buzzwords and frightening paradigms.[1] We need to educate many of our most-dedicated people before we have a chance of educating anyone else.

The bulk of the American people sense something is wrong but don't really know what it is or what to do about it — and in their uncertainty, they turn to the establishment pundits for solutions. The pundits give them "solutions" — good and hard. "Higher taxes, more government control — and disarm all those extremists who are trying to tell you not to listen to us."

I'm not saying we can't win. I'm saying that we have an uphill fight to recapture the minds and hearts of the people. But right now, the people are *not* on our side, and to pretend that they are is a miscalculation that can lead to our making false moves and being silenced.

The people suffer statism right now because they don't have the will to resist it. They do not have the will to resist it because they think what they have is as good as it's going to get. A few living libertarian science-fiction writers have tried writing novels showing how it could get better and what it would look like if it does. I'm one of them. So is L. Neil Smith, Victor Koman, Brad

Linaweaver, F. Paul Wilson, Robert Anton Wilson, Robert Shea,[2] and Victor Milan. Our literary forbears include Ayn Rand, Robert Heinlein, and C.S. Lewis, and before them, Mark Twain and Sinclair Lewis.

We've gotten through to a few people. But the literary establishment is doing a pretty good of marginalizing us — denying our most ideological books the sort of push behind them that makes for bestsellers — so we tend to preach to the already-converted.

By all means, press forward with educational efforts to tell people that they have rights. But if some of us choose to attempt to preserve some fractions of our rights and freedoms by having the statists grant us a certain measure of privileges and immunities, so that we can continue to live, work, and function at all, I would hope that you will understand the context of our actions. Please do not assume that we have lost sight of the ultimate issues and accuse us of selling out to the State.

We may differ on strategy, but we both seek freedom.

— May 7, 1993

Footnotes:

1 My self-description as an "anarchist" may even fall into this category. The word has gotten bad press through association of the word with anti-state terrorism and nihilism, doctrines which only a few Russian anarchists such as Bakunin and Kropotkin endorsed, and only a very few anarchists ever acted upon. Modern libertarian anarchism, drawing upon the works of Nineteenth Century American philosophers such as attorney Lysander Spooner, and modern libertarians such as free-market economist Murray Rothbard, often find themselves more emotionally resonant to Bart Simpson than to Emma Goldman.

2. Sadly, no longer living. Shea died in March 1994.

Ripostes and Counters

The people who don't like guns have a lot of media resources to call upon. That puts gun-rights activists in the position of playing defense most of the time.

Ah, but that's just another opportunity for a clever attack, if you know how.

Remember: you're never outnumbered. You just have a "target rich" environment.

— JNS

KNX Editorial Replies

Broadcast January 9, 1992:

KNX's call for fewer incidents of irresponsible gunplay is one no sane person can disagree with. But the reasonable-sounding laws KNX endorses undercut the individual right to own firearms in this country, so wider anti-gun laws can be passed later.

Take the legal requirement that you need to pass a government safety test before you're allowed to buy a gun. What reasonable person can oppose gun safety? The problem is, it makes gun ownership a privilege instead of a right. It expands government power to decide who *can't* own guns.

If unchecked government power doesn't frighten you, consider that when Germany passed laws making Jews turn in their guns, it became possible for the Nazis to send them to death camps. Consider that it was armed soldiers who massacred unarmed students at China's Tien an men Square a couple of years ago.

Then ask yourself whether the massive civil disobedience that thousands of Californians are committing, by refusing to register their so-called assault rifles with the state, is "irresponsible." Just maybe it's a higher responsibility to the U.S. Constitution, the Second Amendment of which tells the government, "the right of the people to keep and bear arms shall not be infringed."

Power-hungry officials understand the threat contained in the Second Amendment. That's why they often lie about it. It's the threat to all tyrants written by Thomas Jefferson in the Declaration of Independence. It tells us that governments are instituted to secure life, liberty, and the pursuit of happiness, and "That whenever any Form of Government becomes destructive of these ends, it is the Right of the People to alter or to abolish it."

Broadcast July 15, 1993:

KNX General Manager George Nicholaw asks why it takes a tragedy in a San Francisco high rise for there to be a chorus of outrage demanding stricter gun control. I'll answer that question. It's because the choir is the news media themselves.

When a lunatic misuses firearms to commit multiple murders and suicide, it's headline news, every hour on the hour. Then, for weeks afterwards, pundits capitalize on the tragedy with calls for more restrictive gun laws, based on the charge that firearms can only be used to murder the innocent.

But that's just not true. According to a study by Professor Gary Kleck, Criminologist at Florida State University, Americans use their privately owned firearms — handguns, rifles, and shotguns — 1.4 million times every year to *save* innocent lives. Let me say that another way. Three thousand, eight hundred times a day, an American firearm owner uses her or his firearm to prevent a rape, a robbery, or a burglary. In 99% of those thirty-eight hundred daily firearm defenses, no one is shot at all — and because non-violence is non-news, *you* never hear about it.

Let me put this statistic in perspective. During the fifteen-minute period in which a psycho murdered nine people at a San Francisco law office, forty *ordinary* Americans used their privately owned firearms to *stop* a crime, without shooting anyone.

The bitter tragedy in San Francisco is that some of those nine murders could have been stopped if anyone at that law office had kept a firearm locked in her or his desk for protection.

We do have a problem with firearms in this society. It's not that too many criminals and lunatics have a gun handy when *they* need one, it's that too many victims *don't*.

Broadcast October 6, 1993

KNX General Manager George Nicholaw wants the LA Police Department to restrict licenses to carry concealed firearms to a small elite who can demonstrate a "clear and present danger" ... but he also thinks that simple fear of violence isn't enough. Under that standard, he says — and this is a direct quote — "every city resident would qualify."

Amen to that!

Mr. Nicholaw also says — another direct quote — "Let's be careful not to turn the 'City of Angels' into an armed camp of gun-toting vigilantes."

Mr. Nicholaw seems to be more afraid that you might legally carry a firearm for protection than he is of the carjackers, ATM-robbers, and rapists who are already carrying them illegally.

This paranoia about ordinary citizens turning into vigilantes just isn't supported by states where civilians are already commonly carrying firearms.

Pennsylvania, Oregon, Washington, Georgia, and New Hampshire are among the states where it's easy to get licensed — and none of those states have problems with ordinary civilians carrying firearms. Vermont doesn't even require a license for anyone to carry a concealed firearm. Have you seen any stories on *60 Minutes* about vigilantes being a big problem in Vermont?

But Florida is the best example because they're a big state and keep good records.

Florida issues a license to carry a concealed firearm to any adult who can meet minimal requirements. In the last six years, Florida has issued almost 120,000 new licenses to carry — and only 16 Floridians lost their licenses because they violated Florida's laws regarding the use of that firearm. That's a compliance with the law of 99.99987 percent.

And even though 120,000 concealed-weapons carriers aren't all that many in a state with 13 million people, it just might be enough of a reason why criminals in Florida are attacking tourists whom they know are a lot less likely to shoot back.

Excerpts from a Letter to Nadine Strossen, President, ACLU

October 11, 1991

Dear Ms. Strossen:

I'm a member of ACLU writing to ask your assistance in a matter where ACLU Of Southern California is, itself, violating my civil rights.

In the light of recent court decisions which have been narrowing civil liberties one after another, I joined ACLU with the intention of bringing my activism to ACLU. I have been impressed by ACLU's work in the areas of the first and fourth amendments, its fourteenth amendment work in the area of equal protection, and its pro-privacy work (including pro-choice and gay rights), but there were major gaps where the government has been running roughshod over civil rights where I felt my energies, and those of like-minded people, could be of maximum value. Specifically, these are the fundamental human right to autonomy over one's own body, as violated by drug prohibition and FDA interference with the purchase of vitamins and drugs, and the right to keep and bear arms, as protected by the 2nd amendment, and violated by statutes prohibiting or restricting ownership, trade, possession, and carrying of defensive weapons. (Let me note here that the Second Amendment is included in the copy of the Bill of Rights which ACLU of Southern California mailed me as part of the membership information kit, and again as part of the membership kit when I joined. What on earth are they thinking?)

I read the literature mailed to me by ACLU of Southern California carefully, noting that chapters could be formed not only by region, but also by special interest — for example, there's a Gay and Lesbian Rights Chapter. I then called Gary Mandanach, President of ACLU of Southern California, and spoke with him several times, telling him that I have been recruiting new ACLU memberships with the intention of forming an ACLU of Southern California chapter, to be focused on 9th and 2nd amendment issues, including drug privacy and right to keep and bear arms. I requested his assistance in the formation of such a chapter, and he said he would bring up the issue at the next board meeting.

Today he informed me that ACLU of Southern California would not recognize any chapter I formed on these issues, since the board has a pro-gun-control policy. I asked how I could appeal this decision, or bring about its change, and he told me in essence, "There is no way."

I am shocked, dismayed, and outraged. It's the precise equivalent to me as if I was a newspaper reporter who approached ACLU with the intention of protecting the right of free press, and was told that the board of ACLU had a policy calling for government control of newspapers.

We have here a situation where I was (and am) ready to bring hundreds of new members into ACLU of Southern California, to support Constitutionally-protected civil rights — and ACLU of Southern California has not only told me to buzz off, but it has informed me it is in league with those who would narrow civil liberties. I do not intend to allow this corruption of ACLU policy to hinder the important work of defending civil liberties.

This letter is a formal request for national ACLU to grant me the right to recruit new ACLU members nationally, and to invite current ACLU members, for a new national ACLU affiliate to be called the Unabridged Bill of Rights Chapter. This would be unaffiliated with any regional affiliate of ACLU.

I believe that with proper publicity, I can bring in several thousand new members to national ACLU for this chapter, and restore the luster which has been tarnished by an ACLU affiliate's attempt to fight for government restriction of civil rights rather than the constitutional rights of the people.

I look forward to hearing from you as soon as possible, so that we can discuss the proper procedures I need to go through to form this chapter.

Sincerely,
J. Neil Schulman

Nadine Strossen replied to this letter and told me she'd forwarded my reply to the ACLU of Southern California; she told me to write her again if I found their response unsatisfactory. Since Gary Mandanach of the ACLU of Southern California told me in polite language to buzz off, I wrote back to Nadine Strossen, and followed up with phone calls and faxes that were never acknowledged. **— JNS**

Letter to *Scientific American*

The following letter was sent to *Scientific American*. They elected not to publish it. — JNS

October 28, 1991

Franklin E. Zimring's article in the November 1991 *Scientific American*, "Firearms, Violence and Public Policy," has no proper place in any publication with the name "science" on its masthead, much less a publication with the prestige of *Scientific American*. It is pure political advocacy covered with a thin veneer of statistics to make it appear scientific to the naive.

Zimring's claim that "[T]he percentage of gun-related crimes in an area is related to the proportion of owners of firearms in that area" is not even supported by comparing Zimring's own charts on "Crimes with Guns by Region in 1990" and "Homicides by Region in 1990" with his "Households with Guns by Region in 1991." These clearly show that while the Midwest has the second highest percent of households owning at least one gun, it has the lowest per capita number of crimes with guns and per capita gun homicides of any region.

That Zimring begins with an ideological point of view, and chooses to study only that which might tend to support his conclusions, is borne out by the absence from his study of any data comparing armed crimes against the unarmed with armed crimes against the armed. Zimring asks only how reducing the number of guns in criminal hands affects violence; he never asks the obvious corollary, as any *scientist* would, of how increasing the number of guns available to potential crime victims at the point of attack would affect the sociology of violence. His omission is not without intent: if Zimring has looked into anything on this question at all, he would be aware of the book *Point Blank: Guns and Violence in*

America (1991) by Gary Kleck, and "The Value of Civilian Arms Possession as a Deterrent to Crime or Defense Against Crime," by Don B. Kates Jr., in *American Journal of Criminal Law*, Volume 18, #3 (1991). Both clearly show, by interviews with criminals convicted of violent attacks, and with statistics comparing criminal attacks against unarmed persons with criminal attacks against armed persons, that the number of successful criminal attacks and homicides are far lower when criminals are met by armed defense.

Nor is Zimring's premise, that reducing the number of gun deaths is a social goal that justifies curtailing the legal right of Americans to keep and bear arms, borne out by statistics from the National Center for Health Statistics that rate gun homicides as less than one-half percent of the yearly causes of death in this country and only three percent yearly of *accidental* deaths, or by FBI statistics showing that yearly criminal misuse of firearms involves only four-tenths of one percent of handguns, or by comparisons between U.S. cities with restrictive handgun laws and lenient handgun laws showing that the per capita rate of homicide and robbery average *four times as high* in cities with restrictive gun laws, or that each year, handguns are successfully used to repel more crimes than handguns used to commit crimes.

When political propaganda is labelled as science, it both discredits science in the minds of the public, and stands as evidence for the Luddites among us that scientists are mere technicians in the hire of the politically powerful.

J. Neil Schulman, Chair
The Committee to Enforce the Second Amendment

A Reply to Joyce Brothers

From Dr. Joyce Brothers' column of Nov 11, 1991 titled "Man May Equate Guns With Power":

> Men who have a love affair with guns often feel threatened or insecure...Men who are insecure about their sexual identity often equate guns with sexual power. In fact, *gun* is sometimes used verbally as another word for the male sex organ. Typically, this kind of man is usually a defender of sexual stereotypes. He places high value on the use of force and on maintaining the status quo, both sexually and politically.

November 11, 1991

Dear Dr. Brothers:

You are mistaken in stereotyping gun-owners as "a defender of sexual stereotypes [who] places high value on the use of force and of maintaining the status quo, both sexually and politically."

Thirty-five million Americans own handguns. Twelve million of them are women, including the president of the San Francisco NOW chapter, Helen Grieco. While currently gun ownership rises both with education and income, the population segment buying the most new handguns is black women living in crime-infested neighborhoods.

A recent survey of 1500 police officers show 92.2 percent feel that because of limited police manpower, citizens should retain the right to own firearms for self-defense at home or business, and with good reason. More private handguns are used in a year to prevent or end a crime than to commit one, and convicted armed robbers say they fear private gun owners more than they fear the police. As for accidental gun deaths, they represent one-and-a-half percent of the accidental deaths in this country, rating half as high as medical mishaps, and only three percent as high as auto accidents.

Finally, if you must invoke the Freudian image of a gun as a symbol of the male sexual organ, you might at least note that Freud described pencils, nail files, umbrellas, and trees as phallic symbols as well.

J. Neil Schulman, Chair
The Committee to Enforce the Second Amendment

Can You Trust Handgun Control, Inc.?

I got a new mailing last week, under the signature of Jim Brady, asking me to renew my Handgun Control membership.

Here are a couple of excerpts:

> "In his attempt to assassinate the President, John Hinckley — a man with a history of mental problems — had purchased a $29 Saturday Night Special handgun in Texas *where no waiting period or background check is required for gun buyers*. He used that gun to shoot the President, a secret service agent, a policeman and me."

Brady Bill Would Not Have Saved Jim Brady

Interesting that Brady doesn't mention that Hinckley bought his gun months earlier, so that even if the Brady Bill had been in place, Hinckley still would have had plenty of time to buy his gun and attempt the assassination. Moreover, Hinckley's mental problems would not have been discovered by any legally possible background check — instantaneous or combined with a waiting period — because of the constitutional guarantee of privacy which shields psychiatric patients.

Here's another excerpt:

> "ASSAULT WEAPONS BAN — Machine guns, assault pistols and other rapid-fire weapons were designed for one thing: *killing*. They have no place on our streets or anywhere in our country. Yet, the NRA fights any proposed limits on these killing machines as a violation of 'gun owner's rights.'"

Wow. Hard to believe there can be so many misstatements in three sentences. Let's take it one piece at a time.

HCI: "Designed For One Thing: *Killing*."

Since a gun is potentially lethal, it can be used to threaten lethality without having to kill. If the person threatening the lethality has criminal intent, the gun can be used to obtain a victim's compliance for robbery, rape, or other extorted behavior. If the person threatening the lethality has a non-criminal intent, the gun can be used to obtain a criminal's surrender before, during, or after a crime is attempted or committed.

In addition to killing, a gun can be used to produce a cone of shock force sufficient to incapacitate a person who would otherwise be able to deliver a lethal attack. This is technically called "stopping power," and is the reason that police and others who obtain guns for non-criminal purposes prefer larger caliber, higher-power firearms, which can drop an attacker quickly. The intent of shooting an attacker is not to kill; it is to instantly incapacitate. With certain wounds sufficient to stop, however, the wound is sometimes also fatal. Nonetheless, the death of the attacker is a by-product of the force needed to stop a lethal attacker; the attacker's death is not the intent of a defensive shooting.

Stopping Versus Killing

Stopping power and killing power are two different things. The "phasers on stun" of *Star Trek* illustrate effectively the concept of "stopping power at a distance" with a sufficiently advanced technology that there is a low mortality rate to the entity so stopped. Unfortunately, we don't live in that fantasy world, where stopping without high risk of mortality is possible. In the real world, if a person is threatening lethal force and needs to be stopped from attacking, the only effective way to stop them quickly from a safe distance is to shoot them, usually at the center of body mass, with around 150 or more grains of metal. Handguns are optimized to do this: they are engineered to be "machines that stop lethal attackers before they can murder."

That murderers misuse them to murder tells us no more about the engineered purposes of handguns than the fact that kitchen knives, icepicks, rat poison, baseball bats, and water can also be misused as implements of death.

A Gun Defined By Function, Rather Than Purpose

What is the function of a gun? It is to shoot something. An electron gun, for example, shoots electrons onto a plate so to emit photons and produce a visible image. This is called television.

The function of a firearm is to fire a projectile. The purposes to which that object may be put depend (a) on the qualities of design engineered into it and (b) the actual purposes to which it is put by the end-user.

For example, a baseball bat is *designed* to hit baseballs. That is its intended purpose by its designers and manufacturers. That may or may not be the purposes of the persons using it, depending on whether they are baseball players or rioters in South Central Los Angeles.

The Manufacturers' Intended Purpose For The Guns They Make

The primary purpose of firearms designed and manufactured by Colt, or Smith & Wesson, or Glock, is entirely limited to end-users who wish them for defensive combat or threat of such against criminal attackers, or for sporting purposes. Firearms manufacturers are unhappy when their products are used by gangsters for drive-by shootings, or to rob the clerks of a 7-11, and if they knew a way to prevent criminals from getting their hands on them without depriving honest people from getting them also, they would encourage it.

Arms As The Empowerment Of The Citizenry

In addition to uses of defensive firearms in combat, firearms can also be used as part of the force necessary to secure the political sovereignty of the private citizen in a democracy.

The concept of liberty is that of a society organized on the basis of universal individual rights — rights which are equally held by every individual in that society.

What do we mean by a "right"? It is the moral authority to do something without needing prior permission from another to do it.

No matter what the institutions are of a given society, or what names they are called, the fundamental question is whether rights in that society are universally held by all the people, or whether they are reserved to those with the political power to get their own way.

Other Uses Of Arms

Firearms can be used to hunt animals, for the ecologically sound purpose of controlling their population so that they don't breed themselves into greater numbers than can be supported by the food supply available to them, causing them slow death by starvation, or causing them to attack humans or domesticated pets to obtain food.

Firearms can also be used for target shooting, a sport which many enjoy as much as other hand-eye competitions, such as baseball, cricket, archery, golf, bowling, or video games.

So it is clearly demonstrable that guns have other purposes than killing. And, in fact, 99.4% of firearms are used for purposes other than killing.

I am not arguing that guns can't kill. I am arguing against Handgun Control, Inc.'s contention that this is the *only* purpose to which they can be put. Guns, as inanimate objects, have no purposes of their own. To impute a purpose to them implies that they were engineered to perform a certain function by purposeful beings.

This is not an academic or trivial point. The rhetorical phrases " ... were designed for one thing: *killing*" and "killing machines" are misstatements with political purpose: to deny that guns have moral or otherwise lawful functions, particularly by others than police or armies.

So, when I point out that guns can threaten instead of killing, I am both describing a function to which they can be put and a lawful and moral purpose for which a person might wish to obtain them.

A Big Lie Told To Discredit One's Opponent

Handgun Control, Inc.: "Machine guns, assault pistols and other rapid-fire weapons were designed for one thing: *killing*. They have no place on our streets or anywhere in our country. Yet, the NRA fights any proposed limits on these killing machines as a violation of 'gun owner's rights.'"

The truth:

The self-loading, semi-automatic firearms that Handgun Control is trying to ban are not machine guns or machine pistols; they are handguns and rifles with firing capabilities no better than revolvers and hunting rifles in use for a century. Fully automatic machine guns have been illegal to own without a rare and expensive federal license since 1933, and no new licenses have been issued since 1986.

And the National Rifle Association of America and its lobbying arm, the Institute for Legislative Action, does not "fight any proposed limits on these killing machines as a violation of 'gun owner's rights'" because that particular battle was lost half a century ago.

In other words, Handgun Control is attempting to persuade its constituency that there is a danger from machine guns on the streets in order to mislead them into thinking that proposed legislation against "assault weapons" is needed, and that NRA is opposing it.

There is no such danger and the "assault weapons" legislation is not aimed at it: it is aimed at the self-loading single-shot-per-trigger-pull rifles, shotguns, and pistols which Americans have been owning for self- defense, recreation, and animal-population control for over a century. And lying about the existence of machine guns on the streets and charging that NRA is attempting to keep them there is a Big Lie that Hitler or Stalin would have used.

— February 9, 1993

The following article appeared in the *Orange County Register* of Sunday, July 18, 1993.

The Mark of Kane Is on Firearms Reporting

In the classic film *Citizen Kane*, newspaper publisher Charles Foster Kane is arguing with his wife. Kane's wife begins a sentence, "The public will think ..." and Kane ends it, "what I *tell* them to think."

When it comes to print and broadcast news treatment of firearms, Kane's attitude is everywhere.

In the April 24, 1993 issue of *Editor and Publisher*, former *Boston Globe* editor Thomas Winship calls for "a sustained newspaper crusade" against firearms that Kane would have been proud to engineer. "Ask editorially whether small arms producers should be licensed more strictly or even shut down ... Investigate the NRA with more vigor ... Support all forms of gun licensing; in fact, all the causes NRA opposes."

Mr. Winship is late; the news crusade against civilian firearms has been on the march for years. A 1989 form letter sent out by *Time Magazine* to readers charging *Time* with biased reporting in a July 17, 1989 cover story on gun-related deaths, stated, "[T]he time for opinions on the dangers of gun availability is long since gone ... our responsibility now is to confront indifference about the escalating violence and the unwillingness to do something about it."

As in all crusades, factual correctness is sacrificed to political correctness. When the Glock 19 pistol, which replaces some steel parts with polymer, entered the American market, newspapers crusaded against terrorists' plastic guns which could evade airport metal detectors and X-rays. They failed to note that the Glock 19 contains over a pound of metal which sets off alarms, looks identical to any other gun in an airport X-ray ... and that no undetectable plastic guns exist.

News media eagerly jumped on former San Jose Police Chief Joseph McNarama's crusade against teflon-coated "cop killer" bullets which could defeat police body armor. The reports failed to note that such ammunition was created as a *police* round and was not available to the general public ... and no cop had ever been killed by one, anyway. The broadcast news about this issue, however, endangered police by graphically showing criminals that police were *using* body armor, and that they should shoot at unarmored body parts such as the head. Out of this crusade came legislation to ban armor-piercing bullets which would also have banned most ordinary rifle ammunition, since most body armor is no protection against it. When NRA opposed such legislation, the media then charged NRA with opposing legislation which would have protected the police. Again, Citizen Kane would have beamed approvingly.

The language of firearms reporting is itself intended to persuade rather than inform. Newspapers dub inexpensive handguns "Saturday Night Specials," even though three-quarters of criminals don't care about the price of the guns they use in crimes since they steal them or buy stolen guns anyway. Crusades against "assault weapons" deliberately confuse semi-automatic civilian firearms with similar-looking machine guns available only to the military, and only rarely note that law-enforcement studies show that these classes of firearms are hardly ever used in crimes.

Mark Twain said in his autobiography, "There are three kinds of lies — lies, damned lies and statistics." The news media have taken Twain to heart by making sure that the only statistics they use prove that private firearms are destructive and that the public wants them banned. The media quotes medical statistics on the number of criminally-caused firearm-related injuries and deaths but hardly ever quote criminological studies which show that gun owners use firearms 1.4 million times each year to stop or deter a crime, without anyone being wounded 99% of the time. That's two bloodless gun-owner defenses for each time a criminal uses a firearm in an attack.

Network TV programs such as *60 Minutes* focus on the tragedy of children killed in firearms accidents, while failing to note that firearms are involved in only 3% of the accidental deaths of children 14 or younger each year. Other news stories also routinely use statistics which inflate such figures by including suicides and gang-related homicides that include statistical groupings up to age 25.

Neither do the press note that firearms accidents in general are down 40% in the last ten years, and down 80% in the last fifty years.

Editorials trumpet a new Louis Harris survey claiming that 52% of Americans want private handgun ownership banned — extremely unlikely, since half the homes in this country already keep firearms — but fail to note that this same Louis Harris survey finds that 67% of gun owners would refuse to comply with such a ban, even with a $200-per-gun buy-back program, making the law an instant dead-letter.

Showing further press bias, only three reporters show up at a June 10, 1993 Washington D.C. news conference announcing the results of a new study by Luntz-Weber Research which shows that 88.8% of Americans believe a citizen has the right to own a gun, and only 4% see lack of gun control as a root cause of violence. The reason the press conference was ignored? The Luntz-Weber study was commissioned by the press's favorite scapegoat, the NRA.

Headlines routinely focus on criminal use of firearms, and editors bury stories where a civilian successfully uses a firearm defensively. When postal clerk Thomas Terry saved a restaurant from a takeover robbery in Alabama two months after the restaurant massacre in Killeen, Texas, the story was almost universally ignored. When ex-prizefighter Randy Shields did the same at a 4 n 20 Pie Shop in Studio City last September, newspaper readers had to look for the story in the *Los Angeles Times*'s sports section.

Political scandals related to abuse of civilian firearms rights are similarly ignored. Since 1974, the Los Angeles Board of Police Commissioners has refused to issue any private person a license to carry concealed firearms, even though state law requires them to do so, hewing to a policy which states, "[E]xperience has revealed that concealed firearms carried for protection not only provide a false sense of security but further that the licensee is often a victim of his own weapon or the subject of a civil or criminal case stemming from an improper use of the weapon." When this writer revealed in testimony at the November 2, 1992 police commission meeting that Commissioner Michael Yamaki had secretly obtained such a license to carry a firearm from Culver City — demonstrating that when it came to his own family's safety even a police commissioner didn't believe that policy — what few news stories appeared were buried in routine reports on the commissioners meeting, and the press unanimously honored Yamaki's refusal to discuss it.

Finally, there is outright, deliberate manufacture of news film footage to distort the truth about firearms' capabilities. Shortly after Patrick Purdy used a semi-auto AK-47-lookalike to murder schoolchildren in Stockton, NBC News ran footage showing a range officer using such a firearm to explode a melon into smithereens. The footage was faked; a Beretta 9 millimeter pistol with hollow-point expanding ammunition had to be used to make the melon explode: the full-metal-jacketed AK-47 round had merely made a dime-sized and unexciting hole in it.

This past February, Los Angeles TV station KABC pulled a similar stunt. In a report intended to show the awesome rapid fire accuracy of semi-auto handguns being carried by LA gangs, film showing LA County Sheriff's Department Sergeant Hugh E. Mears rapidly firing a 9 millimeter pistol from seventy-five feet away was intercut with footage showing the rounds hitting a target's bullseye. The film was faked: the rapid-fire shots at seventy-five feet had spread widely. The footage showing the repeated hits had been achieved by Sgt. Mears also being requested to provide an example of aimed fire at twelve feet — and this was the footage that KABC intercut.

With a deliberate media campaign of distortion, suppression of vital facts, and outright lying, it's no wonder that the fifty percent of Americans who don't know about guns from personal experience might begin to wonder whether the Second Amendment was a mistake. But more to the point: if reporters and news editors are willing to lie to the public to achieve the public opinion on firearms they desire, then how can representative democracy become anything but covert aristocracy?

"You provide the prose poems," Citizen Kane said to his correspondent. "I'll provide the war."

Indeed he has.

Excerpts from a Letter to David Glass, CEO, Wal*Mart Stores

December 23, 1993

Dear Mr. Glass:

I have heard that as of February 1, 1994, Wal*Mart will no longer be selling handguns in its stores. I can understand, in the light of the recent shooting at a Wal*Mart in Oklahoma, why Wal*Mart might wish to climb onto the political bandwagon favoring reducing the number of firearms for sale to the civilian population. However, I think you need to be made aware of why this decision by Wal*Mart will impact negatively both on public policy and Wal*Mart's stature as a leading retailer.

Over the course of my research for the last few years, I have learned that most of what passes for news and information in the mass media is distorted to give the impression that the availability of privately held firearms makes the United States a more violent and dangerous society than it would be if firearms were more restricted. This is a popular belief among many persons in the media, and they promote it to politicians and other opinion leaders, even though the best available research proves quite the contrary.

[Excerpts from Kleck survey.]

Since the number of times that a firearm is used criminally in the United States in a year is, at most, 800,000 times, the use of firearms by American gun-owners to prevent or stop a crime is three times as high as the number of times criminals use firearms to commit a crime.

As I said, this isn't widely reported on by the news media, whose personnel have their own prejudices on the subject for obvious reasons. A TV news slogan is, "If it bleeds, t leads." Crimes committed with firearms fit that election criterion. Civilian firearms defenses, the great majority of which are accomplished without anyone at all being shot, do not, and are therefore not reported on.

The Kleck survey, and other data collected by other prominent criminologists, clearly document the important role of privately-owned firearms in protecting lives and property from criminals and the criminally insane.

American firearms owners find themselves currently in a political and media battle to protect their right to own and carry firearms for defense against criminals. Anti-firearms politicians are daily introducing new legislation to restrict entire classes of firearms which are useful for defensive purposes; to tax ammunition; to transfer the choice of whether or not one can own or carry a firearm from the civilian population to political authorities. All of this is counter to the American tradition of relying on the people themselves as a force against crime, and adopting the European and Asian tradition of relegating the legal use of arms only to government officials. It is this sort of thinking that disarmed Europe's Jews and made them vulnerable to the Nazis sending them to death camps. American gun owners do not wish to see the same vulnerability to tyranny happen here.

It is vitally important that retailers of the prominence of Wal*Mart not abandon America's 70 million responsible firearms owners at a time when their rights are under attack by headline-seeking demagogues. If Wal*Mart discontinues the sale of handguns in its stores, it is implying that the American people cannot be trusted to buy guns and use them responsibly. This is a political message that is already being capitalized on by the opponents of civilian firearms ownership.

I strongly recommend that it is in Wal*Mart's interest to reexamine its decision, and decide whether it wishes to offend 70 million firearms-owning Americans by implying that they are not responsible individuals who are a bulwark in the defense against crime and tyranny, but are instead irresponsible children who need to be disarmed for their own good by a wise and paternalistic government.

Sincerely,
J. Neil Schulman

Following:
Interview with Gary Kleck
A Massacre We Didn't Hear About
Gunfight at the 4n20 Pie Shop
The Mark of Citizen Kane is On Firearms Reporting

And, here is David Glass's reply:

WAL-MART®

WAL-MART STORES, INC.
CORPORATE OFFICES
BENTONVILLE, AR 72716-8071

David Glass
President and
Chief Executive Officer
501-273-4198

January 4, 1994

Mr. Neil Schulman
P.O. Box 94
Long Beach, CA 90801

Dear Mr. Schulman:

Thank you for your recent letter regarding our decision concerning the sale of handguns in Wal-Mart stores. All of us at Wal-Mart pride ourselves on being customer oriented--not only listening to our customers but doing our very best to respond to their suggestions. While our policy beginning February 1, 1994, is to no longer carry handguns in our stores, we are making manufacturers' catalogs available for customers who wish to purchase handguns from Wal-Mart after meeting all state, federal and local laws.

This decision is designed to satisfy as large a segment of our customer base as possible, and in no way is intended to reflect a company position on the actual handgun controversy.

Again, thank you for your inquiry. We continue to value you as a Wal-Mart customer.

Sincerely,

David Glass
President and CEO

DG\SB\14\66120

When Doctors Call For Gun Seizures, It's Grand Malpractice

Abraham Lincoln once told a visitor to the White House, "It is true that you may fool all of the people some of the time; you can even fool some of the people all of the time; but you can't fool all of the people all the time."

We in the United States are about to test Lincoln's wisdom, and our own. While lying for political purpose is nothing new, it's hard to think of another time in our national history when the most trusted of all professionals, medical doctors, were willing to deliberately lie about the conclusions of supposedly unbiased scientific research for political purpose.

Anybody who's studied the stock market knows it's common knowledge that when women's skirts have gone up, the prices of stocks have gone up also, but no one is foolish enough to claim that by shortening women's skirts we can cause a stock market boom.

That sort of common sense, however, doesn't seem to hold when the subject is the so-called epidemiology of "gun violence," and medical researchers are sniffing for statistics to prove their predetermined conclusion that gun control is desirable public policy.

The point to this research is the contention that doctors can study firearms-related violence as an epidemiologic health issue apart from the motives of the people who pull the trigger ... which is the proper study of that branch of sociology known as criminology. By this premise alone, epidemiologists discard the humanistic premise of personal volition in favor of a mechanistic view of human behavior which denies a fundamental difference between the contagion of microbic cultures and human cultures: microbes don't act on their value-judgments and people do.

The latest outbreak of statisticitis emerges from the study led by Arthur L. Kellermann, M.D., published in the October 7, 1993 issue of the *New England Journal of Medicine*, and financed by the Center for Disease Control. A previous Kellermann-led study published in the June 12, 1986 *NEJM*, also financed by the CDC, gave us the factoid that you are 43 times likelier to die from a handgun kept in the home from homicide, suicide, or accident than you are to kill a burglar with it.[1] By the time this factoid turned into the mega-soundbyte used by gun-control advocates in the media and Congress, you were supposedly 43 times as likely to die from a handgun kept in the home than to protect yourself from a burglar with it.[2]

Kellermann, himself, cautioned against that conclusion saying,

> Mortality studies such as ours do not include cases in which burglars or intruders are wounded or frightened away by the use or display of a firearm. Cases in which would-be intruders may have purposely avoided a house known to be armed are also not identified. We did not report the total number of nonlethal firearm injuries involving guns kept in the home. A complete determination of firearm risks versus benefits would require that these figures be known.

Kellermann's latest "population-based case-control study" of homicides throws such caution to the wind. He attempts to quantify "firearm risks versus benefits" by comparing households where a homicide occurred with households where no homicide occurred in three counties, chosen for their convenient location to the researchers. After correcting for several other risk factors such as alcohol or illicit-drug-use, previous domestic violence, and persons with criminal records in the 316 matched households ultimately compared, Kellermann determined that households where "homicide at the hands of a family member or intimate acquaintance" occurred were almost three times likelier to have kept a loaded handgun in the home than control households where such a homicide did not occur. From this determination, Kellermann concludes,

> Although firearms are often kept in the home for personal protection, this study shows that the practice is counterproductive. Our data indicate that keeping a gun in the home is independently associated with an increase in the risk of homicide in the home.

An immediate technical problem with Kellermann's methods is raised by David N. Cowen, Ph.D., in a discussion with National Rifle Association staffers. Cowen charges that Kellermann's research grouped together socially dysfunctional people — for example, the chronically unemployable — with normal people, and thus *any* other risk factors would be inseparable.

Another problem is that by relying on a case study of households with homicide victims, Kellermann is looking at almost twice as many black households as white, and only a handful of Asian households — far too few to be statistically useful. African-Americans are homicide victims way out of proportion to other racial or ethnic groupings, and any case study of homicides has to live with this demographic distortion. The problem is that studying homicide within the African-American culture may not produce conclusions which are generalizable to other racial or ethnic groups. According to Don Kates, a criminologist with the Pacific Research Institute, "African-Americans have greater death rates than other population groups for drowning, other accidents, and diseases." Other sociological studies note crude differences between African-Americans and Asian-Americans in divorce rates, school drop-out rates, father-absent households, and so forth.

A more basic problem with Kellermann's conclusion is that it attempts to draw a reverse implication from a set of facts. Certainly it will be true that people who own parachutes will die more frequently in falls from airplanes than people who don't — but does that mean that parachute-ownership constitutes an increased risk factor for death by falling from an airplane? Wouldn't logic tell us that the risk of dying as a result of falling from an airplane would be far greater by those people who fall from airplanes who d*on't* have a parachute handy?

Kellermann tells us, "We found no evidence of a protective benefit from gun ownership in any subgroup, including one restricted to cases of homicide that followed forced entry into the home and another restricted to cases in which resistance was attempted."

This is where Kellermann's study is completely disingenuous, and indicates — as does his financing and publication by gun-control zealots James Mercy at the Center for Disease Control and Jerome P. Kassirer, editor of the *New England Journal of Medicine* — that the intent of these studies is to produce pro-gun-control soundbytes for Sarah Brady rather than scientific knowledge.

Kellermann is studying only those persons living in a household with a loaded handgun where a handgun fa*iled* to save the victim's life. We're being shown only the *murder victims*, not gun-owners whose firearms saved their lives. Kellermann's study didn't document whether a firearm used in a particular homicide was the same one kept in the home, or whether it might have been carried in by the murderer. Kellermann doesn't even tell us whether the murder weapon belonged to the victim or the murderer. And Kellermann still doesn't ask the questions he, himself, said would be necessary for "a complete determination of firearms risks versus benefits": "cases in which burglars or intruders are wounded or frightened away by the use or display of a firearm ... Cases in which would-be intruders may have purposely avoided a house known to be armed [and] the total number of nonlethal firearm injuries involving guns kept in the home."

Dr. Kellermann can't study such questions because these are the proper focus not of medical doctors, but of criminologists. And when we shift from the medical paradigm of "gun violence" as a health issue, to the criminological paradigm of "offenders and victims," we get a completely different vision.

Immediately we discover that the cases in which Kellermann perceives an increased risk factor — "homicide at the hands of a family member or intimate acquaintance" — are, according to both the FBI's *Crime in the United States*, 1992, and *Murder Analysis*, 1992 by the Detective Division of the Chicago Police — only around 10% of the yearly homicides in this country. In the Chicago study, 36.8% of the homicides occurred in or around the home — including public housing. In the three counties in which his study was conducted, Kellermann tells us that 23.9% took place in the home of the victim. Kellermann also tells us, "Guns were not significantly linked to an increased risk of homicide by acquaintances, unidentified intruders, or strangers."

What this adds up to is that while home is where you are far less likely to be murdered by a stranger — not surprising since homes usually have locks to keep such people out — the great majority of murders that do take place at home are at the hands of those who have a key. The caution here might well be that if you live with someone whom you think might possibly murder you, you might want to move out if they also keep a loaded handgun. Or, if the loaded handgun is yours, you might want to keep it somewhere where you can get to it faster than he or she can.

The thrust of Kellermann's contention, that the mere availability of a loaded handgun is an increased risk factor to the general population, is also countered by comparing the 69% increase in the number of handguns in private hands from 1974 to 1988 to the 27% *decrease* in handgun murders during that same period.[3] Therefore even though the increase in handguns and handgun murders were found the previous 15-year time period, no conclusion regarding cause and effect can be drawn.

The answer which Kellermann says we need to discover — the overall usefulness of firearms in self-defense — is to be found in the definitive analysis of a dozen studies in the book *Point Blank: Guns and Violence in America* (Aldine de Gruyter, 1991), by Gary Kleck, Ph.D., professor of criminology at Florida State University. Unlike Kellermann, Professor Kleck has carefully avoided taking funding from advocates in the gun-control debate, and Kleck's impeccable liberal Democratic credentials — membership in Common Cause and Amnesty International, for example — preclude a presumption of conservative or pro-NRA bias. Kleck's analysis of these studies had produced an estimate of around 650,000 handgun defenses per year, and over a million gun defenses if one included all firearms.

Kleck's latest research, his Spring, 1993 National Self- Defense Survey of 4978 households, reveals that previous studies had underestimated the number of times previous survey respondents had used their firearms in defense. The new survey projected 2.4 million gun defenses in 1992, 1.9 million of them with handguns, and about 72% of these gun defenses occurred in or near the home. This indicates a successful gun defense with no dead body for Dr. Kellermann to find about 1,728,000 times a year. Even if we were to accept Dr. Kellermann's reverse implication that a home-dweller who lives with a loaded handgun suffers a three-fold increased risk of homicide from a family member or intimate acquaintance, the handgun's usefulness in warding off potentially lethal confrontations against burglars is enormous.

Murder Analysis, 1992 by the Detective Division of the Chicago Police tells us that 72.39% of the murderers they studied in 1992 had a prior criminal history and, interestingly, 65.53% of the murder victims did as well.

Further, a recent National Institute of Justice analysis finds, "It is clear that only a very small fraction of privately owned firearms are ever involved in crime or [unlawful] violence, the vast bulk of them being owned and used more or less exclusively for sport and recreational purposes, or for self- protection."[4]

Criminologist Don Kates concurs in his book *Guns, Murder, and the Constitution:* "Concurrently, it has been estimated that 98.32% of owners do not use a gun in an unlawful homicide (over a 50-year, adult life span)."

Here is the essential truth about the risk of homicide which all the talk about violence as a health problem, rather than a criminal problem, is attempting to ignore: overwhelmingly, violence isn't a matter of ordinary people killing because a firearm is handy, but of criminals committing violence because violence is a way of life for them. The National Rifle Association has been saying this for years, but anti-gun crusaders just don't want to listen.

When the federal Center for Disease Control starts defining bullets as "pathogens" and declares that honest gun owners are the Typhoid Marys of a "gun-violence epidemic," the medical profession has lent its scientific credibility to a radical political agenda which threatens to increase the overall violence in our society by shifting the balance of power toward the well-armed psychopath, and destabilize our system of government by restricting the people's arms, which are a fundamental check on ambitious tyrants.

That this propaganda is being engineered by a committed gun-control advocate at the Federal Center for Disease Control, James Mercy, who is diverting taxpayers' money away from the study of *real* diseases such as AIDS, makes this politicized science even more shocking.

Those who decide that a handgun is a useful tool for protection against the criminals among us can rest assured that the risks of being victimized with that firearm by their husbands, wives, and other loved ones are still massively outweighed by their firearm's ability to keep evil strangers at bay.[5]

Advocates of the right to keep and bear arms need to be especially aware that *gun owners* are the intended targets of the Center for Disease Control's disinformation campaign against privately held firearms. James Mercy and his tax-financed minions are well aware that with half the households in the United States keeping firearms, the American people can't be disarmed without their co-operation. The only way they can gain that cooperation is by tricking gun owners into thinking that their firearms, and their neighbors' firearms, are more of a danger than they are an effective defensive tool.

In this particular gunfight, the best ammunition is the truth.

Footnotes:

1. Thirty-seven of those 43 deaths were suicide; eliminating suicide immediately drops the claimed figure to "six times likelier."
2. On the syndicated TV *Mo Show*, in January, 1994, a spokeswoman for the Center to Prevent Handgun Violence even asserted that a gun kept in the home was "43 times as likely to kill a child than to offer protection against a burglar."
3. *Point Blank: Guns and Violence in America* (Aldine de Gruyter, 1991), by Gary Kleck, Ph.D.
4. J. Wright & P. Rossi, NIJ Felon Survey 4.
5. Oddly enough, even Dr. Kellermann agrees. In the March/April 1994 issue of *Health* magazine, Kellermann is quoted as saying, "If you've got to resist, your chances of being hurt are less the more lethal your weapon. If that were my wife, would I want her to have a thirty-eight special in her hand? Yeah."

What It Takes to Get Me to Put on a Yarmulke

If you haven't already seen *Schindler's List*, see it. Then ask yourself whether it was better for a thousand Jews to be saved by a righteous gentile, or whether it would have been better for millions of Jews not to *need* saving because they had fought like the ancient Israelites against the Nazis.

I do not understand how any Jew can walk out of the theater, after seeing a graphic and historically accurate portrayal of Jews being exterminated like rodents, and not wish every Jew to own a fully-automatic assault rifle and plenty of ammunition.

To die as a warrior fighting for one's people has, at least, nobility to recommend it.

The modern Israelis understand this. They manufacture and possess excellent assault rifles.

For the most part, American Jews don't understand this. I hope they get wise before it's too late and history repeats itself.

It is my belief that if the Jews of Europe had believed in and prepared for armed resistance against the Nazis, then the night known as *Kristallnacht* would have been the beginning of the end for the Nazi expansion over Europe. The Jews of the Warsaw Ghetto held out against the Nazis for weeks longer than all of Poland did. If even thousands more Jews had made the taking of their lives expensive, it might have cost Hitler's war machine enough that Germany might have suffered an early defeat.

When I have expressed that opinion before, I have been charged with engaging in idle speculation.

I have gotten awards for engaging in idle speculation. I'm very good at it.

A science-fiction writer is just a prophet with a pocket calculator. Ignore us at your peril.

—JNS

[Note: This speech is being reprinted in the book *Guns in America*, Jan Dizard, editor, being published this year by Amherst College.

—JNS]

Talk at Temple Beth Shir Shalom
Friday, April 30, 1993

Just to introduce myself. I'm a novelist, screenwriter, and journalist. I'm also a graduate of the PC-832 reserve police training program at Rio Hondo Police Academy. I was asked to speak here tonight because I've written about firearms for the *Los Angeles Times* opinion page. I should also mention that one of my articles convinced Dennis Prager[1] to change his views about guns. And just for the record, I'm a member of the National Rifle Association, Handgun Control, Inc., and the American Civil Liberties Union. So I have all bases covered.

I'd like to start by asking you a question. How many of you can correctly quote me the Sixth Commandment?

It's not "You shall not kill" but "You shall not mu*rder*."

There's a big difference between killing and murdering. Killing means purposely ending a life. Murdering means purposely ending an *innocent* life. If you kill someone who's trying to murder you or some other innocent person, that's not murder. As a matter of fact, it's a moral *requirement* to defend the innocent by killing if that's the only way you can do it.

I'm going to spend about two minutes correcting the lies you hear about guns on TV and in the newspapers.

You're told the lie that gun control will stop criminals from getting guns. The truth is that according to a Bureau of Alcohol, Tobacco, and Firearms study titled "Protecting America, Yes," criminals get 37% of their guns on the black market and another 34% from burglaries and robberies. That means that 71% — almost three out of every four guns a criminal uses — won't be stopped by gun control. If you pass gun restrictions, criminals will still gets their guns for murder, robbery, burglary, and rape — but you won't be able to get a gun to stop them.

You're told that a gun kept in the home for protection is more likely to kill someone you know than a burglar. That's a distortion of the truth, which is that a gun kept in the home is *far* more likely to capture or chase away a burglar without having to kill anyone at all.

You're told the lie that gun accidents are killing children at unprecedented rates. The truth is that gun accidents account for less than 300 deaths of children under age 14 each year — less than 3% of children's accidental deaths. Car accidents kill around 3700 children each year, 1200 drown, and 1000 die in fires. In general, firearms accidents are down about 40% from ten years ago and down 80% from fifty years ago. You can thank NRA's gun safety training programs for that. If NRA's gun safety courses were taught in all schools, we could probably get it down to a quarter of that.

Yes, there are teenagers — usually gang members — murdering other teenagers with guns. But those young murderers are already forbidden by law to have guns; laws don't stop them for an instant. Matter of fact, the Bloods and the Crips are required to commit a murder to advance rank in their gangs. That's why there are so many drive-by shootings.

You hear that assault rifles are major crime guns. The California Department of Justice has admitted that was a politically motivated lie — the truth is that fewer than 2% of the guns used in crime fall into the prohibited categories.

I could go on refuting these lies for hours. I'm not going to bother. It's beside the real point.

Let me tell you some things you don't hear about on TV or in the newspapers. According to figures compiled from around eight different studies, private citizens in this country use a firearm about a million times each year to stop or prevent a crime.

My father is a concert violinist who was a member of the Boston Symphony Orchestra and the Metropolitan Opera Orchestra in New York. He carried a gun to protect himself in Boston and New York for fifteen years — and on around five separate occasions, carrying that gun saved him from gangs of robbers.

My father couldn't count on the police to save him, and neither can you. Under California law, which is like the laws of the rest of the country, no one in the government is legally responsible for protecting you — *no one.*

California Government Code, Section 845, states, "Neither a public entity nor a public employee is liable for failure to establish a police department or otherwise provide police protection service or, if police protection service is provided, for failure to provide sufficient police protection service."

But the California Constitution says the following in Article I, Section 1: "All people are by nature free and independent, and have certain inalienable rights, among which are those of enjoying and *defending* life and liberty; acquiring, possessing, and *protecting* property; and pursuing and obtaining *safety*, happiness, and privacy."

California law merely reflects reality: when you're attacked, the only person you can count on to protect you is *you.*

During the Los Angeles riots, police were completely unable to stop arson, shootings, and looting for three days, until another fifteen thousand army and National Guard troops showed up. A few months later, Hurricane Andrew left parts of Florida without electricity or phone for almost three months — and no one could call the police for help. A major earthquake here could do the same.

I know that some of you are thinking that the more guns you have, the more violence you have. That's another one of those lies. Switzerland has one of the lowest murder rates of anywhere on Earth. Yet the Swiss keep machine guns and anti-tank weapons in their homes, and Swiss citizens regularly carry their machine guns on bicycles and trains to the ranges where they practice. Why is it that the Swiss have hardly any murderers? The answer is simple. The Swiss take their responsibility to defend themselves very seriously. Every able-bodied male in the country is in the Swiss army or reserve and the Swiss have been eliminating their violent criminals regularly until their criminals are an endangered species.

It comes down to competition. If you're running a business today, you know that you'll go under if you don't have competitive technology. You wouldn't run an office today with typewriters when other businesses are using computers. The same is true regarding your life and property, which the criminals are in competition for. The criminals are arming themselves with 9 millimeter semi-auto pistols which can easily be smuggled in across the Mexican border. If you are going to survive, you'd better not be armed with anything less effective.

As Dennis Prager says, there are only two races of people: the decent and the indecent.[2] Laws should stop indecent people who use guns to commit violent crimes. That means the decent people need to be better armed than the criminals, or the criminals will win.

And that's the real issue. As Jews, we know that from the destruction of the Second Temple of Solomon two millennia ago, until 1948 when the State of Israel was created, Jews have been persecuted. Jews stopped being victimized when they took up arms and started fighting back. The first major battle was fifty years ago this month, when the Jewish militia of the Warsaw Ghetto fought a battle with the Nazi SS. Almost all the Jews in the Warsaw ghetto died in that battle, but the lesson lived on, and Jews learned they needed to fight for survival.

Jews in America have been blessed. We have been less oppressed in this country than anywhere else in modern history. But that's made a lot of us complacent and lazy.

The price of liberty is eternal vigilance. You can't count on things always being good. Jews in Germany thought they were safe because Germany was a modern, enlightened, industrialized country where they had been safe for hundreds of years. In a short twenty years that turned around. Jews in Germany submitted to Nazi gun control laws and allowed themselves to be disarmed. And because they'd lost the will to fight, a third of the Jews on this planet were murdered.

I am here to tell you that peaceful submission to evil is not only *not* a higher morality, it is not morality at all. It is a moral atrocity. Those among us who tell us to be unarmed are setting us up to be victims of the next Adolf Hitler to come to power — and if you ask me, they want us disarmed because they intend for *them-*

selves to be the ones in absolute power over our lives and property.

Maybe one of you is going to quote Gandhi to me about non-violent resistance. Gandhi chose that strategy in his fight to chase the British out of India because the British had already disarmed the Indians, and non-violent resistance was the only strategy Gandhi had left. Here's what Gandhi had to say about it: "Among the many misdeeds of the British rule in India, history will look upon the Act depriving a whole nation of Arms, as the blackest."

Adolf Hitler agreed with Gandhi's assessment — but from the other side. "The most foolish mistake we could possibly make," Hitler said, "would be to allow the subject races to possess arms. History shows that all conquerors who have allowed their subject races to carry arms have prepared their own downfall."

If the Jews of Germany had listened to Hitler, they might have saved Earth a Second World War.

Jews in Israel understand this. They are armed to the teeth — and have as low a murder rate as Switzerland. A few weeks ago, the Israeli Chief of Police called for all Israeli citizens to carry their guns with them at all times. Can you imagine what would have happened here if Chief Gates had done that a year ago during the LA riots?

But Israel is dependent upon the continued freedom of the United States for its own survival. If Jews in America do not actively support the right of the American people to keep and bear arms for their individual and common defense, then the American civilization is open to political dictatorship, and the next Holocaust of the Jews is just a short step behind.

We are already well down the road to Nazi Germany. Did you know that we have had the Nazi gun-control laws in America since 1968? There is strong evidence that the 1938 Nazi Weapons law was the basis for the 1968 Gun Control Act. The two laws are structurally very similar. The 1938 Nazi Weapon's Law disarmed Germany's Jewish citizens and made it possible for the democratically-elected German government to murder millions of innocent people. Don't tell me it can't happen here.

Never again. Take up arms. Learn to use them properly and

teach your children to use them properly. You can't have a peaceful or civilized society if good people won't fight to preserve it and practice with the weapons needed to do it.

Defend the constitutional provisions that legally protect those who keep and bear arms to preserve peace and civilization. Demand the impeachment of all government officials — police, judges, and legislators — who lie about the right to bear arms and try to disarm us. It's not the government's job to defend society from gangsters and potential dictators: it's *yours*. It's the moral responsibility of every one of us who is able to do so.

Thank you.

Footnotes

1. See my parenthetical comments which lead off the first section of this book containing my *LA Times* Op-Eds. Prager, whom I've mentioned several times, is a popular Los Angeles radio talk-show host on top-rated KABC AM. He is also a former teacher, newspaper columnist, and an author of several books on Judaism. He is an internationally known lecturer, and is considered one of the most prominent spokespersons for modern Judaism, and writes a newsletter titled *Ultimate Issues* devoted to the promotion of ethical monotheism.

2. On his radio program, Dennis attributes this paradigm to Viktor Frankl's book *Man's Search for Meaning*. I read that book years ago but didn't remember the quote until I heard it again from Dennis on a program before I gave this talk, and didn't remember the quote was from Frankl until Dennis attributed it on a subsequent program.

More Stopping Power

Stopping Power didn't have the power to stop me from writing more about firearms issues. About a year and a half after the original publication of this book, I authored another collection of my writings titled *Self Control Not Gun Control.* The first section of that book, titled "The Politics of Gun Control," added twenty-one new articles on the gun issue. But even that didn't stop me.

So here are a few of my most-recent musings on why, when it comes down to it, a gun is a lot more useful to keep around than a liberal if you need to hang on to your liberty.

— JNS, 1999

A Rude Awakening

They thought that sort of thing happened only in America, didn't they? Sure, in Killeen, Texas, you could have a madman with a gun start randomly shooting dozens of people, then turn the gun on himself. In Stockton, California, you could have a whacko with an "assault" rifle go into a school and start massacring innocent children.

But not in Dunblane, Scotland, for God's sake! They had gun control laws so strict that Sarah Brady of the American Handgun Control, Inc., could only dream about them, and use the low British gun-homicide rate in their fund-raising letters.

Maybe the Americans hadn't outgrown the Wild West, but this was supposed to be *civilization*.

It has taken the deaths of sixteen children at the hands of a madman, who then used the gun to kill himself also, to alert the townspeople of Dunblane, Scotland that irrational violence doesn't respect national borders, or the Marquess of Queenberry rules, or sweet innocence itself.

Had enough yet?

How many more innocent people must die this way before those who count on the goodness in people to keep them safe wake up to some fundamental truths about the human species?

We are not good by nature. Character resides in the individual capacity for choosing between good and evil, right and wrong, self-control or its opposites, tyranny and dissipation. There are wild people among us who will not exercise self-restraint, and we must live with the expectation that at a time and place of *their* choosing, not of ours, they will explode upon us.

So if you are through playing "if only" and "if I had my way" with public policy, are you ready to take a hard look at our options of how to deal effectively with random, savage violence against the most vulnerable among us?

Sarah Brady might as well pack up shop now. Stricter gun-control laws than she has been fighting for were in place in Scotland, and they were unable to keep a resolute madman from getting a gun.

We can always try to solve the problem of lawlessness by becoming a police state. We can surround ourselves with police and throw more people into prison, throwing away the key after them. In Japan, there is no constitutional Bill of Rights which prevents the police from searching your home at random, holding you as long as they like before trial, and torturing a confession out of you. The criminal conviction rate in Japan approaches 100%, most of them by "confessions." And it works, if preventing crime is your only goal. The Japanese homicide rate is a fraction of ours, as Sarah Brady will eagerly tell you.

But the Japanese suicide rate is twice the American rate — high enough that the combined homicide-suicide rate in both countries is the same — and included in these Japanese suicides are incidents where a father kills his whole family then kills himself — not too different from the gunman's actions in Dunblane. Laws and police can't frighten a man who doesn't expect to be alive by the time the police show up, anyway.

Or, we can get used to the idea that there are terrorists living among us, political or otherwise, and the Framers of the Constitution of the United States understood that when they wrote the Second Amendment. It says, "A well-regulated Militia being necessary to the security of a free State, the right of the people to keep and bear Arms shall not be infringed."

The militia the authors of the Second Amendment were talking about wasn't a National Guard or a police department. It was every decent adult who knew how to use a gun. There are about 70 million Americans today who own guns. A substantial number of them are qualified with handguns, and if well-intentioned idealists hadn't written laws subverting the intent of the realists who wrote our constitution, these gun-owners could be carrying their guns with them wherever they go. And, yes. Some of these gunowners are even schoolteachers, who could conceal a gun on them while they are in the classroom.

A few weeks ago in Israel, a terrorist drove his car into a crowd of civilians, intent on mass murder. The Israelis are far more pragmatic than their Jewish cousins here, many of whom support civilian disarmament as public policy. When the terrorist tried to kill innocent civilians, the innocent civilians took out their guns and defended themselves. Result: living innocent people and a dead terrorist. It's happened in Israel before, in Jerusalem in April, 1984 and in Ashod in February, 1994. The results in all these cases show that our Founding Fathers knew what they were doing: when innocent people are armed so that they can protect themselves, those with the intent to commit random acts of violence don't live long enough to get away with it.

A popular saying among gun-owners is a quote from the late science-fiction author, Robert A. Heinlein: "An armed society is a polite society." That is true, but I think Heinlein was thinking of Switzerland, which has had five centuries of being an armed society to eliminate the "impolite."

In the meantime, it is becoming increasingly obvious that an armed society is the only one which stands a chance of dealing with the terrorism that a gun in the wrong hands can create.

The following letter was sent October 19, 1996 to *The Economist* magazine in response to an editorial in the October 19, 1996 issue titled "A Tale of Two Lobbies." An edited version of this reply was the lead letter in the November 9th-15th issue.

A Letter to *The Economist*

Economist Misrepresents American and British Gun Violence

"A Tale of Two Lobbies" demonstrates the anti-gun bias the writer has of seeing the firearms issue from the usual British and European perspective-the perspective which is also represented in the mainstream American media.

The availability of legal firearms is not a factor in the presence or absence of violence, in either Britain or America. In the nineteenth century, both Britain and America enjoyed universal gun availability and the violent crime rate in both countries was a fraction of what it is today in either country. As recently as 1963—when any American could anonymously purchase any firearm (except for machine guns or sawed-off shotguns) through the mail, the homicide and violent crime rate in the United States was half what it is today.

Further, a recent study at the University of Chicago by criminologist John Lott, Jr., and economist David Mustard has found that homicide, assault, rape, and robbery are lower in areas of the United States where the public is allowed easy access to carrying concealed firearms in public. The areas of the United States where violent crime is the highest are also the areas with the strictest gun controls. Washington D.C. has a complete ban of legally-owned handguns. It also consistently ranks among the U.S. cities where the homicide rate is the highest.

The homicide rate in the United States varies not according to availability of guns, but according to ethnic and cultural differences. Japanese-Americans enjoy a low homicide rate comparible to the Japanese in Japan; African-Americans and Hispanic-Americans living in the inner cities suffer high rates of homicide, yet legal gun ownership among African-Americans and Hispanic-Americans ranks well below that of Anglo-Americans, who have lower rates of homicide and violence. A study comparing homicide rates along the American-Canadian border states and provinces, among ethnically and culturally similar populations, finds that homicide rates are similar to both each other and to Great Britain, also.

In America, where we have well-armed criminal gangs who use their arms to enforce drug-selling territories, restrictions on legal firearms serve only as unilateral disarmament of the potential victims of violence, and increases violent crime by shifting the balance of power to the illegally-armed criminal.

If Great Britain ever develops a violent criminal class equivalent to that which already exists in America, Brits may need to rethink the gun issue-much as the post-Soviet Russians are doing, now that their criminal classes have been unleashed to terrorize the public.

J. Neil Schulman

Cease Fire, Ed Asner!

Been watching TV recently? Or picked up a magazine? You've probably seen a TV spot with Ed Asner ("Lou Grant") speaking in somber tones, or a full-page ad in *Time* or *The National Enquirer*, warning you about gun violence. This campaign is being run by a group calling itself Cease Fire, and they're trying to convince you that keeping a gun at home is more likely to cause harm to you or to someone in your family than it's likely to protect you from a criminal who invades your home.

Ed Asner tells you about a young boy who "accidentally" shoots his brother with a handgun he's been playing with. Of course Asner doesn't mention that, according to the National Safety Council, firearms accidents account for only 3 percent of accidental deaths for children aged 14 or under — far fewer deaths than those due to auto accidents, drownings, or fires.

Cease Fire's ads claim that a gun kept in the home increases the chance of a homicide in that home by three times. Of course they never mention that, according to the 1993 National Self Defense Survey conducted by criminologists at Florida State University, 1.7 million times each year a gun kept in the home protects an American family from a criminal intruder. That's 216 times more often than a gun kept in the home takes the life of an innocent resident of that home.

That's the whole trick which advocates of banning guns use to convince the public that guns are too dangerous to keep around. They just choose what they think will scare you the most. They never tell you what Paul Harvey calls "the rest of the story."

Statistics are funny things. They tell you only what you ask them about. Suppose you wanted to convince people that guns are too dangerous to keep in their houses. You'd look at death statistics until you noticed that while lots of Americans who commit suicide at home do it with a gun, very few criminals who break into houses are killed with guns. So you'd take these suicides and just for good luck throw in the occasional accidental gun death and family murder which uses a gun, and — lo and behold! — you have a "study" by Dr. Arthur Kellermann published in the June 12, 1986 *New England Journal of Medicine* which says that a gun kept in the home for protection is 43 times as likely to kill a family member than to kill a burglar. By the time the news media are done with their spin-doctoring, pundits tell us that a gun kept in the home is 43 times as likely to murder a family member than to protect you from a burglar.

I'm not exaggerating. A few weeks ago I participated in a TV news discussion of gun control with Molly Selvin, who sits on the editorial board of the *Los Angeles Times*, and Sandy Cooney of Handgun Control, Inc. Molly Selvin misquoted that Kellermann article in precisely that way.

Of course Molly Selvin probably never read Kellermann's article closely enough to discover that 37 of those 43 non-burglars are those Americans who used a gun to kill themselves. She undoubtedly is also unaware that five separate studies of suicide show that people who are determined to kill themselves just choose another way to die if their first choice isn't available. In a study by Rich et al reported in the March 1990 issue of *The American Journal of Psychiatry,* Canadians who wanted to commit suicide but found guns harder to come by due to recent gun control instead jumped off bridges. The unavailability of guns was statistically irrelevant. Further, in Japan it's almost impossible for anyone to get hold of a gun, yet twice as many Japanese kill themselves than Americans.

Cease Fire's campaign doesn't tell you that in the overwhelming majority of cases where a gun is used in defense against a criminal, the gun is never even fired, much less is used to shoot or kill the criminal. So if you're only counting up the criminals killed by guns for your comparison, as did Kellermann, you're leaving out all the criminals who didn't complete their intended crime — burglary, rape, or even a serial murder — because the criminal's intended victim had a gun and was prepared to use it in defense.

The funny thing about the people who tell you these statistics is that even when you prove to them that their statistics are deceitful, they still refuse to believe it. So, when two criminologists at Florida State University released the results that the National Self Defense Survey had determined 2.45 million private gun defenses in America during the preceding year (the 1.7 million is just those that occurred in or around the gun-defender's own home), gun-ban advocates did everything they could to attack the results.

In that same TV news show with Molly Selvin and me, Handgun Control, Inc.'s, Sandy Cooney called the National Self Defense Survey "obscene" and threw ad hominem slurs at its lead researcher, professor of criminology, Dr. Gary Kleck. Mind you, since Kleck is an impartial social scientist with no links to gun advocates or manufacturers — in fact he's a liberal Democrat — it appears that Kleck's only sin is doing research which produces results that challenges the gun-control agenda of Handgun Control, Inc., and Cease Fire.

On that program opposite me, when I argued defensive-gun-use statistics from the National Self Defense Survey, Cooney charged that Kleck, the lead criminologist who designed the study, had kept changing his figures. That is simply wrong. Kleck had previously only analyzed the results of a dozen surveys conducted by others including Democratic Party pollsters and *Time* magazine. This had already produced estimates of a million gun defenses per year. Kleck included his analysis in his book *Point Blank: Guns and Violence in America* (Aldine de Gruyter, 1991). When Kleck analyzed the data from the National Self Defense Survey, he found that the number of yearly gun-defenses was simply higher than previously reported due to the incompleteness of each of the previous surveys, none of which attempted to quantify gun defenses comprehensively.

Cooney also charged that the results of the National Self Defense Survey had never been peer-reviewed. But it was my fault that he believed that. In 1993 when the survey was first conducted, I convinced Gary Kleck to give me preliminary results of the survey in a newspaper interview I did with him, because his previous analysis was being widely quoted in other news articles. Dr. Kleck generously allowed me to include some of these figures in my interview with him in the September 19, 1993 *Orange County Register* [*] and these preliminary results, drawn from my interview, were widely quoted, including in testimony before the House Subcommittee on Crime in March, 1995. Because of the slowness of the academic publishing and peer-review process, the formal report on the survey titled "Armed Resistance to Crime: The Prevalence and Nature of Self-Defense with a Gun" by Gary Kleck and Marc Gertz, was only just published in Northwestern University Law School's *Journal of Criminal Law and Criminology,* Volume 86, Number 1, Summer, 1995 issue...and it wasn't actually printed until December, 1995. If that's not tediously slow enough for you, when I spoke to Dr. Kleck on January 3, 1996 he still hadn't received his personal copy in the mail.

But the foremost criminologist in the country, Dr. Marvin E. Wolfgang, director of the University of Pennsylvania's Sellin Center for Studies in Criminology and Criminal Law, wrote in that issue of the *Journal of Criminal Law and Criminology*:

"I am as strong a gun-control advocate as can be found among the criminologists in this country. If I were Mustapha Mond of *Brave New World*, I would eliminate all guns from the civilian population and maybe even from the police ... What troubles me is the article by Gary Kleck and Marc Gertz. The reason I am troubled is that they have provided an almost clearcut case of methodologically sound research in support of something I have theoretically opposed for years, namely, the use of a gun in defense against a criminal perpetrator. ...I have to admit my admiration for the care and caution expressed in this article and this research. Can it be true that about two million instances occur each year in which a gun was used as a defensive measure against crime? It is hard to believe. Yet, it is hard to challenge the data collected. We do not have contrary evidence. The National Crime Victim Survey does not directly contravene this latest survey, nor do the Mauser and Hart Studies. ... the methodological soundness of the current Kleck and Gertz study is clear. I cannot further debate it. ... The Kleck and Gertz study impresses me for the caution the authors exercise and the elaborate nuances they examine methodologically. I do not like their conclusions that having a gun can be useful, but I cannot fault their methodology. They have tried earnestly to meet all objections in advance and have done exceedingly well."

That, Mr. Cooney, is called "peer review."

Because I was one of the first laymen to discuss the results of the National Self Defense Survey with Dr. Kleck, and consequently have been thinking about these results for longer than other writers, every once in a while I've been calling Dr. Kleck and asking for other comparisons between the criminal uses of guns and their defensive uses. Usually, Dr. Kleck would either tell me the figures were in his book *Point Blank*, or he told me that nobody had studied the particular question I was asking and, to the best of his knowledge, nobody knew the answer.

Today I did somewhat better. I said to Dr. Kleck, "We're always being told by gun-ban advocates that the majority of homicides in this country are committed with guns. Has anybody looked at the percentage of justifiable homicides committed with guns ... that is, a number which tells us how often guns are legitimately used by a private individual to kill a criminal in self-defense as opposed to other types of weapons?"

It turned out that these figures were available. At my request, Dr. Kleck took them out of the Federal Bureau of Investigation's "Supplementary Homicide Reports public use tapes," distributed by the Inter-University Consortium for Political and Social Research, National Archive of Criminal Justice Data, P.O. Box 1248, Ann Arbor, MI 48106-1248.

According to Dr. Kleck's analysis of this FBI data reporting civilian (non-police) justifiable homicides in the United States between 1976 and 1991, 87.3 percent of justifiable homicides are accomplished using a gun. Of those justifiable homicides where the type of gun was recorded, 78.6 percent of these justifiable homicides was conducted with a handgun.

Compare this with homicides in general (65.1 percent use a gun) or other-than-justifiable civilian homicides, where only 64.7

percent of the homicides involved the use of a gun.

So here's a brand new sound bite for you, courtesy of my question today to Dr. Kleck, and his analysis of FBI statistics:

"Almost nine out of ten times that Americans had to kill a criminal in defense, they used a gun. And that's about 25 percent more often than guns are the weapon of choice for a murder."

Got all that, Ed Asner? "Lou Grant" always told the truth. You may not be a newspaperman, but you played one on TV. I'm eagerly awaiting the TV spots in which you do what newspapers do when they learn they've made a mistake: issue a retraction and inform the American people that you didn't tell them the whole story.

[*] Reprinted earlier in this book.

The Unconstitutional Bill of Rights

What does it mean to be an American?

This is a question patriots are going to have to start asking themselves, seriously, for the first time since the end of the Civil War on April 9, 1865, six score and eleven years ago.

That war, the most costly in American lives of any in U.S. history, was made inevitable by the decision of the Supreme Court of the United States announced on March 6, 1857 in the case of Dred Scott v. Sanford. Scott was a slave purchased by a U.S. army surgeon, John Emerson, in 1833, while in the slave state of Missouri. In 1834, Scott accompanied Emerson to Illinois, a free state, and thereafter to the northern part of the Louisiana Purchase, a free territory. The two returned to Missouri in 1838. In 1846, Emerson having died and title to the slave Dred Scott having passed to John F.A. Sanford of New York, Scott sued the out-of-stater Sanford in Federal court, his antislavery lawyers arguing that because Scott had been a resident in a free state and a free territory, he was a free man. The Supreme Court ruled in the Dred Scott case that Negroes were not citizens of the United States and did not have legal standing to sue in the federal courts.

"Standing," in the legal sense, is the first issue that any court must look at as a legal issue. Could a lawyer go into court representing a redwood tree's right not to be cut down? The court would first have to decide whether the tree had legal standing to bring a petition or lawsuit to the court. Does a fetus have the right to sue a mother to prevent the mother from aborting? The court would first have to decide whether the fetus was an "it" or a legal person. The Supreme Court in Dred Scott asserted that Scott was not a "he" but an "it": mere property.

The Supreme Court having ruled on March 6, 1857 that the Constitution of the United States allowed slavery, and that the American Declaration of Independence was incorrect when it stated on July 4, 1776 that "all men are created equal, that they are endowed by their Creator with certain unalienable Rights, that among these are Life, Liberty and the pursuit of Happiness," it was a matter of a short four years and five weeks before the conflict between those Americans who believed that the Declaration of Independence applied to all men found themselves in a shooting war with those who believed it applied only to white men, when pro-slave-state Confederates fired on Fort Sumter on April 12, 1861.

One can easily argue that the decision by President Abraham Lincoln to preserve the jurisdiction of the Constitution of the United States over Southern States who had voted to secede was a Pyrrhic victory, in that it was brute force rather than love of liberty which defeated the South — and the balance of power between the states and the federal government has never been right since. Nevertheless, the Southern States had also first seceded from Britain under the Declaration of Independence's premise, "That to secure these rights, Governments are instituted among Men, deriving their just powers from the consent of the governed, — That whenever any Form of Government becomes destructive of these ends, it is the Right of the People to alter or to abolish it, and to institute new Government, laying its foundation on such principles, and organizing its powers in such form, as to them shall seem most likely to effect their Safety and Happiness."

Dred Scott was not consenting to be a slave. The Southern states could try to secede from the Constitution of the United States. They could not secede from Dred Scott's natural rights as stated in the Declaration of Independence.

Why this history lesson? Why now?

We have had controversial Supreme Court decisions in the years since the Dred Scott case. *Brown v. Board of Education*. *Roe v. Wade*. But there now comes a case as important as Dred Scott, and it cannot be allowed to stand without forcing American patriots who love liberty to ask themselves what sort of country the United States of America has become, where an obvious right, enshrined in the Constitution of the United States, can be summarily dismissed by a federal appellate court on the same grounds as the Dred Scott case: that a citizen of the United States doesn't have standing to bring suit in federal court when officials violate his constitutionally protected rights.

The case is *Hickman v. Block*, and the ruling was announced April 5, 1996 by the United States Court of Appeals for the Ninth Circuit.

Douglas Ray Hickman, owner of a Southern California security firm, had repeatedly applied for a license to carry a concealed firearm, and had repeatedly been denied, by public officials including Los Angeles County Sheriff, Sherman Block. The merits of Hickman's applications are no longer at issue, since Hickman later obtained such a license from the City of Los Angeles as part of a separate lawsuit filed in California state courts. But Hickman first sued in federal court, citing his right under the Second Amendment to "bear arms." The Second Amendment to the Constitution of the United States reads, "A well-regulated militia being necessary to the security of a free state, the right of the people to keep and bear arms shall not be infringed." The sole question remaining before the Court of Appeals for the Ninth Circuit when it issued its ruling was: did Douglas Ray Hickman have legal standing to sue in federal court for any injury that might arise from violation of his rights under the Second Amendment?

The United States Court of Appeals for the Ninth Circuit said no. It said, "Hickman lacks standing to sue for a violation of the Second Amendment." The Court's reason? "The question presented at the threshold of Hickman's appeal is whether the Second Amendment confers upon individual citizens standing to enforce the right to keep and bear arms. We follow our sister circuits in holding that the Second Amendment is a right held by the states, and does not protect the possession of a weapon by a private citizen. We conclude that Hickman can show no legal injury, and therefore lacks standing to bring this action."

The ruling was issued by a three-judge panel of the Ninth Circuit: Cynthia Holcomb Hall, John T. Noonan, and William B. Shubb. Before Hickman asks the Supreme Court of the United States to grant a further hearing, Hickman's attorneys will ask the complete Ninth Circuit to take another look at the case.

They could do so or not. The Supreme Court of the United

States could issue a summary affirmation of the Ninth Circuit's ruling, or it could deny certiorari — which means they could decide not to listen to the case and let the ruling stand as the law of the land for the federal district in which the lawsuit was filed — or the Supreme Court could agree to hear this case and tell us whether Douglas Ray Hickman has as little standing to ask for his rights as Dred Scott, which is what the Court of Appeals for the Ninth Circuit has ruled.

There are at least seventy million Americans now living to whom this question is not theoretical but immediate and meaningful: they are the seventy million Americans who are estimated to own guns. That is about half the adults in the United States, a much larger part of the population than the ethnically black African population of the United States on March 6, 1857. If a federal appeals court can get away with telling seventy million Americans that they don't know how to read a plain English sentence with a single unrestricted clause in it — "the right of the people to keep and bear arms shall not be infringed" — and that the authors of the Bill of Rights were illiterates who wrote "people" when they really meant "states" … then what?

Another Civil War four years and five weeks from now? A mass protest movement equivalent to the Civil Rights protests of thirty years ago? Mass civil disobedience, as gun-owners find themselves subject to the legislative whims of the Charles Schumers and Dianne Feinsteins in Congress, and the Bill and Hillary Clintons in the White House?

Make no mistake: this court ruling was decided on political grounds, not judicial grounds. It will take a political mass movement to overturn it. This election year is as good a time as any to start.

The candidates for president, and for Congress, must be shown this decision and they must take a position on it. They must have questions shouted at them about it at press conferences and signs asking them about it at their public rallies. The presidential candidates must be asked whether they will appoint federal judges who will rule that there is an individual right to keep and bear arms under the Second Amendment. Candidates for the United States Senate must be asked whether they will vote to confirm an appointment of a candidate who does not pledge to support the Second-Amendment.

You see, we patriots have to start deciding what we are going to do if we find ourselves with no Second Amendment. There are already legislative and court attacks on the rest of the Bill of Rights: anti-terrorism legislation which attacks the Fourth, Fifth, and Sixth amendments; a Communications Decency Act which threatens the First Amendment. Ultimately, protections written on parchment are only as good as the will, and power, of the people to enforce them.

Are you willing to live in a United States of America where you have no legal standing to sue for violation of your Constitutional rights? If you are, you and I have nothing further to discuss.

But if you are not willing to live in a country where a federal court can say you have as few rights as a slave — then what are you willing to do about it?

The Supreme Court of the United States denied certiorari, allowing the appelate court ruling to stand. Welcome to post-constitutional America.

— JNS

Guns and Self-Defense
by Gary Kleck, Ph.D.

This afterword is abridged from chapter five of *Targeting Guns: Firearms and Their Control* Copyright © 1997 by Walter de Gruyter, Inc., New York. Used by permission of the publisher, Aldine de Gruyter, and the author.

Citations have been deleted and the original chapter should be consulted for all references.

Gun ownership for self-protection, and defensive gun use, must be distinguished from other forms of forceful activity directed at criminals, such as private vigilantism, or the activities of the criminal justice system, such as police making arrests. All of these can be coercive and all may be done by armed persons. However, vigilantism and criminal-justice activity share a purpose that self-defensive actions do not—-retribution. Whereas the criminal-justice system and the vigilante both seek to punish wrong-doers, the defensive gun user seeks to protect the bodily safety and property of himself and others. Retribution is neither an essential nor even necessarily common part of self-defense actions. Further, the vigilante proactively seeks out contact with criminals, while the defender typically reacts to actions initiated by criminals. The true vigilante acts collectively, in concert with like-minded individuals, whereas the defender ordinarily acts alone. It therefore is an oxymoron to refer to a defensive gun user as a "lone vigilante." Further, gun ownership is largely passive self-protection—-once a gun is acquired, the owner only rarely does anything defensive with it. Only a minority of defensive owners actually use their guns for self-protection; most of the rest just keep the gun in a bureau drawer or similar location, where it is available for use should the need arise. This contrasts sharply with neighborhood crime control strategies, that may require considerable investment of time and effort from each participant.

Although gun ownership costs more money than simple measures such as locking doors, having neighbors watch one's house, or avoidance behaviors such as not going out at night, it costs less than buying and maintaining a dog, paying a security guard, buying a burglar alarm system, or relocating one's residence to an area with less crime. Consequently, it is a self-protection measure available to many low-income people who cannot afford more expensive alternatives. Gun ownership is not a replacement or substitute for these other self-help measures, nor for criminal-justice-system activities, but rather is more accurately thought of as a complement to them—-an additional measure that might prove useful, for at least some crime victims, some of the time.

At least 12 national and 3 state-wide surveys have asked probability samples of the general adult population about defensive gun use. The surveys differ in many important respects. The two most sophisticated national surveys are the National Self-Defense Survey done by Marc Gertz and myself in 1995 and a smaller scale survey done by the Police Foundation in 1996.

The National Self-Defense Survey was the first survey specifically designed to estimate the frequency of defensive gun uses. It asked all respondents about both their own uses and those of other household members, inquired about all gun types, excluded uses against animals or connected with occupational duties, and limited recall periods to one and five years. Equally importantly, it established, with detailed questioning, whether persons claiming a defensive gun use had actually confronted an adversary (as distinct from, say, merely investigating a suspicious noise in the backyard), actually used their guns in some way, such as, at minimum, threatening their adversaries (as distinct from merely owning or carrying a gun for defensive reasons), and had done so in connection with what they regarded as a specific crime being committed against them.

The National Self-Defense Survey indicated that there were 2.5 million incidents of defensive gun use per year in the U.S. during the 1988-1993 period. This is probably a conservative estimate, for two reasons. First, cases of respondents intentionally withholding reports of genuine defensive-gun uses were probably more common than cases of respondents reporting incidents that did not occur or that were not genuinely defensive. Second, the survey covered only adults age 18 and older, thereby excluding all defensive gun uses involving adolescents, the age group most likely to suffer a violent victimization.

The authors concluded that defensive uses of guns are about three to four times as common as criminal uses of guns.

The National Self-Defense Survey confirmed the picture of frequent defensive gun use implied by the results of earlier, less sophisticated surveys.

A national survey conducted in 1994 by the Police Foundation and sponsored by the National Institute of Justice almost exactly confirmed the estimates from the National Self-Defense Survey. This survey's person-based estimate was that 1.44% of the adult population had used a gun for protection against a person in the previous year, implying 2.73 million defensive gun users. These results were well within sampling error of the corresponding 1.33% and 2.55 million estimates produced by the National Self-Defense Survey.

The one survey that is clearly not suitable for estimating the total number of defensive gun uses is the National Crime Victimization Survey. This is the only survey that has ever generated results implying an annual defensive-gun-use estimate under 700,000. Not surprisingly, it is a favorite of academic gun-control supporters. If one is to make even a pretense of empirically supporting the claim that defensive gun use is rare in America, one must rely on the National Crime Victimization Survey, warts and all.

That the National Crime Victimization Survey estimate is radically wrong is now beyond serious dispute. Ultimately, the only foundation one ever has for knowing that a measurement is wrong is that it is inconsistent with other measurements of the same phenomenon. There are now at least 15 other independent estimates of the frequency of defensive gun uses and every one of them is enormously larger than the National-Crime-Victimization-Survey estimate. Unanimity is rare in studies of crime, but this is one of those rare cases. Apparently, however, even unanimous and overwhelming evidence is not sufficient to dissuade the gun control advocacy organizations, such as Handgun Control, Inc., and the Coalition to Stop Gun Violence, that the National Crime Victimization Survey estimate is at least approximately valid and that defensive gun use is rare.

The numerous surveys yielding contrary estimates strongly support the view that the National-Crime-Victimization-Survey estimate is grossly erroneous.

There has probably been more outright dishonesty in addressing the issue of the frequency of defensive gun use than any other issue in the gun control debate. Faced with a huge body of evidence contradicting their low defensive-gun-use position, hardcore gun-control supporters have had little choice but to simply promote the unsuitable National-Crime-Victimization-Survey estimate and ignore or discount everything else. Authors writing in medical and public health journals are typically the most crudely dishonest—-they simply withhold from their readers the very existence of a mountain of contradictory evidence.

Adherents of the rare-defensive-gun-use thesis also use another tactic, in addition to simply pretending that the contrary evidence does not exist. On those rare occasions when they briefly and very partially address some of the contrary evidence, they counter evidence with one-sided speculation rather than better empirical information.

Even if some of these speculations had been correct and consequential, it is not productive or legitimate to speculate only in one direction, in this case speculating only about flaws that supposedly pushed defensive-gun-use estimates up. If one is not willing to seriously consider errors in both directions, one is simply engaging in "adversary scholarship" or "sagecraft," an enterprise aimed not at discovering the truth, but rather at buttressing predetermined positions.

Speculation about the flaws in surveys estimating large numbers of defensive gun uses resemble UFO buffs' beliefs that the federal government captured aliens from other worlds at Roswell,

New Mexico in 1947. The reason most people do not share these beliefs is not that they can be proven false; they cannot, since it is impossible to prove a negative. Rather, most people reject them because there is no credible evidence that they are true. It is the same with speculations about the gun surveys' supposed flaws. Since it is impossible to prove a negative, one cannot prove that massive misreporting of nonexistent defensive gun use incidents did *not* occur in the gun surveys. There is, however, no evidence whatsoever that such massive misreporting *did* occur.

Faced with such overwhelming survey support for the idea that defensive gun uses are common, some pro-control scholars belatedly adopted the view that surveys simply cannot yield useful information about how often they occur. Faced with defeat on the field of empirical evidence, they suddenly developed a radical skepticism toward *all* survey estimates.

Most uses of guns for either criminal or defensive purposes are less dramatic or consequential than one might think. Only 3% of criminal gun assaults involves anyone actually being wounded, even nonfatally, and the same is true of defensive gun uses. More commonly, guns are merely pointed at another person, or perhaps only referred to ("I've got a gun") or displayed, and this is sufficient to accomplish the ends of the user, whether criminal or noncriminal. Nevertheless, most gun owners questioned in surveys assert that they would be willing to shoot criminals under the right circumstances. A 1989 *Time*/CNN survey found that 78% of gun owners said they would shoot a burglar if they felt threatened by that person.

Despite this stated willingness of gun owners to shoot under certain circumstances, most defensive uses of guns do not in fact involve shooting anyone. Data from the National Self-Defense Survey indicate that no more than 8% of the 2.5 million annual defensive gun uses involved a defender who claimed to have shot their adversaries, or about 200,000 total. The 8% figure, however, should be taken with a grain of salt because it is based on a sample of only 213 cases, 17 of whom reported a wounding, and because the respondants were not asked how they knew they had wounded the criminals. In cases where the criminal escaped, these reports may often have been based on favorable guesses about the shooter's marksmanship skills. As Marc Gertz and I noted, the claimed "hit rate" of shooters in the National-Self-Defense-Survey-reported incidents was higher than that of police officers, an unlikely level of shooting skill under stress.

Regardless, there is nothing even mildly implausible about 200,000 annual nonfatal woundings linked with defensive gun uses, in light of the estimated 150,000 annual medically treated gunshot woundings. There could also easily be just as many more that went untreated because they involved criminals wounded by their victims during a criminal attempt. Criminals wounded in the course of attempting a crime against an armed victim are almost certainly a set of persons lying largely *outside* the set of persons receiving medical treatment for gun-shot wounds, and thus the size of the latter set can tell us nothing about how large the former should be.

The rarest, but most serious form of self-defense with a gun is a defensive killing. The FBI does not publish statistics on self-defense killings *per se*, but it did start publishing counts of civilian justifiable homicides gathered through their Supplementary Homicides Reports program in their 1991 issue. For a variety of reasons, the FBI counts of civilian justifiable homicides represent only a minority of all civilian legal defensive homicides. FBI-counted civilian justifiable homicides were used to estimate total civilian legal defensive homicides. FBI counts of police justifiable homicides are also reported here. Regardless of which counts of homicides by police are used, the results indicate that civilians legally kill far more felons than police officers do. The figures imply that, of 24,614 civilian (not by police) homicide deaths in the United States in 1990, about 1400 to 3200, or 5.6% to 13.0% were legal civilian defensive homicides.

This estimate was independently confirmed by the only national study of homicide dispositions done to date. Analysis of 231 homicides occurring in the U.S. in the first week of May, 1989 indicated that between 15 (6.5%) and 28 (12.1%) were ruled justifiable.

Nonfatal gun woundings are far more frequent than fatal shootings. In 1985 Cook reviewed data that indicate that about 15% of assault-linked gunshot wounds known to the police are fatal, implying a ratio of about 5.67 (85/15) reported nonfatal assaultive gun woundings to each fatal one. Assuming the same applies to legal civilian defensive shootings, there were between 6,300 and 15,300 reported nonfatal, legally permissible woundings of criminals by gun-armed civilians in 1990. Combining the defensive killings and nonfatal woundings, there are about 7,700 to 18,500 reported legal shootings of criminals a year, which would be less than 1% of all defensive gun uses. The rest of defensive gun uses, then, involve neither killings nor woundings but rather misses, warning shots fired, or guns used to threaten, by pointing them or verbally referring to them.

That defensive gun uses, with or without a wounding, are so common is not surprising in view of how many Americans own guns for defensive reasons and keep them ready for defensive use. A 1989 national survey found that 27% of gun owners have a gun *mainly* for protection, and 62% said that protection from crime was at least one of the reasons they owned guns. This translates into about 16 million people in 1993 who had guns mainly for protection, and about 36 million in 1993 who had them at least partly for protection.

Further, many gun owners, and almost certainly a majority of those who own guns primarily for protection, keep a household gun loaded. The 1989 survey found that 24% of gun owners always keep a gun loaded, and another 7% had a gun loaded at the time of the interview although they did not do so all the time, for a total of 31%. Guns were most commonly kept in the bedroom, where they would be ready for nighttime use.

Are gun defenders really vengeful vigilantes, seeking out criminals to inflict punishment on them? If this were true, we would expect defenders to express more punitive views towards criminals. Results from the National Self-Defense Survey did not support this imagery. Both with regard to support for the death penalty and opinions concerning whether the courts are sufficiently harsh towards criminals, gun defenders were essentially identical to nondefenders. Instead, gun defenders were drawn from the ranks of groups with higher-than-average risks of criminal victimization: males, young adults, minorities, and big-city dwellers. And, of course, gun defenders were more likely to own guns and to carry them for protection.

Before addressing the objective effects of actual defensive uses of guns, a more subjective issue should be addressed. If some people get guns in response to crime or the prospect of being victimized in the future, does a gun make its owner feel safer?

A December 1989 CNN/*Time* national survey of 605 U.S. gun owners asked the following question: "Does having a gun in your house make you feel more safe from crime, less safe, or doesn't it make any difference?" Of the gun owners, 42% felt more safe, 2% felt less safe, and the rest said it made no difference. Results were virtually identical in a May 1994 survey for *U.S. News and World Report.* When asked "Overall, do you feel comfortable with a gun in your house or are you sometimes afraid of it?," 92% of gun owners said they were comfortable, 6% were sometimes afraid, and 2% were not sure.

In sum, most gun owners, including many who do not even have a gun for defensive reasons, feel comfortable with guns, feel safer from crime because of them, and believe their guns actually do make them safer.

Another way of approaching this issue is to ask people how they would feel if guns were eliminated. If widespread gun ownership was currently making people feel less safe, then eliminating guns should make them feel more safe. An August, 1994 Gallup poll asked: "Suppose a law were passed which you were certain would remove all handguns from the possession of all citizens other than the police. Would you feel more safe, less safe, or wouldn't it make any difference?" While 32% said they would feel more safe, 41% said they would feel less safe, and the remainder felt it would make no difference. Since there are more who would feel less safe than who would feel more safe, the net effect on the population as a whole of eliminating guns would be to make the population feel less safe.

Do gun owners' feelings of greater security, however real in emotional terms, have any factual foundation? Even proponents of stringent gun control who assert that guns are not effective defensive devices for civilians nearly always make exceptions for police officers and the like. The rationale for police having guns is based at least partly on the idea that police need and can effectively use guns for defending themselves and others. Doubts about the defensive utility of guns, then, appear to rest on any of three beliefs: (1) civilians do not need any self-protective devices, because they will almost never confront criminals, or at least will almost never do so while they have access to a gun, or (2) they do not need guns because they can rely on the police for protection, or (3) civilians, unlike police, are not able to use guns effectively, regardless of need.

Regarding the first belief, National Crime Victimization Survey estimates indicate that 83% of Americans will, sometime over the span of their lives, be a victim of a violent crime, all of which by definition involve direct confrontation with a criminal. Although it cannot be stated what share of these incidents will transpire in a way that would allow the victim to actually use a gun, it is clear that a large share of the population will experience a violent victimization.

The second idea, that citizens can depend on police for effective protection, is clearly erroneous. It implies that police can serve the same function as a gun in disrupting a crime in progress, before the victim is hurt or loses property. Police cannot do this, and indeed do not themselves even claim to be able to do so. Instead, police primarily respond to crimes after they have occurred, questioning the victim and other witnesses in the hope that they can apprehend the criminals, make them available for prosecution and punishment, and thereby deter other criminals from attempting crimes. Police officers rarely disrupt violent crimes or burglaries in progress; even the most professional and efficient urban police forces rarely can reach the scene of a crime soon enough to catch the criminal "in the act."

The third idea, that civilians are not generally able to use guns effectively, requires more extended consideration. Gun-control proponents sometimes argue that wielding guns effectively in self-defense requires special training, skills, and emotional control that only police have. They hint that would-be gun users are ineffectual, panic-prone hysterics, as likely to accidentally shoot a family member as a burglar, occasionally citing a few illustrative anecdotes for support.

Incidents in which householders shoot family members mistaken for burglars and other criminals have occurred, but they are extremely rare. Studies indicate that fewer than 2% of fatal gun accidents involve a person accidentally shooting someone mistaken for an intruder. With 1409 fatal gun accidents in 1992, this implies that there are fewer than 28 incidents of this sort annually. Compared with about 2.5 million annual defensive uses of guns, this translates into about a less than 1-in-90,000 chance of a defensive gun use resulting in this kind of accident.

It has also been claimed that many people who attempt to use guns for self-protection have the gun taken from them by the criminal and used against them. Although this type of incident is not totally unknown, it too is extremely rare. In the 1979-1985 National-Crime-Victimization-Survey sample, it was possible to identify crime incidents in which the victim used a gun for protection and lost a gun to the offender(s). At most, 1% of defensive gun uses resulted in the offender taking a gun away from the victim. Even these few cases did not necessarily involve the offender snatching a gun out of the victim's hands. Instead a burglar might, for example, have been leaving a home with one of the household's guns when a resident attempted to stop him using another household gun. Thus, the 1% figure probably represents an upper limit.

Some people have misinterpreted data on police killings as indicating that even trained police officers can have their guns taken away while attempting to use them for self-defense. With about 600,000 sworn officers carrying guns on duty, and an average of about 68 killed per year, about eight of which per year were killed with their own weapons, this would imply an annual risk of

1.4 police officers killed with their own guns per 100,000 officers.

More misleading still was the suggestion that these rare killings bore on the issue of the risks of defensive gun use. In a detailed study of killings of officers, the FBI found that, among 11 officers who were killed with their own guns, only one involved a gun taken from the victim officer's hand. Since actually using a gun for self-defense would have to involve an officer holding the gun, this implies that cases of officers killed with their own guns almost never involve an attempt by the victim officer to use the gun for self-defense. Instead guns were typically taken from the officer's holster or vehicle. Police officers are almost never killed by offenders who took their guns away while the officers were trying to use the guns defensively. Police killings therefore offer no support for the notion that using guns for self-defense is risky.

Based on nationally representative samples of crime incidents reported in the National Crime Victimization Surveys, victims who use guns for self-protection were less likely to be injured or to lose property than otherwise similar victims who used other forms of self-protection or who did not resist at all. For example, among robbery victims who used guns, only 17% were injured and only 31% lost property, compared to 25% inury rates and 88% property loss rates among victims who did not resist at all, and 33% injury rates and 65% property loss rates among all robbery victims.

Some police officers advise people to refrain from armed resistance should they be confronted by a criminal. For example, Joseph McNamara, then the Chief of the San Jose Police Department, testified before a Congressional committee: "We urge citizens not to resist armed robbery, but in these sad cases I described, the victims ended up dead because they produced their own handguns and escalated the violence. Very rarely have I seen cases in which the handgun was used to ward off a criminal."

Given the foregoing evidence, McNamara's factual premises are clearly wrong.

Why, then, do some police give such advice? While some, like McNamara, a strong gun control advocate, may simply be motivated by political considerations, there is no evidence that this is true for all officers. Instead, police advice may well logically follow from the resistance experiences of victims with whom officers have had contact. The problem with relying on this sample of resistance cases is that it is substantially unrepresentative of the experiences of crime victims in general—-the cases McNamara and other police officers have seen are not like those they have not seen, and the latter outnumber the former by a wide margin.

Most crimes are not reported to the police, and the crimes most likely to go unreported are the ones that involve neither injury nor property loss, i.e., those that had successful outcomes from the victim's viewpoint. For example, among robberies reported to the National Crime Victimization Surveys, only 24% of those with no injury or property loss were reported to police, whereas 72% of those with both were reported. Likewise, assaults without injury are less likely to be reported than those with injury. By definition, all incidents involving successful defensive gun uses fall within the no-injury, no-property-loss category, and thus are largely invisible to the police.

Consequently, police never hear about the bulk of successful defensive gun uses, instead hearing mostly about an unrepresentative minority of them containing a disproportionately large number of failures. Further, even when they do receive a report of a crime that in fact involved a gun-wielding victim, the victim has strong legal reasons for leaving their own gun use out of their account of the crime. Since most defensive gun uses occur away from the victim's home, and few victims have the required permits for carrying concealed weapons in public, most gun uses probably involved a crime on the part of the victim.

To conclude that armed resistance is ineffective or dangerous, based on the experiences of this sort of unrepresentative sample of victims, can be called, in honor of Chief McNamara, "the Police Chief's Fallacy."

At present, advising victims to not use guns to resist criminal attempts seems imprudent at best, dangerous at worst.

Another variant of this fallacy concerns the frequency of defensive gun uses rather than their effectiveness. It is the belief that because defensive gun uses are rarely recorded in police reports of crimes, they rarely occur. This is fallacious not only because many incidents involving a defensive gun use would not be reported to police at all, but also because even when the crime is reported, victims are unlikely to mention their own legally controversial actions or their possession of legally questionable guns.

When gun-control advocates and public health scholars consider whether keeping a gun for defensive purposes is sensible, they frequently bring up one variant or another of the most nonsensical statistic in the gun control debate.

In 1975 four physicians published an article based on data derived from medical examiner files in Cuyahoga (Cleveland) County, Ohio. They noted that during the period 1958-1973, there were 148 fatal gun accidents (78% of them in the home) and 23 "burglars, robbers or intruders who were not relatives or acquaintances" killed by people using guns to defend their homes. They stated that there were six times as many home fatal gun accidents as burglars killed. (This appears to have been a miscomputation—the authors counted all 148 accidental deaths in the numerator, instead of just the 115 occurring in the home. Although the value of the number does not matter much, the correct ratio was five rather than six.)

On the basis of these facts alone, the authors concluded that "guns in the home are more dangerous than useful to the homeowner and his family who keep them to protect their persons and property" and that "the possession of firearms by civilians appears to be a dangerous and ineffective means of self-protection."

Eleven years later, Arthur Kellermann and his colleagues unwittingly replicated the Rushforth findings, finding that "for every case of self-protection homicide involving a firearm kept in the home, there were 1.3 accidental deaths, 4.6 criminal homicides, and 37 suicides involving firearms." The authors then concluded, just as Rushforth *et al.* did, that "the advisability of keeping firearms in the home for protection must be questioned."

While conceding that they had made no effort to count "cases in which burglars or intruders are wounded or frightened away," the authors never acknowledged a far more pertinent and serious omission: lives saved by defensive gun use.

The basic problem that makes these ratios nonsensical is that they are presented as risk-benefit ratios, but in fact do not reflect any benefits of keeping guns for self-protection. If one sets out to assess only the costs of a behavior, but none of its benefits, the results of such an "analysis" are a foregone conclusion. What is so deceptive about the ratio is the hint that killing burglars or intruders is somehow a "benefit" to the householder. This is both morally offensive and factually inaccurate. Being forced to kill another human being, criminal or not, is a nightmare to be suffered through for years. Even police officers who take a life in the course of their duties commonly suffer the symptoms of post-traumatic stress syndrome.

Gun owners do not keep guns for the sake of having a chance to "bag a burglar." Instead, the benefit of defensive gun ownership that would be parallel to innocent lives lost to guns would be innocent lives *saved* by defensive use of guns.

As previously noted, less than one in a thousand defensive gun uses involves a criminal being killed. Few purportedly life-saving defensive uses of guns involve killing the criminal, and, conversely, killings of criminals do not necessarily involve saving the life of a victim. Therefore the number of criminals killed does not in any way even approximately index the number of lives saved. It is, however, impossible to directly count lives saved, i.e. deaths that did *not* occur, so it will never be possible to form a meaningful ratio of genuinely comparable quantities.

This implied cost-benefit ratio is so meaningless that it can fairly be dubbed the "Nonsense Ratio."

To briefly summarize:

Defensive gun uses by crime victims are three to four times more common than crimes committed with guns;

Victim gun use is associated with lower rates of assault or robbery victim injury and lower rates of robbery completion than any other defensive action or doing nothing to resist;

Serious predatory criminals perceive a risk from victim gun

use that is roughly comparable to that of criminal-justice-system actions, and this perception may influence their criminal behavior in socially desirable ways.

A deterrent effect of widespread gun ownership and defensive use has not been conclusively established, any more than it has been for activities of the legal system. Given the nature of deterrent effects, it may never be convincingly established. Nevertheless, available evidence is consistent with the hypothesis that civilian ownership and defensive use of guns deters violent crime and reduces burglar-linked injuries.

Economic injustice, a history of racism, and other factors have created dangerous conditions in many places in America. Police cannot realistically be expected to provide personal protection for every American, and indeed are not even legally obliged to do so. Although gun ownership is no more an all-situations, magical source of protection than the police, it can be a useful source of safety in addition to police protection, burglary alarms, guard dogs, and all the other resources people exploit to improve their security. These sources are not substitutes for one another. Rather, they are complements, each useful in different situations. Possession of a gun gives its owner an additional option for dealing with danger. If other sources of security are adequate, the gun does not have to be used; but where other sources fail, it can preserve bodily safety and property in at least some situations.

People sympathetic toward gun control yet skeptical about its likely impact sometimes note that although a world in which there were no guns would be desirable, it is also unachievable. The evidence raises a more radical possibility—that a world in which no one had guns would actually be *less* safe than a hypothetical one in which nonaggressors had guns and aggressors did not.

If gun possession among prospective victims tends to reduce violence, then reducing such gun possession is not, in and of itself, a social good. To disarm noncriminals in the hope that this might indirectly help reduce access to guns among criminals is a very high-stakes gamble, and the risks will not be reduced by pretending that crime victims rarely use guns for self-defense.

Sources and Recommended Reading

Books

The Second Amendment and the Right to Keep and Bear Arms

The Right to Keep and Bear Arms:
Report of the Subcommittee on the Constitution
of the Committee on the Judiciary
United States Senate, Ninety-Seventh Congress
Superintendent of Documents, U.S. Government Printing Office, 1982

That Every Man Be Armed: The Evolution of a Constitutional Right
by Stephen P. Halbrook
University of New Mexico Press, 1984

A Right to Bear Arms
by Stephen P. Halbrook
Greenwood Press, 1989

Contexts of the Bill of Rights
Edited by Stephen L. Schechter and Richard B. Bernstein
New York State Commission
on the Bicentennial of the United States Constitution, 1990

Gun Rights Fact Book
by Alan M. Gottlieb
Merril Press, 1988, 1989 (revised)

The Rights of Gun Owners
by Alan M. Gottlieb
Merril Press, 1981, 1983, 1991 (revised)

To Keep and Bear Arms: The Origins of An Anglo-American Right
by Joyce Lee Malcolm
Harvard University Press, 1994

For the Defense of Themselves and the State: The Original and Judicial Interpretation of the Right to Keep and Bear Arms
by Clayton E. Cramer
Praeger Publishers, 1994

Gun Control and the Constitution:
Sources and Explorations on the Second Amendment
Edited by Robert J. Cottrol
Garland Publishing, 1994

Firearms Criminology

Under the Gun: Weapons, Crime, and Violence in America
by James D. Wright, Peter H. Rossi, Kathleen Daly
Aldine Publishing, 1983

Restricting Handguns: The Liberal Skeptics Speak Out
Edited by Don B. Kates, Jr.
Foreword by Senator Frank Church
North River Press, 1979

Armed and Considered Dangerous:
A Survey of Felons and Their Firearms
by James D. Wright and Peter H. Rossi
Aldine de Gruyter, 1986

Guns, Murder and the Constitution
by Don B. Kates, Jr.
Pacific Research Institute, 1990

Point Blank: Guns and Violence in America
by Gary Kleck
Aldine de Gruyter, 1991

The Journal of Criminal Law & Criminology, Vol. 86, No. 1, 1995
Northwestern University School of Law
Includes "Armed Resistance to Crime: The Prevalence and Nature of Self-Defense with a Gun," by Gary Kleck and Marc Gertz, and "A Tribute to a View I have Opposed" by Marvin E. Wolfgang

Targeting Guns: Firearms and Their Control
by Gary Kleck
Aldine de Gruyter, 1997

More Guns, Less Crime
by John R. Lott, Jr.
University of Chicago Press, 1998

Firearms & Self-Defense

In the Gravest Extreme
by Massad F. Ayoob
Massad F. and Dorothy A. Ayoob/Police Bookshelf, 1980

The Armed Citizen
Edited by Joseph P. Roberts, Jr.
National Rifle Association of America, 1989

Armed & Female
by Paxton Quigley
E.P. Dutton (hc), 1989; St. Martins (pb.), 1990

Effective Defense: The Woman, The Plan, The Gun
by Gila May-Hayes
Foreword by Massad F. Ayoob
The Firearms Academy of Seattle, 1994

Not an Easy Target: Paxton Quigley's Self-Protection for Women
by Paxton Quigley
Illustrated by Liz Kelsey
Fireside/Simon & Schuster, 1995

How to Own a Gun and Stay out of Jail
by John Machtinger
Gun Law Press, 1994 (and updated yearly by state)

Personal, Sociological, and Historical Issues

The Gun Grabbers
by Alan Gottlieb
Introduction by Senator Steve Symms
Merril Press, 1986

The Gun Control Debate: You Decide
Edited by Lee Nisbet
Prometheus Books, 1990

The Gun Culture and Its Enemies
Edited by William R. Tonso
Second Amendment Foundation/Merril Press, 1990

To Ride, Shoot Straight, and Speak the Truth
by Jeff Cooper
Illustrated by Paul Kirchner
Gunsite Press, 1990

"Gun Control": Gateway to Tyranny
by Jay Simkin and Aaron Zelman
Jews for the Preservation of Firearms Ownership, 1992

The Samurai, The Mountie and The Cowboy: Should America Adopt the Gun Controls of Other Democracies?
by David B. Kopel
Prometheus Books, 1992

Gun Control: The Consuming Debate
by Donald D. Hook
Merril Press, 1993

Things You Can Do to Defend Your Gun Rights
by Alan M. Gotlieb and David B. Kopel
Merril Press, 1993

Firing Back
by Clayton E. Cramer
Krause Publications, 1994

Guns, Crime, and Freedom
by Wayne LaPierre
Foreword by Tom Clancy
Regnery Publishing Inc., 1994

Lethal Laws: "Gun Control Is the Key to Genocide"
by Jay Simkin, Aaron Zelman, and Alan M. Rice
Jews for the Preservation of Firearms Ownership, 1994

Guns — Who Should Have Them
Edited by David Kopel
Prometheus Books, 1995

Self Control Not Gun Control
by J. Neil Schulman
Afterword by Brad Linaweaver
Synapse-Centurion, 1995

Tennessee Law Review, Volume 63, Fall 1995, No. 1
Includes "Luna Law: The Libertarian Vision in Heinlein's *The Moon is a Harsh*

Mistress"
by Dmitry N. Feofanov

No More Wacos: What's Wrong with Law Enforcement and How to Fix It
by David P. Kopel & Paul H. Blackman
Prometheus Books, 1997

The Great American Gun Debate: Essays on Firearms & Violence
by Don B. Kates, Jr. and Gary Kleck
Pacific Research Institute, 1997

Pro-Gun Control/Anti NRA

National Rifle Association: Money, Firepower & Fear
by Josh Sugarmann
National Press Books, 1992

Under Fire: The NRA and the Battle for Gun Control
by Osha Gray Davidson
University of Iowa Press, 1998

For Children

Learn Gun Safety with Eddie Eagle (videotape, coloring books, teacher's materials)
Hosted by Jason Priestly
National Rifle Association, 1993
800-231-0752

"Gran'pa Jack" illustrated pamphlet series
by Aaron Zelman
Jews for the Preservation of Firearms Ownership, 1996, 1997, 1998

Pro-Firearms Fiction

Alongside Night
by J. Neil Schulman
Crown Publishers, 1979
Near future portrayal of Second American Revolution.

The Probability Broach
by L. Neil Smith
Del Rey, 1980

Shows alternate history in which George Washington lost the Whiskey Rebellion and government grew smaller thereafter.

Red Planet (Restored Edition)
by Robert A. Heinlein
Del Rey, 1990
Story of secession from despotic Earth government by human colonists on Mars. Written as a Young Adult novel, but *all* Heinlein novels are intellectually suitable for an adult readership as well.

Pallas
by L. Neil Smith
Tor Books, 1993
The *Uncle Tom's Cabin* of the Sagebrush Rebellion. Direct in-your-face confrontation between armed individualism and victim disarmanent.

The Mitzvah
by L. Neil Smith and Aaron Zelman
(forthcoming in 1999)

Firearms Rights Periodicals

The New Gun Week
P.O. Box 488, Station C
Buffalo, NY 14209
Voice: 716-885-6408
Fax: 716-884-4471
Subscriptions: $32/year ($40 foreign)

Women and Guns
P.O. Box 488, Station C
Buffalo, NY 14209
Voice: 716-885-6408
Fax: 716-884-4471
Introductory Subscription: $10/5 issues

The American Guardian
(included with membership)
National Rifle Association of America
11250 Waples Mill Road
Fairfax, VA 22030
703-267-1000
Membership inquiries: 800-672-3888
Membership & subscription: $25/year/12 issues

Firearms Rights Organizations

National Rifle Association of America
11250 Waples Mill Road
Fairfax, VA 22030
703-267-1000
Membership inquiries: 800-672-3888
http://www.nra.org
Largest firearms organization in the world, currently with 3 million members. Institute for Legislative Action focuses on protecting firearms owners' rights, while NRA itself focuses on firearms training, safety, and competitive programs.

The Second Amendment Foundation
James Madison Building
12500 NE 10th Place
Bellevue, WA 98005
206-454-7012
Gun Rights Hot Line: 800-426-4302
http://www.saf.org
Publishes books, magazines, and monographs on firearms issues, including *The New Gun Week, Women & Guns, Gun News Digest* and J*ournal on Firearms and Public Policy.*

Citizens Committee for the Right to Keep and Bear Arms
12500 NE 10th Place
Bellevue, WA 98005
206-454-4911
http://www.ccrkba.org
Second largest firearms rights activist organization with approximately 500,000 members. Organizes yearly Gun Rights Policy Conference.

Gun Owners of America
8001 Forbes Place, Suite 102
Springfield, VA 22151
Voice: 703-321-8585
Fax: 703-321-8408
http://www.gunowners.org/
Uncompromising defenders of gun owners rights. Vilified by ATF in affidavit used to raid Branch Davidians

Jews for the Preservation of Firearms Ownership
2872 S. Wentworth Avenue
Milwaukee, WI 53207
Voice: 414-769-0760
Fax: 414-483-8435
http://www.jfpo.org/
Publishes research and position papers on firearms rights, with a particular emphasis on moral and Biblical issues. You don't have to be Jewish to join.

Center for the Study of Crime,
Randall N. Herrst, President
16645 Taylor Court
Torrance, CA 90504
310-715-2812
Organizes research materials on all aspects of firearms and firearms rights. Provides specific training to high-profile individuals who need to be accurate in their discussion of firearms-related issues and technology. Available as technical advisors to motion picture and television productions on rare and unusual aspects of firearms.

World Wide Web Gun Defense Clock
http://www.pulpless.com/gunclock
Minute-by-minute, calculates the number of gun defenses from January 1st of each year to the present moment. Includes links to other criminological information on firearms self-defense.

Doctors for Integrity in Research and Public Policy
5201 Norris County Road, Suite 140
San Ramon, CA 94583
510-277-0333
Internet Email: edgarsuter@aol.com
Specializes in correcting inaccurate claims made by physicians, particularly epidemiologists, on firearms/health issues.

AWARE (Arming Women Against Rape and Endangerment)
P.O. Box 255
Maynard, MA 01754
508-443-5404
http://www.aware.org
Advocates preserving the option of arming women against rape and endangerment.

Law Enforcement Alliance of America
7700 Leesburg Pike
Falls Church, VA 22043-2618

703-847-COPS
http://wwwlargo.org/LEAA.html
Publishes the LEAA Advocate. For law-enforcement officers and others interesting in defending victims rights and supporting civilian firearms ownership.

National Association of Federal Licensed Firearms Dealers
2455 East Sunrise Blvd., 9th floor
Fort Lauderdale, FL 33304
305-561-3505
http://www.amfire.com/
Lobbies for firearms rights.

Academics for the Second Amendment
P.O. Box 131254
St. Paul, MN 55113
Dedicated to giving the right to keep and bear arms its proper, prominent place in Constitutional discourse and analysis.

The Independence Institute
14142 Denver West Parkway, Suite 101
Golden, CO 80401-3134
Voice: 303-279-6536
Fax: 303-279-4176
http://www.i2i.org/
Publishes research on firearms rights issues, among other libertarian issues.

Libertarian Second Amendment Caucus
c/o 736 Eastdale Drive
Fort Collins, CO 80524
Voice: 303-484-6824
The single most uncompromising gun-rights organization, bar none. These guys are perfectly willing to elect anti-gun Democrats if it means trashing wimpy sell-out Republicans.

Firearms Instruction

In addition to the National Rifle Association, which offers firearms safety and proficiency instruction throughout the United States, the following individuals are one's I've heard especially good things about. Caveat: I have not personally taken instruction from any of these organizations or individuals.

Massad F. Ayoob
Lethal Force Institute
P.O. Box 122
Concord, NH 03301
800-624-9049

Peter Alan Kasler
Threat Management Institute
800 West Napa Street
Sonoma, CA 95476
Voice: 800-750-4-TMI (Calif. only) or 707-939-0303
Fax: 707-939-8684
Internet: tmi@crl.com
TMI Computer BBS: 707-935-1713

Paxton Quigley's Personal Protection (women only)
9903 Santa Monica Blvd., #300
Beverly Hills, CA 90212
310-281-1762

Kent Turnipseed's Enhanced Weaver Stance
610 N. Alma School Road, Suite #18-213
Chandler, AZ 85224
(602) 802-0346
www.turnipseedstance.com

About J. Neil Schulman

J. Neil Schulman is the author of two Prometheus award-winning novels, *Alongside Night* and *The Rainbow Cadenza*, short fiction, nonfiction, and screenwritings, including the CBS *Twilight Zone* episode "Profile in Silver."

Stopping Power: Why 70 Million Americans Own Guns was his first nonfiction book. It was published hardcover in June, 1994, by Synapse-Centurion, and has made the Amazon.Com most-requested list for political titles. It was quoted from by witnesses on both sides in the March, 1995 hearings on firearms before Congress's House Subcommittee on Crime.

Schulman's next book, *Self Control Not Gun Control,* picked up where *Stopping Power* left off with an exploration of the uses and abuses of both personal and political power.

Dr. Walter E. Williams, talk show host, newspaper columnist, and Chairman of the Department of Economics at George Mason University, says of *Self Control Not Gun Control*, "Schulman interestingly and insightfully raises a number of liberty-related issues that we ignore at the nation's peril. His ideas are precisely those that helped make our country the destination of those seeking liberty. The book's title says it all: personal responsibility, not laws and prohibitions, is the mark of a civil society."

His most recent book is *The Frame of the Century?* which asks the question, "Was O.J. Simpson framed for murder by his biggest fan?" *The Cincinnati Enquirer* calls it, "A compelling circumstantial argument" for Simpson's innocence.

The Robert Heinlein Interview and Other Heinleiniana, just released by Pulpless.Com, Inc., has been called by Virginia Heinlein "a book that should be on the shelves of everyone interested in science fiction."

Schulman has been published in the *Los Angeles Times* and other national newspapers, as well as *National Review*, *New Libertarian, Reason*, *Liberty*, and other magazines. His *L.A. Times* article "If Gun Laws Work, Why Are We Afraid?" won the James

Madison Award from the Second Amendment Foundation; and in November, 1995, the 500,000-member Citizens Committee for the Right to Keep and Bear Arms awarded Schulman its Gun Rights Defender prize. Schulman's books have been praised by Nobel laureate Milton Friedman, Anthony Burgess, Robert A. Heinlein, Colin Wilson, and many other prominent individuals. His short story "The Repossessed" was the lead story in *Adventures in the Twilight Zone*, edited by Carol Serling; and his short story "Day of Atonement" appeared in the shared-world anthology *Free Space* edited by Brad Linaweaver and Ed Kramer, a Tor hardcover published in July, 1997. These and seven other stories, including his first fiction dealing with the subject of gun rights, "When Freemen Shall Stand," are collected in *Nasty, Brutish, and Short Stories.*

Schulman is a popular speaker on a variety of topics, and a frequent talk show guest for such hosts as Dennis Prager, Michael Jackson, Oliver North, and Barry Farber. He was on ABC's *World News Tonight* as an expert on defensive use of firearms during the 1992 Los Angeles riots, and was chosen to debate Los Angeles County Sheriff Sherman Block on UPN Channel 13 News Los Angeles on the topic of the repeal of the federal "assault weapons" ban.

J. Neil Schulman is a pioneer in electronic publishing, having founded in 1987 the first company to distribute books by bestselling authors for download by modem. He is currently Chairman and Publisher of Pulpless.Com, Inc., which operates the Pulpless.Com web site—"We Make Books—Paper Optional"—on the World Wide Web at www.pulpless.com, and his personal web site is at www.pulpless.com/jneil/. His internet address is jneil@pulpless.com.

All of Mr. Schulman's books are available for download from these web sites.